W9-BAL-540

10996216

AMERICAN JOBS AND THE CHANGING INDUSTRIAL BASE

AMERICAN JOBS AND THE CHANGING INDUSTRIAL BASE

Edited by
Eileen L. Collins *and*
Lucretia Dewey Tanner

Ballinger Publishing Company • Cambridge, Massachusetts
A Subsidiary of Harper & Row, Publishers, Inc.

Copyright © 1984 by Ballinger Publishing Company. All rights reserved. No part of this publication may be reproduced, stored in a retrieval system, or transmitted in any form or by any means, electronic, mechanical, photocopy, recording or otherwise, without the prior written consent of the publisher.

International Standard Book Number: 0-88730-017-0

Library of Congress Catalog Card Number: 84-14495

Printed in the United States of America

Library of Congress Cataloging in Publication Data

Main entry under title:

American jobs and the changing industrial base.

Includes index.
Contents: Introduction / Eileen L. Collins — High tech and the structural employment problems of the 1980s / Eileen Appelbaum — Automation and its effect on employment and income / Faye Duchin — [etc.]
1. Labor supply — United States — Effect of technological innovations on — Addresses, essays, lectures. 2. United States — Occupations — Forecasting — Addresses, essays, lectures. I. Collins, Eileen L. II. Tanner, Lucretia Dewey.
HD5724.A56   1984   331.12′0973   84-14495

ISBN 0-88730-017-0

RIDER COLLEGE LIBRARY

To Our Parents

CONTENTS

LIST OF FIGURES

LIST OF TABLES

PREFACE

Lucretia Dewey Tanner

Throughout its history, the United States has been in the forefront of technological innovation, eager to adopt or design new processes to produce more and better-quality products. Its agricultural productivity continues to astound the world, and it is one nation with policies that attempt to limit production, not increase it. Yet in recent years, it has appeared that the old flame has died and that the country is suffering, if not from old age, then at least middle-age lethargy. Productivity outside of agriculture has lagged, advancing a respectable 3 percent annually in the two decades following World War II but dropping to less than 2 percent in the 1965–73 period and remaining stagnant from 1978 to 1982. Nevertheless, reports for 1983 and projections through the turn of the century indicate that perhaps a resurgence will occur.

The economic decline during the 1970s was steep, brought on by a number of factors, including the oil price shocks of 1973 and 1980. This—coupled with demographic changes and the influx of baby-boomers, women, and new groups of immigrants, both legal and illegal—brought on high rates of unemployment. At the same time, changes occurred on other fronts as well. Imports increasingly penetrated domestic markets, interest rates were volatile and rising, capital investment sagged, and technology was swiftly changing. The term "structural change" reentered the language as a popular explanation for what was taking place, reminiscent of the interest of the early 1960s' fear of automation.

Viewed in retrospect, the researchers of the 1960s — with their gloomy forecasts of how automation would displace people — could be classified as alarmists, since the growing economy subsequently absorbed most of the new job entrants. Turmoil is clearly evident now, however, as advances in technology occur in tandem with corporate restructuring — such as merger mania, joint U.S.-foreign ventures, the rise of entrepreneurial small business, and government's reassessment of its responsibilities.

But are we once more sounding a false clarion and identifying problems where none really exist? Are we looking at today's rate of unemployment — holding steady well above the full employment goal of 4 to 5 percent — and projecting this to higher levels at a time when the economy stands on the threshold of another great expansion, one equal to the agricultural and industrial revolutions? As citizens we hope for nothing more, yet as social scientists we must caution against unbridled optimism. At the very least, we must prepare and plan for the problems caused by change as they develop. Viewing history as one great continuum, we see improved living standards in each succeeding generation as technology advances, yet change has not been without substantial costs to some segments of the population. Herein lies our concern.

Economists talk in terms of "cost," which the nontechnicians often call "hardships." Change, even if for the greater long-term good of the economy, potentially brings for some the economic hardships of lost jobs, reduced earnings, and underemployment, as well as the psychological damage of forced relocation, acceptance of lower-status jobs, or dependency on other members of the family. (Marriage breakups, wife batterings, and child abuse might also serve as economic indicators of the nation's well-being.)

While the contributors to this volume foresee substantial benefits from technical advance, they also identify problems, express concerns, and present creative ideas for lessening the impact of change for those adversely affected. The authors of this book attempt to assess through rigorous analysis and use of the new computer-based technology their projections and recommendations for adapting to the changing industrial base. They point out that real hardships can be created with structural change and ask, Who will bear the burden: those already on the lower economic rung, blue-collar workers in smokestack industries, women, and minorities? Even in industries that have attempted to minimize displacement through attrition, a smooth transition has not always been possible. How then to cope with structural change?

One of the prime responsibilities of the federal government is promoting and sustaining economic growth, but prescriptions for policy differ on how to do this. Reasoned disagreement exists as to the best approaches to follow in dealing with technical change and worker displacement. For example, answers differ to the questions, "Should industry or government or a combination of both provide leadership for coping with change?" "Is collective bargaining and closer labor management cooperation sufficient, or are additional programs necessary?" "Can government programs help?" The most basic questions raised by a number of authors are, "If emphasis has and will be placed on training, will the jobs be there?" "Will technical change create good highly skilled professional jobs or bad low-skilled ones?" The authors suggest that we can consider alternative approaches. For example, technology can produce a variety of jobs through flexible job design.

In summary, this book offers the informed policymaker approaches for understanding and dealing with technological progress and the disruption that is all too frequently the companion of change.

ACKNOWLEDGMENTS

We owe a general debt of gratitude to the authors of this book without whom the project would not have been possible. Thanks are due our colleagues and friends whose comments and questions helped sharpen our work.

We are grateful to Harvey Gram whose ideas about the relationships between economic theory and policy issues prompted us to undertake this project, to Rolf Piekarz for provocative discussion, to Hermann Anton for practical advice, and to Carole Grider for research and secretarial assistance.

E.I.C.
L.D.T.

INTRODUCTION

Eileen L. Collins

Increasing interdependence among nations, shifting patterns of international trade, and increased innovative pressures from abroad are intertwined with a significant restructuring of the U.S. economy to which American workers and firms must adjust. Public discussions of these interrelated shifts have often focused on methods and strategies for improving productivity growth and stimulating technical advance. In such discussions, labor is often viewed as a factor of production, and wages are viewed as an input price. This book takes a larger perspective—one that treats the effect of technical change on workers.

In view of the many dimensions and consequences of technical change, it is not surprising that many different views are expressed about how it should be managed and what it can do. This book brings together analyses that examine different aspects of technical advance, employ different techniques for assessing its effects, and as a group help to explain the interrelationships between technical change, structural shifts in the domestic and international economies, and the employment prospects of American workers.

Any opinions, findings, conclusions, or recommendations expressed in this chapter are those of the author and do not necessarily reflect the views of the National Science Foundation. The author thanks H. Anton, H. Gram, R. Piekarz, L. Pike, and the authors of this book for helpful comments and discussion and C. Grider for research and secretarial assistance.

1

This introductory chapter provides an overview of succeeding chapters and untangles their points of agreement and disagreement in terms of differences in underlying assumptions and analytical approach: In other words, it sorts out differences in the mechanics that drive each chapter's argument. The first part below provides a general outline of the book. The second part summarizes the question addressed in each chapter, the approach used to address the question, and key findings of the analysis. The third part sorts out major points of agreement and disagreement in terms of differences in underlying assumptions and approach. Policy implications are drawn in the final part.

GENERAL OUTLINE OF BOOK

Chapter 1, by Eileen Appelbaum, presents an overview of the changing industrial base and implications for American employment prospects. Chapter 2, by Faye Duchin, provides a comprehensive framework for tracing the effects of technical change on the composition of future labor demand and the distribution of income. Chapter 3, by Robert A. Levy, Marianne Bowes, and James M. Jondrow, and Chapter 4, by Lucretia Dewey Tanner, examine the introduction of new technology in specific industry sectors. Chapter 5, by John Vrooman, analyzes how the benefits of technical progress differ for workers in different market segments. Chapter 6, by Peter S. Albin, assesses the role of improved job design in promoting productivity growth and quality of working life. Chapter 7, by Kenneth McLennan, and Chapter 8, by Markley Roberts, provide industry and labor perspectives on the changing industrial base. The concluding chapter, by Larry M. Blair, provides a comprehensive review of specific private and public mechanisms that have been and/or could be used to facilitate labor adjustment to technical change.

CHAPTER SUMMARIES

Eileen Appelbaum, in "High Tech and the Structural Employment Problems of the 1980s," provides an overview of structural shifts in the American economy of the 1970s that have set the stage for the evolution of American industry and labor prospects in the 1980s.

Appelbaum's analysis of the 1970s begins with the slowdown in U.S. investment, which led to slower growth in capital per worker and labor productivity and contributed to the erosion of U.S. international competitiveness in many old-line manufacturing sectors. Reduced international competitiveness in traditional manufacturing sectors, including steel, automobiles, rubber, and apparel, has in turn curtailed employment growth in those industries and in some instances actually created job loss. As traditional manufacturing in the northeast and north central regions has declined, employment has grown in the service sectors generally and in both manufacturing and services in the south and west; the regional shift has been due less to firm migration to the sunbelt than to growth in industries already located there, in particular, electrical and electronic equipment, defense, and space-related sectors.

Appelbaum provides a detailed picture of the consequences of the shifting pattern of employment and concludes that, on balance,

1. There has been relative employment decline in regions and industries where organized labor is strong and wages are above the average in manufacturing, and employment growth in regions and industries where organized labor is weak and wages are below the average in manufacturing;
2. As we moved from the 1970s to the 1980s, a process was already in motion that was slowing the growth in average American wages and eroding the relative wage of American workers compared to workers in other developed countries;
3. The composition of American employment has been shifting toward a greater proportion of poorly paid jobs that are frequently sex-stereotyped as female; and
4. Male blue-collar workers in the frostbelt displaced by technical change or changing patterns of international trade are not likely to find comparable employment in the expanding service and manufacturing industries of the sunbelt, and if social discrimination persists, black workers will be hardest hit.

Appelbaum argues that the erosion of employment opportunities should not be dismissed as a temporary phenomenon and observes that the costs of black poverty today can be traced to the earlier displacement of agricultural workers by machinery and the failure of a growing manufacturing sector to reabsorb significant numbers of displaced farm workers.

Appelbaum next considers the pattern of employment in emerging high-tech sectors. If current patterns continue, high tech alone will not provide comparable earnings opportunities for displaced blue-collar workers. This is partly because a different set of skills is required and partly because high tech is contributing to increased bipolarization of employment opportunities—that is, increased employment in well-paid professional, technical, and managerial jobs at the top and in low-paid clerical, sales, and nonprofessional service jobs at the bottom, but erosion of the sorts of midlevel jobs now held by blue-collar manufacturing workers. Appelbaum concludes that solving the structural employment problems of the 1980s will require not only training and relocation programs but also programs to transform the characteristics of poor jobs, antidiscrimination policies, and new initiatives in macroeconomic employment policy.

Faye Duchin, in "Automation and Its Effect on Employment and Income," argues that the specific and global effects of automation can be systematically investigated—not by purely theoretical considerations or informed speculation but through a detailed, integrated model of the economy that captures not only the direct effects of technical change in specific subsectors but also indirect effects transmitted through interlinkages among subsectors. Duchin develops such a model, states it in compact mathematical notation, and provides a nontechnical explanation of how it works and how it can be used to analyze the impacts of technical change. The production equations of the model, a dynamic input/output model with extensions, describe interlinkages among production subsectors; how input coefficients (that is, input per unit of output for each input in each subsector) shift when a new technology is introduced; and the process of economic growth. The model's price equations track how changes in input coefficients and input prices influence the earnings of each factor of production in each subsector. An adding-up equation describes how the specific effects of technical change in individual subsectors add up to shifts in the distribution of income and the composition of output.

After tracing historical movements in capital and labor use and income shares, Duchin explores potential effects of computer-based automation on U.S. employment through the year 2000. In particular, the production equations of the model were used to project the composition of output, investment, and labor requirements of the U.S. economy in terms of about ninety production sectors and over fifty occupations under alternative assumptions about technical change. Duchin reports initial work with three scenarios. Scenario one, a reference scenario, is based on the assumption that no technological change occurs after 1980. Scenario two assumes the fastest rates at which the American economy might be expected to absorb computer-based automation up to the year 2000. The same moderate rate of growth of final deliveries (essentially consumption goods) is assumed in both scenarios. Under the rapid-automation scenario, aggregate labor productivity turns out to be about 13 percent higher and aggregate labor requirements about 20 million worker-years lower for the year 2000 than under the reference scenario. Although sharp reductions in direct labor requirements show up under the rapid-automation scenario, these are partly offset by the assumption of a moderately increasing standard of living and the additional labor required to produce and service the additional capital inputs associated with the adoption of new technology.

A third scenario is used to project the growth in consumption goods that would be possible over the next two decades if the labor force (as currently projected) were fully employed under the technical assumptions of the rapid-automation scenario. Under the full-employment rapid-automation scenario, public plus private consumption could grow at about 2 percent per year in the 1980s and 0.5 percent to 1 percent per year in the 1990s.

Duchin observes that computer-based automation alone is not likely to proceed so rapidly that a dramatic decline in employment opportunities will necessarily follow. However, she sounds a cautionary note. Other factors in combination with computer-based automation could lead to significant labor displacement. Moreover, the occupational composition of labor demand can be expected to shift significantly over the next two decades, including sharp declines in the relative demand for clerical workers and middle-level managers and increases in relative demand for computer programmers and analysts and most categories of engineers. Consequently, public training efforts, including reassessment of current school curricula, will almost certainly be required to supplement industry training efforts.

Robert A. Levy, Marianne Bowes, and James M. Jondrow, in "Technical Advance and Other Sources of Employment Change in Basic Industry," develop an econometric model (which is described in nontechnical terms) of industry behavior in order to untangle the effects of technical change from the influence of other variables in the steel, automobile, aluminum, iron ore, and coal industries. Levy, Bowes, and Jondrow set out to capture both the direct and indirect effects of technical change on employment. The direct effects operate through reductions in the inputs, including labor inputs, required to produce a given level of output. The indirect effects, which the authors call the output-enhancement effect, operate through the cost-saving effects of technical change that allow a company to sell at a lower output price, thus increasing total sales and employment.

Estimates of the direct effects of technical change are based on a model in which a company in competitive equilibrium is assumed to minimize production cost, given input prices, the level of output, and the level of technology. Estimates of the output enhancement effect are based on a model in which demand for an industry's product is conditioned against the presence of a competing but not perfectly substitutable import. Improved domestic technology is assumed to reduce domestic production cost and selling price, but import prices are not treated as responding.

Key findings of the Levy, Bowes, and Jondrow work include the following:

1. Over the last two decades, the direct effects of technical change on labor demand have been the substitution of other inputs for labor in all five industries. However, the effects have proceeded gradually, and the impacts on employment have been far smaller than reductions due to shifts in relative wage rates and the level of production, especially in the recession years of 1979 and 1980.
2. Although the output enhancement effect in the steel industry has been insignificant (since the rate of productivity growth attributable to technical change has been close to zero), the effect in the other four industries has been positive and sufficiently large to offset much of, and in some instances more than, the entire negative direct effects.
3. When both the output enhancement effect and the direct effects of technical change are accounted for, any net decline in employment due to technical change has been relatively small and pro-

ceeded gradually at a lower rate than the average industry quit rate.

Based on the experience of the 1960s and 1970s, Levy, Bowes, and Jondrow are relatively optimistic about the future. They observe that technical change alone is not necessarily a cause of aggregate labor displacement—although layoffs can occur, for example, if employment reductions are concentrated in particular geographic areas or cyclical downturns overwhelm attrition as means of accommodating reduced labor demand.

Lucretia Dewey Tanner, in "Modernizing the Federal Government: Effect on Its Employees," examines the introduction of new technology in the federal government. She integrates results of studies to assess the impact of technological change on employees and productivity in a number of different government settings, including the introduction of computer processing by the Internal Revenue Service in the late 1960s and the continuing increased mechanization and computer-assisted control technology used by the U.S. Postal Service to handle the mail.

Tanner finds that the varied experience of government agencies demonstrates the problems and opportunities created by technical change in the service sectors and suggests that efficient adaptation to change is sensitive to its institutional setting. In the Postal Service— which operates in some ways as a private corporation and which permits collective bargaining on wages and working conditions (unlike most federal agencies)—management and labor have worked jointly to introduce labor-saving equipment and to ease the effect of reduced work requirements. Tanner reports that Postal Service productivity is high and that although automation efforts in other agencies are relatively less advanced, overall government productivity is twice that of the private-sector service economy.

John Vrooman, in "Effect of Technology on the Distribution of Labor Income," integrates two seemingly divergent explanations of the determinants of labor income in order to identify differential effects of technology on the earnings of different labor-market groups. Vrooman builds on both a supply-side model, which emphasizes the human-capital characteristics of workers, and a demand-side model, which stresses the segmentation of labor markets based on the technology of jobs, to construct a model of the effect of technology on the returns to investment in human capital.

Under the combined approach, the labor market is composed of three basic market segments. The upper-tier primary segment provides the best jobs; jobs in this segment are highly paid and prestigious and require professional skills that are obtained through formal education and that can be applied in different industry settings. For the upper-tier primary market, formal education provides professional skills that are required for entry, are enhanced by work experience, and are not tied to industry-specific technology.

The lower-tier primary segment provides jobs that are stable and well paid but not necessarily prestigious; these jobs are highly structured and require firm-specific or industry-specific skills that are acquired on the job. For the lower-tier primary market, formal schooling fosters the discipline and regular work attendance that workers will need to learn firm- or industry-specific skills on the job.

In marked contrast, the secondary market contains jobs that are unskilled, unstable, poorly paid, and nonprestigious. In the secondary market, workers need few skills to enter and have acquired few skills when they leave.

Vrooman concludes from a pilot study that the process of earnings determination differs in the three market segments. Some key findings are as follows:

1. In the secondary market, returns to postschool accumulation of employment experience are virtually nonexistent, regardless of the level of technology in the industry where a worker is employed.
2. In the lower-tier primary market, returns to employment experience are significant, but only in industries characterized by high productivity.
3. In the upper-tier primary market, returns to experience are significant and not related to the level of productivity in the industry where a professional is employed.

An implication of Vrooman's work is that programs intended to improve the earnings potential of unskilled or structurally unemployed workers cannot rely on institutional training alone. The returns to investment in human capital through formal training programs may not be realized if a secondary market segment persists in isolation from technical advance.

Peter S. Albin, in "Job Design within Changing Patterns of Technical Development," analyzes a component of technical advance generally neglected in economic analysis: the role of job design in the use of and adaptation to new technology. He explicitly examines changing job design in basic metalworking and draws implications for American employment prospects and economic growth.

Albin finds that turn-of-the-century Taylor job-design principles, which included centralized control and specialization of labor at the work station, were reasonable adaptations to the limited computational capacity of the time. However, rigid application of Taylor principles today does not make efficient use of dramatic computational advances. In particular, using the new computer-based control technologies to downgrade skill requirements at work stations and increase control at the center (in the hands of the engineer/programmer) may provide a short-run saving in labor cost, but it also erodes opportunities for future productivity enhancement. An alternative, more flexible approach is to reduce central control and to increase work-station responsibility and skill requirements. This allows greater scope for handling shifts in the flow or specifications of work, trouble shooting production problems, and developing innovative improvements on the shop floor, and contributes to improved quality of working life.

Albin attributes part of Japanese industrial success to wider application of the more flexible approach. U.S. industry has been slow to adopt more flexible job-design principles, especially in basic manufacturing and even in some high-technology sectors. Albin notes that a conditioning factor in Japan is the relatively stronger tie between a firm and workers, which allows a firm to internalize more of the benefits (as well as the costs) of the human-capital investments required by the more flexible approach.

Albin argues that wider use of state-of-the-art job-design principles is a necessary component to reviving U.S. productivity growth. A modest policy initiative would be to develop labor education, training, and placement programs *in coordination* with programs to inform and encourage adoption of efficient job-design strategies. Complementary government efforts would include macroeconomic policies to maintain full employment and reconstruction finance.

Kenneth McLennan, in "Industry Perspectives on Adjustment to Economic Change," observes that the success of business enterprise depends on its ability to adapt to and take advantage of continuous economic change. A sense of continuous competitive pressure is the driving force in business operating decisions, assessments of the economic environment, and the perceptions of appropriate public policy. McLennan notes that although not all of business agrees on specific aspects of policy for dealing with structural change, there is general agreement on overarching points. McLennan sets out business perceptions of the current economic environment and the appropriate policy response.

Business views are conditioned by recent economic experience. The recent erosion of American international competitiveness in some older manufacturing sectors reflects excessive increases in unit labor costs relative to productivity growth for which, in some industries, both management and labor were responsible. Also reflected are international competitive pressures, which are becoming more not less pronounced both in traditional manufacturing and high-technology sectors.

To fend off foreign competition and protect American jobs, a number of strategies are required. Business is taking steps to improve efficiency and increase productivity, including greater investment in technological innovation. However, resources are needed to finance the investment, and time is needed for the investment to bear fruit. To enable business to make the necessary investment, government policy should be used to provide a healthy, noninflationary economic environment; to remove legislative impediments to market forces (for example, overregulation and the consumption bias in the existing tax code and in the composition of government expenditures); and to act with governments of other nations to reduce trade barriers and eliminate unfair trade practices.

Business does not state a position on the appropriate structure for collective bargaining. McLennan observes, however, that the expansion of international trade over the last two decades may mean that pattern-setting wage agreements may no longer be desirable for labor or management. Bargaining at the local level would allow wage agreements to reflect a specific plant's productivity and local labor-market conditions and thus would reduce labor-market dislocations.

Finally, business cites research evidence showing that on balance technological innovation creates jobs rather than destroys them. When shifts in the structure of the economy occur — for example, the increasing proportion of employment in service-sector occupations — the adjustments have been accomplished without major labor-force dis-locations. Nevertheless, business realizes that some workers can face permanent dislocation. Some employers have negotiated adjustment provisions in collective bargaining agreements, and some have uni-laterally provided adjustment assistance. All agree that government should provide adjustment assistance for permanently dislocated workers but are critical of earlier government efforts that often im-peded labor-market adjustment. A second role for government is en-couraging revised school curricula to prepare students for future jobs in high-technology industry.

Markley Roberts, in "A Labor Perspective on Technological Change," sets out the attitudes of workers and their unions toward both the problems and opportunities presented by the introduction of new technology. He draws on studies of union response to technical change that indicate that the most common response of American labor unions has been willing acceptance of new technology and that col-lective bargaining can allow labor and management to work together to mitigate adjustment costs. Techniques that have been used include attrition or no-layoff protection, early warning of job displacement, "red-circle" pay protection, shorter work weeks or work years, trans-fer rights, retraining, and relocation assistance. In addition, a secure union can work with management to enhance the joint benefits of technical change through programs to improve productivity, work-place safety, and quality of working life.

Also of concern is the evolving pattern of American wages. In-creasing employment in service-sector occupations relative to manu-facturing occupations is contributing to a downward shift in the over-all wage base and segmentation of the labor force into high-skill and low-skill jobs with decreasing opportunities in the middle. Moreover, the skill mix offered by high technology seems to be continuing the process of bipolarization. A consequence could be erosion of the con-sumer buying base for the economy and increased social instability.

Roberts argues that a national industrial policy is required to deal in a comprehensive way with structural shifts in the domestic and international economics, slow economic growth, persistent unemploy-ment, and the complexities of technical change. An appropriate policy would include

1. participation by business, labor, and government in developing programs to revitalize ailing industries and stimulate new ones;

2. channeling private pension funds to finance revitalizing investments (while maintaining adequate fund security);
3. removing tax and trade policy incentives that encourage the export of American technology, capital, production, and jobs; and
4. controlling imports that raise unemployment and weaken the industrial base.

Policies specifically directed to labor adjustment to technical change
would include

1. a systematic data-gathering program to improve understanding
   of the process and impacts of technical change;
2. a data clearing house to provide information that unions and employers can use to develop cooperative solutions to the complex
   problems of technical change;
3. training and relocation programs; and
4. legislated protection for workers whose jobs cannot be saved.

Roberts concludes that a healthy, expanding, full-employment economy is an essential environment within which workers and their
unions can obtain the dignity and enhancement of human values that
come from income protection, advancement opportunities, and productive jobs.

Larry M. Blair, in "Worker Adjustment to Changing Technology:
Techniques, Processes, and Policy Considerations," provides a comprehensive review of the specific private and public mechanisms that
have been and/or might be used to facilitate worker adjustment to
technical change. Blair's discussion of the relative advantages and
disadvantages of various private mechanisms is organized around six
major groupings: (1) training, transfer, and worker mobility; (2) job
protection; (3) work sharing; (4) income security measures; (5) reemployment aids; and (6) collective bargaining procedures. Analysis
of the relative strengths and weaknesses of public mechanisms includes discussion of: (1) macroeconomic policies to maintain full
employment; (2) job-creation programs; (3) labor-market information
and placement programs; (4) education, training, and relocation programs; (5) income and work maintenance programs; and (6) policies
toward labor/management relations.

The appropriate policy mix depends on the degree of effect that
technical change is expected to have on the level and composition of

labor demand, the mix of private mechanisms already in operation, and the objectives of adjustment policy. If policy objectives include not just matching up numbers or workers with numbers of jobs but also qualitative variables such as job satisfaction and general well-being, then a broader set of public mechanisms is required. Blair draws on formal studies of welfare economics (that is, formal studies of relationships between economic variables and social well-being) to suggest an approach for assessing alternative policy strategies.

Key findings of Blair's review are:

1. Technical change alone is not likely to create major labor displacement; however, new technologies will influence job content and skill requirements for a substantial number of workers, and some worker displacement will occur.
2. Retraining programs are an important component of public policy, but there is considerable disagreement about how training programs should be structured and what they should try to do.
3. If technical change unfolds gradually as in the past, continued use of public and private mechanisms, including policies for full employment and labor/management cooperation, seems sufficient to handle the vast majority of worker adjustment problems. However, some extension of existing mechanisms is probably needed to cover pockets of displaced workers and perhaps the special needs of some groups (particularly minorities and the unskilled).
4. Often underlying the generally sanguine assessments of the capacity of existing mechanisms to handle most labor adjustment problems is the assumption that the introduction of new technology will not accelerate or be swamped by other perturbations in labor demand.

POINTS OF AGREEMENT AND DIFFERENCE

The work of this book suggests that technical change can follow more than one path and the adjustment process can be handled in more than one way. Thus, the future course of change depends on the plans and actions of the private sector, the government programs and institutions that condition the social and economic setting within which business and labor operate, and the larger international environment.

Since the distribution of the costs and benefits of new technologies varies for different paths of change and different adjustment programs, it is not surprising that different economic actors have different agendas for technical advance. What is surprising is the degree of implicit (although frequently unacknowledged) agreement among different actors and analysts about the phenomenon of structural change and important aspects of the adjustment process. Disagreements about appropriate policy response stem not so much from major disagreements about what is happening but primarily from examining different consequences of structural change and/or using different criteria for identifying problems and opportunities created by technical advance.

Points of Agreement

Roberts, McLennan, and Appelbaum have examined structural shifts in the domestic and international economies that have eroded U.S. international competitiveness and curtailed earnings growth in some sectors, primarily frostbelt old-line manufacturing sectors such as steel and automobiles. At the same time, employment growth has occurred in the service occupations generally and in sunbelt industries such as electrical and electronic equipment, defense, and space-related sectors.

The shifting pattern of production and employment has resulted in labor displacement for some groups and contributed to an overall decline in the earnings potential of American workers. New technology is one source of labor displacement, but technical change alone has not created massive unemployment; moreover, technical advance has the potential to improve productivity growth, meet competitive pressures from abroad, improve living standards, and enhance quality of working life.

In addition to general agreement on the nature of recent structural shifts, there is agreement that technical advance is an appropriate public policy goal. It is at the next step of the analysis that researchers begin to address different questions and adopt analytical approaches that lead to different policy conclusions.

A Free-Marketeer Approach

McLennan and Levy, Bowes, and Jondrow consider the effect of new technology on the level of employment and the ability of a competitive economy to reabsorb displaced workers. They point out that although technical change can create significant labor displacement for some groups, technical change can save jobs — even create them — by helping to meet innovative competition from abroad. Implicit in their analyses, and in the neoclassical analyses of production efficiency that turn up in Blair's survey, is a model in which markets are perfectly competitive (or at least approximate the outcomes of perfect competition) and thus channel resources to their most efficient use.

Accordingly, the industry view reported in McLennan is that the best employment policy, indeed the best economic policy, is one that removes perceived legislative impediments (especially overregulation) to business efforts to meet the challenge of foreign competition and thus to preserve American industry and jobs. In addition, the perceived consumption bias in government taxing and spending patterns should be removed to enable business to garner the resources necessary for investment in plant, equipment, and new technology. Also needed are a macroeconomic policy to provide a healthy noninflationary environment and international negotiations with other governments to remove trade barriers and eliminate unfair trade practices.

In this view, the level of American wages in some primarily unionized sectors has contributed to industry difficulties in responding to foreign competition (the importance of management investment in productivity growth is also acknowledged), and a reduction in these wage rates, or at least slower wage growth, is part of the solution to structural adjustment problems. Business groups do not state a position on the appropriate structure for collective bargaining, but the current reduction in union strength and a restructuring of collective bargaining would very likely be welcome. Under the free-marketeer approach, reduced use of pattern-setting wage agreements and returning labor/management negotiations to the local level would allow labor and management to negotiate wage agreements based on productivity at the plant level and in the context of local labor-market conditions. In particular, plant workers could express their preferences on the tradeoff between wage levels and layoffs in collective bargaining, and individual workers could relocate from lower-wage areas to higher-wage areas if their preferences differed from those reflected in the negotiated wage agreement and local labor-market conditions. This would reduce labor displacement and facilitate labor-market adjustment.

Free marketeers observe, however, that some workers can experience permanent dislocation. Thus, private industry efforts to facilitate labor adjustment unilaterally or through collective bargaining should be supplemented by government training and relocation programs for permanently displaced workers. These programs should not impede market adjustment but should channel displaced workers to expanding sectors of the economy. Finally, government policy should encourage revised public school curricula to help equip the future labor force with skill requirements appropriate to emerging technologies and the changing industrial base.

Different Sets of Questions

Other authors of this book consider somewhat different questions that lead to alternative assessments of future employment prospects and different strategies for dealing with structural change. Appelbaum, Roberts, and Duchin ask not only whether jobs lost will be balanced by jobs gained but also about the characteristics of jobs in each group. Blair considers adjustment mechanisms not just in terms of allocative efficiency but also in terms of general well-being.

Appelbaum and Roberts observe that emerging technologies and the evolving industrial base are contributing to erosion of union strength, reduced earnings potential for American workers, and increased bipolarization of job opportunities, with increasing proportions of low-paid low-skill jobs at the bottom and well-paid professional jobs at the top but a reduced proportion of job opportunities in the middle. In their view, the emerging reduction in the structure of American wages and the increased bipolarization of employment opportunities are neither necessary or desirable consequences of technical advance.

Appelbum argues that the erosion of U.S. international competitiveness in traditional manufacturing sectors is the result of management failure to equip U.S. workers with sufficient quantity and quality of capital to maintain international competitiveness without eroding workers' wage prospects. Implicit here is the view that there is more than one way to absorb technical change, more than one way to finance the investment needed to develop and install new technological equipment, and more than one pattern of benefits and costs. Other authors pick up several of these threads.

Appelbaum and Roberts consider the different ways in which investment in capital and innovation can be financed — that is, the way in which productive resources can be channeled into augmentation of the capital stock. If the economy is operating at less than full capacity, then additional investment can be financed without a reduction in consumption. In a growing full-employment economy, growing investment can still be financed without a reduction in consumption. Indeed, growing investment and consumption are simultaneously possible.

An eventual purpose of the comprehensive model developed by Duchin is to trace the distributional consequences of technological and growth alternatives. For example, Duchin explores a growth scenario running to the year 2000 in which the American economy is assumed to absorb computer-based automation at the most rapid feasible rate and to provide full employment for the labor force as currently projected. Resources needed for augmentation of the capital stock on that growth path allow sufficient production of consumption goods to permit moderate growth in real living standards throughout the period. Moreover, direct and indirect labor requirements to produce capital that embodies the new technologies help to sustain the level and composition of job opportunities for production workers. But as Duchin points out, this level of economic activity is not a foreordained course.

Appelbaum and Roberts observe that a less felicitous course is possible. Appelbaum suggests, for example, that increased investment can be financed through maintenance of the existing proportion of income voluntarily saved and growth in total income or that investment can be financed through increasing the proportion saved. If the latter is accomplished through an increase in corporate profit rates and a reduction in labor earnings, aggregate investment and consumption may not be sufficient to maintain full employment, thus stifling economic growth. Duchin provides a framework for empirical investigation of this and other possible outcomes.

Duchin, Appelbaum, and Roberts point out that different growth scenarios have profound implications for the rate of economic progress, the distribution of income, and the health of the economy. Implicit here is a model in which markets do not approximate perfect competition, do not necessarily generate best or even second-best solutions, and do not necessarily contain self-correcting adjustment mechanisms. Thus an important component of structural adjustment policy is macroeconomic policies directed to maintaining full employment of labor and capital. By contrast, economic policies directed to reducing the perceived consumption bias in government patterns of taxing and spending could impose consumption levels that are lower than necessary to finance growing innovative investments. Moreover, such policies could be counterproductive if they lead to underutilization of productive capacity.

Albin, starting from a microeconomic perspective, reaches a complementary conclusion. Albin explicitly examines the interaction of technical change and job design in the current management environment that has been conditioned by turn-of-the-century Taylor job-design principles. Albin finds that the Taylor approach contains a degree of centralized control and job simplification that does not exploit the computational and data-handling capacities of emerging computer-based technologies. Efficient exploitation of these technologies requires reduced centralization and increased job responsibility and skills to provide more flexibility at the work station to handle quantitative and qualitative shifts in work flow and more sophisticated trouble shooting when production problems appear. The result is both increased productivity and improved quality of working life. Albin observes that wider recognition of the implications for job design in Japan is one component of Japanese innovative success.

In addition to asking about what the effects of emerging technologies are likely to be for employment prospects generally, Appelbaum also asks, To what degree will high tech ameliorate existing employment problems—including structural unemployment, underemployment of the working poor, persistent discrimination against black workers, and sex stereotyping of low-paying clerical and service jobs? Appelbaum's assessment of the job-creation potential and skill mix of new technologies suggests that high-tech industry alone is not sufficient to ameliorate existing employment problems and that if current trends continue is likely to make them worse.

Vrooman's pilot work yields results consistent with Appelbaum's assessment. Vrooman finds a segmented labor market in which workers in the low-paying secondary market do not collect wage benefits from technical change in their industry. If a secondary labor market persists in isolation from the development of new technology, then technical advance alone is not sufficient to provide decent well-paid jobs for all who wish to work. Design of better jobs is required. Albin's work suggests that this is feasible and, in addition, would yield dividends in terms of improved quality of working life and greater productivity growth.

POLICY IMPLICATIONS

Defining a larger set of criteria for measuring labor-market performance, and examining the qualitative and distributional consequences of technical advance, leads different-sets analysts to consider a broader mix of policies than those emphasized by free marketeers. As noted above, both free marketeers and different-sets analysts generally agree that technical change alone is not likely to lead to major labor-force dislocation, although some groups will experience displacement, and that more generally the labor force will be required to adjust to shifts in the composition of labor demand.

Thus in the free-marketeer view, business efforts to facilitate labor adjustment, either unilaterally or in the context of a collective bargaining agreement, are appropriately supplemented by government training and relocation programs focused on a relatively small group of permanently dislocated workers. These programs should encourage the movement of workers in response to market signals. Fostering revised school curricula to equip future workers for jobs in high tech is also welcome. Beyond that, the adjustments required by both firms and workers in response to the ups and downs of the marketplace are considered an unavoidable fact of life. Government efforts should be small-scale (perhaps even passive) and focus on enabling business to make the capital and innovative investments required to maintain U.S. industry and jobs.

In contrast, different-sets analysts consider qualitative dimensions of employment prospects, including both psychic and economic costs of dislocation, quality of working life, and general well-being. Blair reports an extensive array of private and public mechanisms that have been and can be used to facilitate qualitative and quantitative dimensions of labor adjustment to technical change. Moreover, formal studies of production efficiency and social well-being find that market mechanisms alone do not guarantee an efficient and equitable adjustment process. This does not mean that massive government intervention is required but simply that a broader set of adjustment mechanisms will help to meet a richer set of goals.

In particular, Blair's review suggests that labor participation in collective bargaining can ease adjustment problems and facilitate the adoption of new technology, *provided* there is cooperation not conflict. Work cited by Roberts, and Tanner's review of technical change in the U.S. Postal Service, suggest that labor and management can work together to seek productivity gains and ease adjustment problems.

Like the free-marketeers, different-sets analysts consider that government education, retraining, and relocation programs should supplement private adjustment efforts. Some of the different-sets group are less convinced, however, that structural employment problems are confined just to small groups of workers. Appelbaum cites, for example, persistent unemployment or underemployment of blacks in frostbelt urban centers.

In addition, Appelbaum, Roberts, Albin, and Vrooman are concerned that training alone will not be sufficient to provide decent jobs for the working poor if a secondary labor market persists in isolation from the development of new technology. Antidiscrimination policy and efforts to coordinate training programs with enlightened job design are also required.

Nevertheless, Blair's review of the adjustment literature yields a generally sanguine assessment of the capacity of existing mechanisms to handle most of the adjustment to technical change. This assessment rests on a number of underlying assumptions, including cooperation between labor and management, no marked acceleration in the rate of adoption of new technology, and no simultaneous appearance of major labor-force dislocations from other sources of change. The erosion of union strength associated with the changing industrial base is one way to reduce labor and management conflict, but Roberts and Appelbaum are concerned that it will also reduce the capacity of existing mechanisms to handle labor adjustment problems.

In addition, Roberts, Appelbaum, and many analysts cited in Blair are not convinced that simply enabling the market to work will necessarily yield full employment and efficient economic growth. Both free marketeers and different-sets groups recommend macroeconomic policy to provide a healthy economic climate; however, the free marketeers emphasize a noninflationary environment and some redirection of government taxing and spending patterns toward savings and away from consumption, whereas the emphasis in different-sets analyses is on maintenance of aggregate demand and full employment.

Roberts suggests the most far-reaching policy approach, which includes labor/management cooperation with government to develop an industrial policy for revitalizing old industries and encouraging new ones. Both Roberts and many of the business concerns reported

in McLennan call for government participation in international negotiations to remove trade barriers and eliminate unfair trade practices,
but Roberts adds a strong caveat. Roberts advocates the removal of
perceived tax and policy incentives that encourage the export of U.S.
technology, capital, production, and jobs and the control of imports
that raise unemployment and weaken the industrial base. McLennan
notes that only some firms in some instances support a degree of pro-
tectionism (especially industries affected by perceived unfair trade
practices of foreign governments).

No one policy, set of policies, or industrial policy follows necessarily from the work of this book. Indeed even analysts in what I have
called the different-sets group do not draw identical policy conclusions. What emerges from their combined work is a larger set of tools
for addressing a more varied set of goals.

Although education, retraining, and relocation assistance are generally supported by both free-marketeer and different-sets groups,
these programs alone are not considered sufficient by different-sets
analysts. A number of other strategies are also needed: improved job
design, development of technology that can enhance both productivity growth and quality of working life, application of such technology to replace jobs in the secondary labor market with productive
employment opportunities, antidiscrimination policies, new macroeconomic initiatives to provide a robust and full-employment economy, and increased sway for private enterprise to meet competitive
pressure from abroad *combined with shared* responsibility between
workers and management for an efficient and equitable response to
the challenges and opportunities presented by the changing industrial
base.

1 HIGH TECH AND THE STRUCTURAL EMPLOYMENT PROBLEMS OF THE 1980s

Eileen Appelbaum

Economic malaise, underlined by the sharpness of the recent cyclical downturn, has been a fact of American life and a topic of national concern and debate for more than a decade. Economists have directed the attention of the profession and the public to a single dimension of the problem, the slowdown in productivity growth. Proposed solutions have focused on providing incentives for private investment in order to achieve rates of growth approximating those that prevailed from 1948 to 1968. Details of these solutions vary widely. They range from incentives for private investment to the formation of quasi-public bodies that would shore up private enterprise by implementing the investments in social overhead capital and in desirable but risky ventures that the private sector has been unwilling to undertake. Overlooked in these discussions of economic stagnation, however, has been another dimension of the crisis, as serious perhaps as the productivity slowdown: the increasing inability of private enterprise to allocate labor resources effectively to productive activity. American workers face the distinct possibility that their wages relative to the earnings of workers in other developed countries will decline. In addition, an important segment of industrial workers confronts the

The ideas in this paper were developed in the course of discussions with Leonard Rapping and the members of the seminar on economic restructuring at the University of Massachusetts.

possibility that the economy will find their labor redundant. The initial stages of this process can already be discerned. In the absence of public policy to anticipate and plan for changes in industrial structure, Americans have had to place their faith in a new round of economic growth, powered by the expansion of the high-tech industries, to provide comparable employment opportunities for these workers. Public policy in the United States has adopted a single-minded emphasis on productivity growth that ignores the problems of structural adjustment to economic change and the need for public programs to facilitate the reintegration of U.S. workers into the new international division of labor. Should the economy fail to provide employment for yet another segment of the work force, the prospects for restoring economic prosperity will be seriously jeopardized.

The first part of this chapter documents the recent deterioration in employment prospects for U.S. workers. The next examines whether new developments in high-tech service and manufacturing industries are sufficient to reverse this decline. Policy implications are drawn in the final part.

STRUCTURAL CHANGE IN THE U.S. ECONOMY IN THE 1970s

The argument that the relative wage and employment possibilities of workers worsened during the decade of the 1970s can be stated straightforwardly. It may be most useful to state each point in the argument as a proposition, suggesting the evidence that can be mustered in support of it and then drawing the implications.

The slowdown in investment in the 1970s led to slower growth in capital/labor ratios and in labor productivity in manufacturing and has given Japan an absolute advantage in several important industries.

Economists tend to hedge on the question of whether there has been an actual slowdown in investment. On the one hand, they cite the fact that nonresidential private fixed investment and investment in producers durable equipment both increased as a percentage of GNP during the 1970s.[1] At the same time, they agree that the average annual rate of growth in investment in real terms has slowed substantially since the 1950s. One typical estimate is that the average annual rate of growth in business fixed investment (in 1972 dollars) slowed from 5.9 percent for the 1955–66 period to 4.6 percent for 1966–73, declining to 3.8 percent for 1973–80 (U.S. Congress 1981: 17). There is general agreement that manufacturing industry has been adversely affected. While estimates of the severity of the slowdown in investment in manufacturing differ, one respected analysis of output and productivity growth in manufacturing found a decline in the average annual growth in capital inputs from 2.4 percent for 1958–65 to 1.8 percent for 1973–77 (Berndt 1980: 60–89).

The negative impact of slower growth in investment in manufacturing has been felt in deteriorating capital/labor ratios, especially in older, capital-intensive industries, and in a consequent decline in the rate of growth of labor productivity. Lester Thurow argues that the capital/labor ratio in the United States grew at about 3 percent per year from 1948 to 1965 but slowed after that as the baby boom increased the work force and investment failed to keep pace. Since 1978 the ratio has fallen at about 1 percent per year (Thurow 1980: 3–4). With a higher ratio of investment to GNP and lacking a baby boom, the Japanese have not only achieved higher rates of growth in the capital/labor ratio but appear to have attained absolutely higher capital/labor ratios than the United States in their most modern facilities. Thus, a Japanese study of leading U.S. and Japanese firms (that is, those that rank first in value added in their respective industries) concluded that Japanese businesses outranked their U.S. counterparts in 1977 in both capital/labor ratios and average labor productivity in four important industries in which Japan competes with the United States (ordinary steel, four-wheeled motor vehicles, auto parts, and chemicals) and equalled the Americans in yet another (electric machinery) (MITI 1980: 133).

American jobs in manufacturing are being lost as the United States thus relinquishes its competitive advantage in numerous industries including crude steel, rubber, passenger cars, zinc, cement, synthetic fibers, and a wide variety of apparel industries.

Steel, automobiles, and rubber are the durable goods, and textiles and apparel are the nondurable goods, in which production and employment are believed to have fared most poorly. Brookings economist Robert Crandall argues persuasively that the cost advantage in steel production has passed decisively to the industrializing nations of Latin America and eastern Asia (Crandall 1980). Raw materials costs are approximately equal for coastal facilities in all countries with deepwater ports, the cost of building new integrated steel mills varies narrowly in countries around the world, while sharply lower labor costs ($2 to $4 an hour in 1978 dollars) in the industrializing nations has placed the United States at a serious disadvantage. Ira Magaziner and Robert Reich agree that wage rates at one-eighth U.S. levels and productivity levels about one-half to two-thirds those of U.S. producers have given countries like Brazil and Korea a cost advantage in producing steel. They estimate that developing countries will produce 17 percent of world steel by 1984 (Magaziner and Reich 1983: 166). They argue, however, that the more serious threat to the viability of the U.S. steel industry came from the Japanese steel industry, which overtook the U.S. steel industry by improving its efficiency between 1966 and 1972. As a result of "large, well-directed capital investments and aggressive pursuit of export markets," Japanese mills have increased their cost advantage over U.S. producers despite a rise in Japanese wages relative to U.S. wages (Magaziner and Reich 1983: 159). While spending less on investment than the Japanese, U.S. industry did spend at a sizable rate. The problem, according to Magaziner and Reich, was that "U.S. steel companies made small incremental investments to obtain 'cheap' capacity rather than make the larger, more aggressive, and riskier investments that could have led to superior productivity overall" (Magaziner and Reich 1983: 161). The loss of competitive advantage in steel, they argue, is the result of strategic mistakes and management failure rather than an inevitable outcome due to the operation of the principle of comparative advantage. Despite this deterioration of the U.S. steel industry's competitive position, the Congressional Budget Office contends that there is no danger that the United States will lose the capacity to produce steel; but it points out that the level of steel produced by domestic mills will probably decline at an average rate of about 2 percent annually for the next two decades (Hearings before the House 1981: 302). This in fact is the rate at which the value of output in the steel industry has declined during the period 1966–78. Steel imports rose steadily from 4.7 percent of so-called apparent steel supply in 1961 to 21.8 percent in 1982, while total employment in the steel industry declined from about 572,000 in 1960 to 453,000 in 1979. Average monthly employment dropped to 391,000 in 1981, of which 286,000 were steel workers and 105,000 were salaried employees. During recession-wracked 1982 the average monthly total was reduced to 289,000, of which 198,000 were steel workers and 91,000 were salaried employees (American Iron and Steel Institute 1970: Table 1A; 1982: Tables 1A, 7; American Metal Market 1981: 169; 171). Many steel mills were closed between

1975 and 1982, and while steel is expected to benefit from economic recovery, neither output nor employment is likely to reach its 1979 level. The adoption of new technologies — continuous casting, direct reduction of iron ore, the electric arc furnace — and the shift to technologically advanced, specialized minimills mean that the recovery in employment will be slow. Assuming moderate growth in GNP, the Department of Labor's projection for steel industry employment is 435,000 by 1990 and 447,000 by 1995, but these estimates seem overly optimistic in light of the decline in steel capacity and the adoption of labor-saving technologies expected over this period (Personick 1983: 33, Table 5).

The Commerce Department report on the automobile industry, released in December 1981, confirmed the general perception that by the late 1970s domestic producers were no longer competitive with Japanese producers. The study attributed much of the unemployment in the industry — automobile-industry unemployment was estimated at 300,000 during 1980 with unemployment among auto suppliers and distributors reaching as high as 1 million — to this cause (*New York Times* 1981). Employment in auto manufacturing fell further as the recession worsened and as high interest rates and fuel prices caused new car sales to decline. Total sales are now recovering from recession levels. However, the U.S. auto industry lost a share of its domestic market to imports as a result of strategic errors by auto companies. Having guessed wrong on the shift in consumer demand toward smaller, fuel-efficient vehicles, the industry found itself in 1980 with an inappropriate capital stock and facing a long lead time for conversion to the production of reliable, efficient cars.

Sales of U.S. cars are now improving. However, the increase in the share of the U.S. market accounted for by imports as well as the introduction of industrial robots and foreign production of component parts of American cars mean that automobile employment will remain permanently below its 1978 peak of 1.03 million. Recent Department of Labor projections of employment by industry estimate that under conditions of moderate growth 834,000 workers will be employed in the manufacture of motor vehicles in 1990 and 860,000 in 1995.[2]

Textile and apparel imports in significant quantities began in the 1950s with the entrance of cotton textiles from Asia. The labor-intensive nature of many textile and apparel processes gave low-wage countries a comparative advantage. Capital investments in this industry *were* undertaken during the 1960s and 1970s, thus enabling domestic producers to offset this advantage to some extent. Real output more than doubled since 1957 with no increase in hours worked, however (Hearings before the House 1981: 302). Nevertheless, the U.S. share in world production has declined since 1969 in a wide variety of apparel products including suits, trousers, dresses, skirts, and shorts (United Nations, *Yearbook* 1978, 1979).

In addition to apparel, crude steel, and passenger cars, the U.S. share in world production declined in a number of other important industries during the 1970s. These include zinc, cement, plastics, synthetic rubber, synthetic fibers, and consumer durables like television sets and refrigerators (United Nations, *Yearbook* 1978, 1979). With the exception of synthetic fibers, Japan's share of world output of these products over the same time period (1969–78) has increased (Japanese Government 1970: Table 74; 1980: Table II-1-6). The extent to which these differences can be attributed to strategic differences in investment performance is difficult to ascertain, though this is clearly the case in steel and color television, which have been studied in detail (Magaziner and Reich 1983: Chs. 13, 14). In any event, the curtailment of employment growth in the older manufacturing sectors—and actual job loss in some industries—has serious consequences.

One result of curtailed employment growth has been a regional shift in manufacturing employment within the United States as jobs in steel, rubber, and automobiles have declined while jobs in electrical and electronic equipment (primarily semiconductors) and defense-related industries have increased.

Nationwide, employment increased 24.3 percent between 1968 and 1978 (prior to the recessions of 1980 and 1981–82) from approximately 76 million to 94 million workers. Manufacturing employment, however, grew by less than 700,000 workers, an increase of less than 4 percent. Very slow growth in manufacturing during this period was not the whole story; national figures hide regional differences. Factory employment increased in the south by more than 900,000, in the west by more than 300,000, and in the north central region west of the Mississippi by 200,000, while declining in the northeast by almost 800,000 jobs (Rones 1980: 12–19). This is not intended to suggest that the flight of northern industry to the south has been the major component of southern economic growth, though some textile, apparel, and electronic component firms did make the move. Regional shifts in manufacturing are due in large measure to the growth of employment in manufacturing industries already located in the south and west. Employment in the electronic components and accessories industry, which includes semiconductors and related devices, increased by nearly 250,000 between 1971 and 1981 and has grown slightly since then despite the recession, with much of the growth occurring in the west (*Employment and Earnings* 1971; 1981; 1983: Table B-2). On the other hand, the south had the smallest proportion of its durable goods employment in primary metals, transportation equipment, machinery, and fabricated metals, which have experienced secular declines exacerbated by the recent recessions. Back-to-back recessions reduced manufacturing employment by 2.5 million nationwide. Fifteen of the twenty manufacturing industry components experienced employment declines of 5 percent or more. The largest cutbacks were in nonelectrical machinery, primary metals, fabricated metals, and transportation equipment. Since 1979 these four groups have seen a combined decline of 1.3 million, accounting for over half of the overall manufacturing decline of 2.5 million (U.S. Department of Labor 1982). Most occurred outside the south.

Defense spending patterns have intensified the shift of manufacturing industry out of the northeast and north central regions and into the south and west. The south's share of military prime contract awards increased from 11 to 25 percent of the total, while the west's share increased from 16 to 31 percent between 1951 and 1976 (Rones 1980: 12-19). The development of aerospace and other high-technology industries in California and several southern states, and the nation's growing dependence on high-technology industries for defense needs, has been responsible for the direction of funds to these areas. Funding of the space program in the 1960s and subsequently had a similar effect. Research and development supported by defense and space program funds led to many commercially successful technological advances. Thus, regions that benefitted from such funds have become the manufacturing center for products that include computers, calculators, semiconductors, and scientific instruments (Rones 1980: 12-19).

The regional shift in total employment has been even more pronounced than in manufacturing. Population migration to the south and west resulted in the expansion of industries where demand is largely dependent on local population pressures — services, retail trade, construction of housing and other structures required for residential and industrial development, financial institutions, and transportation.

Total employment grew 24.3 percent nationwide between 1968 and 1978, but the increase was much above this in the south (32.6 percent) and west (39.7 percent), and much below this in the middle Atlantic (8.7 percent), New England (16.4 percent), and east north central (15.4 percent) (Rones 1980: 12–19). Manufacturing employment played a relatively small direct part in the expansion of both the south and the west. Most of the growth was registered in trade, services, financial institutions, transportation, and public utilities, all of which grew as a result of population shifts or because of the residential and commercial requirements attendant on such shifts. Construction, too, grew in the south and west as a result of rapid urban and suburban development, construction of interstate highways, as well as the need for industrial structures that accompanied growth in manufacturing (Rones 1980: 12–19).

The change in the industrial mix contributed to an above-average increase in employment in industries in which significant proportions (often a majority) of workers are female.

Although manufacturing employment grew slowly in the 1970s, three technology-related manufacturing industries registered substantial gains.[3] Approximately 600,000 new jobs were added between August 1971 and August 1982 in electronic computing equipment, communication equipment, and electronic components and accessories. Women accounted for more than one-fourth of the employees in electronic computing equipment, one-third of those in communication equipment, and one-half of those in electronic components and accessories ten years ago (at which time they held 5 percent of the jobs in steel and 9 percent of those in motor vehicles and equipment). Nearly half the new jobs added went to women, increasing the proportion held by women to 35 percent in electronic computing equipment and to 40 percent in communication equipment and leaving the proportion in electronic components and accessories unchanged.

The major employment increases, however, were registered in services and retail trade, primarily in business services, health services, and eating and drinking places. McDonald's fast-food network now employs more people than U.S. Steel (Tippet 1983). More than 6.3 million jobs were added between 1971 and 1981, approximately three-fifths of them going to women. While the recession reduced total employment between fall 1981 and fall 1982 by more than 2 million jobs, the employment of women increased by 100,000.

Important changes, thus, occurred during the 1970s in the structure of employment and output within manufacturing, and between manufacturing on the one hand and services and retail trade on the other. These changes shifted employment toward industries that employ women.

The change in the industrial mix has also resulted in a decline in employment in industries where organized labor is strong and an increase in employment in industries where it is weak.

The declines in manufacturing in the northeast and in steel and automobiles in the Great Lakes region are declines in industries in which union organization is strong. In automobiles, basic steel, and iron and steel foundries, virtually all nonsupervisory personnel are unionized. This is in contrast to union representation in retail trade and services, particularly in fast-food restaurants and health services, which covers only a small proportion of workers. Moreover, the regional shifts in employment have reduced the influence of unions. Among states in the southeast and the southwest, Alabama, Arkansas, Florida, Georgia, Louisiana, Mississippi, North Carolina, South Carolina, Tennessee, Texas, and Virginia are all right-to-work states, in which union representation is far below the national average (U.S. Department of Labor 1980: Table 166). In California, union membership is above the national average though the margin is much smaller than it was in 1970; but workers in the rapidly growing semiconductor industry are virtually unorganized. Nationwide, about 27 percent of semiconductor production workers are unionized; however, 96 percent of them work in the northeast (U.S. Department of Labor 1977: 5).

The overall effect of the change in industrial mix has been a decline in employment in regions and industries where wages are above the average in manufacturing and an increase in employment in regions and industries where wages are below that average.

This has had a direct effect on the wage growth of U.S. workers. Employment growth has been in jobs sex-stereotyped as female, without union coverage, and paying low wages. Thus, in September 1983 average hourly earnings in manufacturing were $8.90, while in eating and drinking places they were $4.29, in nursing homes and personal care facilities they were $5.10, in business services they were $7.40, and in electronic components and accessories they were $7.59. In motor vehicles and equipment, meanwhile, they were $12.34, and in primary metal they were \$11.31 (*Employment and Earnings* 1983: Table C–3).

The consequences go far beyond these direct effects, however. For workers whose pay is strongly affected by local labor-market conditions, location, degree of unionization, and presence or absence of high-paying manufacturing industries are all important factors influencing wages (U.S. Department of Labor 1979). This is especially true of office workers, including clerical and electronic data processing personnel, and of plant workers, including maintenance and unskilled plant workers. Thus, among workers in the seventy metropolitan areas studied by the Bureau of Labor Statistics, unskilled plant workers in Saginaw, Michigan, earned 41 percent above the average of the seventy areas, while those in San Antonio, Texas, earned 33 percent below that average. Office clerical and data processing workers were highest paid in Detroit, lowest paid in San Antonio; while skilled maintenance workers were highest paid in San Francisco, lowest paid in Greenville, South Carolina. This illustrates three points made in the study of the seventy areas:

1. Higher-paying jobs in plants and offices are found predominantly in the north central region and the west; lower paying jobs are in the south with the exception of clerical work in Atlanta and Washington.

2a. The degree of unionization in a region affects hourly earnings. High-paying regions for plant workers all had union coverage of 45 percent or more of those workers. Some had 80 percent or more. Low-paying regions for plant workers all had less than 45 percent of these workers covered.

2b. The degree of unionization in an industry affects the wages of all plant and office workers. All but one of the high-paying industries, machinery, are at least three-fourths unionized. Most low-paying industries are primarily nonunion. Only two, men's and women's suits and coats, are three-fourths unionized.

3. While the presence or absence of manufacturing employment in a metropolitan area does not affect levels of pay in the area, those areas in which a substantial proportion of manufacturing workers are in high-paying industries are generally high-paying areas. Conversely, wages in general are lower in areas where a substantial proportion of manufacturing workers are in low-paying industries.

Thus, the restructuring of employment in manufacturing and its relative decline will have indirect effects on the earnings profiles of workers, office workers in particular, who may not be directly involved.

Two major implications, each with serious ramifications for continued U.S. economic development, can be drawn from these changes. First, a process is already under way that is reducing the growth rate in average wages and eroding the relative wage position of U.S. workers. In recent years, American workers have experienced a slower rate of growth in compensation than workers in other developed countries.

The second implication is that a section of industrialized workers — primarily male, blue-collar workers in the older manufacturing centers — is becoming redundant as the U.S. moves toward an employment structure increasingly dominated by poorly paid jobs that are frequently sex-stereotyped as female. Blue-collar male workers displaced from their jobs by technology or a changing pattern of imports and exports are not likely to find their labor in demand in the expanding service and manufacturing industries of the south and west.

In 1965, U.S. manufacturing workers were earning $2.61 an hour, while those in West Germany earned $1.02, those in the United Kingdom earned $1.01, and those in Japan earned 45½ cents. U.S. workers were making 5.8 times as much as those in Japan and 2.6 times as much as their British or German counterparts (Japanese Government 1970: Table 74). If wages are adjusted for hours *worked* (rather than hours *earned*) in West Germany and the United States to make them compatible with those reported for Japan and the United Kingdom, the U.S. advantage over Japanese workers in 1965 is even greater. U.S. workers earned 6.1 times as much as those in Japan in 1965. By 1970 the wages of U.S. manufacturing workers were only 3.0 times those of Japanese workers and 2.0 times those of West German workers. By 1977 the wages of U.S. workers were just 1.6 times those of Japanese and 1.1 times those of West German workers. The comparison of manufacturing industry workers' wage per actual working hour (ratio of wages in the United States to wages in selected countries) is summarized in Table 1-1. While the Japanese figures cited in the table indicate that U.S. manufacturing workers enjoyed a slight advantage over Germany workers through most of the 1970s, data from the U.S. Department of Labor on hourly compensation for

Table 1–1. Comparison of Workers' Wages in Manufacturing per Actual Working Hour (ratio of wages in United States to wages in selected countries).

	United States Japan	United States West Germany	United States United Kingdom
1965	6.1	2.4	2.7
1970	3.9	2.0	2.8
1975	1.8	1.1	1.9
1976	1.8	1.2	2.2
1977	1.6	1.1	2.3

Source: Derived from Economic Planning Agency, Japanese Government, *Economic Survey of Japan 1977–1978,* Table 4–2–12.

Note: The exchange rate used in these comparisons is an annual average based on IMF, *International Financial Statistics.*

such production workers indicates that by the mid-1970s workers in West Germany and three other countries — Sweden, the Netherlands, and Belgium — were earning more than manufacturing production workers in the United States (Magaziner and Reich 1983: 37).

International comparisons of the average annual percentage of change in hourly compensation tell the same story: Since 1960 hourly compensation of U.S. employees in manufacturing has increased more slowly than in Japan, Canada, or any of the eight nations of Western Europe. Table 1–2 reports average annual percentage of change in hourly compensation in manufacturing for the United States and ten foreign countries.

The effect of slower growth in compensation on the relative standard of living of U.S. workers is difficult to measure, but the Japanese are clearly gaining. In 1969 a Japanese worker worked 57.7 minutes in order to purchase 100 grams of beef compared with 5.7 minutes for an American worker. By 1977 a worker in Tokyo worked 18.5 minutes for the same quantity of beef while a worker in New York worked 5.1 minutes (Japanese Government 1970: Table 77; 1978: Table 4–2–12). Infant mortality rates are often cited in comparisons of the overall quality of life in different countries. By this measure the United States has been slipping: It ranked sixth in 1955, eleventh in 1960, seventeenth in 1970, and eighteenth in 1977 with 14.1 infant deaths per thousand live births. By comparison, Japan ranked second in 1977 with an

Table 1–2. Average Annual Percent Change in Hourly Compensation in Manufacturing.

Country	1960–65	1965–70	1970–77
United States	3.7	6.0	6.1
Canada	3.9	8.3	7.9
Japan	13.1	15.4	15.8
Belgium	9.0	8.4	12.4
Denmark	9.0	9.2	12.5
France	9.5	8.6	10.9
West Germany	13.6	9.3	10.4
Italy	11.4	12.2	15.0
Netherlands	9.5	10.5	13.6
Sweden	7.6	6.9	11.6
United Kingdom	6.4	7.7	11.1
Ten foreign countries	8.7	9.2	11.6

Source. Arthur Neef, "Unit Labor Costs in the U.S. and 10 Other Nations, 1960–1971," *Monthly Labor Review* (July 1972), pp. 3–8; Keith Daly and Arthur Neef, "Productivity and Unit Labor Costs in 11 Industrial Countries, 1977," *Monthly Labor Review* (November 1978), pp. 11–17.gment>

infant mortality rate of 8.9. The U.S. rate has since declined to 11.7, but its relative position is unchanged. Infant deaths in Japan declined to 7.1, about the same as first-ranked Sweden (United Nations, *Demographia* 1978: 286–89; 1981: Table 9).

Not only are American manufacturing workers becoming relatively lower-paid, they face a less hospitable employment situation as a result of the decline in the share of manufacturing employment from 27 percent of employment in 1968 to 22 percent in 1978 and 21 percent in 1983 (*Employment and Earnings* various years: Table B–2). While manufacturing suffered substantial employment declines during the recent recession, the shift away from manufacturing employment and toward employment in service industries has been under way throughout the post–World War II era. Between 1947 and 1982 the number of service jobs increased from 5 to over 19 million, with most of the increase coming in the last decade (U.S. Department of Labor 1982). Much of this recent growth in service industries was in low-wage, short-hour employment preparing hamburgers and caring for the elderly and infirm. Employment prospects for male industrial workers are discouraging.

This is not the first time in recent U.S. economic history that economic development has displaced a labor-force group. While the employment difficulties of blue-collar workers in the Great Lakes and northeast regions of the country are structural, recent history cautions against dismissing these as temporary adjustment problems that the market can be relied on to resolve. The roots of black poverty can be traced to a previous round of economic development, to the displacement of agricultural workers by machinery, and to the subsequent failure of a growing economy to reabsorb significant numbers of those left jobless by changing labor requirements (Mandle 1978). The issue is not technological unemployment but structural unemployment: The improvements in technology that reduced labor requirements per unit of output in agriculture contributed to overall economic growth and to increases in total employment, while still leaving large numbers of displaced workers and their descendants outside the economic mainstream. The evidence suggests that another round of this process may be underway. Like the black agricultural workers after World War II, displaced manufacturing workers in the industrial belt that arches from St. Louis through the Great Lakes region and into the northeast find that their labor is redundant. Their wives and daughters may find employment in low-paying jobs in the sunbelt. Prospects for the men, however, are far less certain. In the absence of U.S. industrial policy it is quite possible that the ranks of the chronically unemployed will expand as wider use of programmable automation technologies (such as robots) and imported components make it likely that a large number of the 2.5 million manufacturing jobs lost since employment in this sector peaked at 21 million in 1979 will never be recovered.

HIGH TECH IN THE 1980s: A SOLUTION TO PROBLEMS OF ECONOMIC DISLOCATION?

Economists tend to be sanguine about this loss of jobs, relying on the possibilities inherent in technological innovation to provide employment growth.[4] It is possible that they are right. The introduction of a major new technology does not simply create some jobs while destroying others. Often it serves as the basis for economic growth, raising average annual rates of growth in both labor productivity and total output. Moreover, periods of rapid technological advance have not usually been periods of high unemployment; rather, they have been periods in which new sources of employment emerged and total employment expanded rapidly. It may happen, therefore, that despite the shifts in distribution of workers by industry and region, real wages will increase along with technologically induced increases in labor productivity, and virtually all of the labor resources released from the production of steel, rubber, automobiles, and other industrial products will find comparably stable and remunerative employment in the production of new commodities and services.

Alternatively, one could postulate a darker view of economic affairs in which technology advances but the structural employment problems persist. The savings necessary to finance the expansion of technologically innovative industries (or processes in older industries) could come not from an increase in the percentage of GNP that is voluntarily saved but from slower growth in compensation of production workers and, hence, in the ratio of consumption to output. Moreover, a significant proportion of male, blue-collar workers (and perhaps their sons as well) displaced from the smokestack industries could remain outside the economic mainstream for years, finding intermittent work in low-paying jobs, despite the overall increase in employment. One might even speculate that racism will once again intrude so that the group most adversely affected will be black males, who comprised one-seventh of the work force in motor vehicles and primary-metals industries in the 1970s (U.S. Department of Labor 1979).

It would be presumptuous to attempt a definitive answer to the question of what the future holds. The enormity of such an exercise can be grasped by imagining an attempt to predict the dynamic economic implications of the telephone in 1886, ten years after its invention, or of the automobile in 1915. Here I shall attempt a more modest task: an examination of the available evidence in order to discern the relationship between high tech and employment over the next ten years.

High technologies are popularly identified with the technologies of information processing, communications, semiconductors, robots, and biotechnology. A more precise definition can be obtained by reserving the high-tech designation for industries in which R&D expenditures as a percentage of total investment and/or the level of scientists, engineers, and technical employees is at least twice the average for all U.S. industries. This definition encompasses 32 manufacturing in-dustries—including computers, communication equipment, electronic components, laboratory instruments, aircraft, space vehicles, drugs, industrial chemicals, and plastics—as well as such service industries as computer programming, data processing, and research laboratories.[5]

Surprisingly, in view of the general perception that high technology has been a major source of employment growth, high-tech manufac-turing industries did not fare better than other manufacturing indus-tries in providing new jobs for U.S. workers in the last decade. Be-tween the cyclical peak years 1969 and 1979 employment in industries with above-average R&D expenditures grew 4.5 percent, while em-ployment in industries with high levels of scientific, engineering, and technical personnel grew 2.0 percent (Tomaskovic-Devey and Miller 1983: 60). These growth rates do not differ much from employment growth in all manufacturing, which measured 4.2 percent over the decade, and compare unfavorably with the growth of total employ-ment, which increased 27.6 percent. It should be noted that a subset of the high-tech manufacturing industries with both high R&D ex-penditures and high levels of scientific, engineering, and technical workers did experience a 26.3 percent growth rate. However, these industries together added only 444,000 new jobs, 2 percent of the 19 million jobs created during the 1969–79 decade (Tomaskovic-Devey and Miller 1983: 60).

High-tech service-sector industries exhibit a rapid rate of employ-ment growth, but the small size of the sector limits the total number of jobs created. Thus, the computer and data processing services in-dustry, largest of the high-tech service industries, has added only about 300,000 jobs since 1969 (*Employment and Earnings* various years: Table B–2). The growth of clerical employment in this industry is slowing as technological advances such as on-line processing and optical character recognition spread.

Looking to the future, Data Resources Inc. estimates that the number of new high-tech jobs created between 1983 and 1993 will be 730,000 to 1 million, less than half the jobs lost in manufacturing be-tween 1979 and 1982 ("America Rushes to High Tech for Growth" 1983: 85). Rapidly rising productivity as the high-tech companies automate, often using their own products to do so, combined with the small size of the high-tech sector constrains the ability of this sector to provide employment. Moreover, assembly jobs in high-tech industries are subject to competition from low-wage labor, particularly in Third World countries like Malaysia, Taiwan, the Philippines, and Mexico, where assembly workers earn as little as 50 cents an hour. Thus, Atari decided in 1983 to move 1,700 assembly jobs from California to Asia, Apple Computer and Wang Laboratories have turned to the Far East for substantial preliminary assembly work on computer components, Hewlett–Packard predicts that its overseas work force will grow faster than its U.S. work force when major plants in Mexico and elsewhere are completed. These jobs follow others implanting metal pins into computer chips for high-tech companies such as Intel and National Semiconductor, which moved to Asia long ago.

Furthermore, the number of additional jobs in high-tech manufacturing industries will, in part, be offset by the number of jobs lost to robots and other programmable automation technologies in traditional industries such as steel and autos. The W.E. Upjohn Institute for Employment Research estimates that the number of robots working in the automobile industry will increase from 2,400 to between 15,000 and 25,000 by the end of the decade. It is expected that 3,000 to 5,000 jobs will be created producing and maintaining the robots, while the robots will replace 30,000 to 50,000 auto workers (Hunt and Hunt 1983: Tables 2–10, 3–1, 4–4).

While employment growth in high-tech user industries in the manufacturing sector is thus expected to be negatively affected by automation, the impact on employment growth in high-tech user industries in the service sector is uncertain. European observers expect the cumulative effects of information-processing technologies and office automation techniques to substantially reduce the growth of employment in the office industries — insurance and finance. Comparable studies for the United States do not exist. There is some evidence from aggregate data on the insurance industry that the introduction of technology between 1960 and 1978 altered the distribution of occupations within the industry but has not slowed the rate of aggregate employment growth. To a large extent this was due to the introduction of new services. In part it was due to the fact that productivity growth took the form of better performance and higher-quality services rather than a reduction in labor requirements. Widespread use of office automation technologies has slowed the growth of clerical employment substantially, but the implications for overall employment growth are difficult to evaluate.

The analysis of the previous section focused on aggregate employment possibilities. To discuss the qualitative aspects of the new jobs' being created — within the high-tech sector and downstream within traditional industries that utilize high-tech products and services — requires that we turn our attention to how labor markets are structured.

It is evident that the U.S. labor market is segmented into a primary labor-market segment in which most of the "good" or "acceptable" jobs are located and a secondary labor-market segment in which most of the "poor" jobs are to be found. A further distinction can be made between autonomous primary-segment jobs (professionals like doctors, lawyers, and professors or craftsmen like plumbers, electricians, and carpenters) and subordinate primary-segment jobs (mail carriers, insurance adjustors, steel workers, and so forth). The difference between a subordinate primary-segment job and secondary-segment job is sometimes based on worker skills and sometimes on non–skill-related job characteristics. The better jobs are those in which the employer values steadiness and low turnover and is willing to reward tenure on the job with promotions and higher pay, or in which the employee is represented by a union that has won decent wages, a pay scale that rewards seniority, and protection against arbitrary treatment. Many of the subordinate primary-segment jobs available for male workers are to be found in the goods-producing sector of the economy, where workers have more union representation than in other sectors of the economy.

The growth of the high-tech sector has provided both good jobs and poor ones. Producer services (advertising, architecture, law, management consulting, computer and data processing, financial) now account for 19 percent of GNP, and high-tech firms in this industry have been a major source of good jobs. This observation is confirmed by the Bureau of Labor Statistics (BLS) study of the computer and data processing services industry (SIC 7372 and SIC 7374), which provides employment primarily for professional/technical workers and office clerical workers.[6] Professional workers are engaged in work at a level that requires knowledge equivalent to that acquired through completion of a four-year college course, regardless of whether they hold a degree. Technical workers are engaged in technical work utilizing theoretical knowledge acquired through formal post–high-school training or through equivalent on-the-job training. Approximately 37 percent of employees in this industry are professional or technical workers. Of these, one-fifth are computer systems analysts, one-fifth are computer operators, and one-eighth are computer programmers. The remainder are employed as computer data librarians, electronics technicians, and peripheral equipment operators. Most of these employees are male, with the majority of women analysts, programmers, and operators in the lowest classification in each of these occupations. Average salaries for computer systems analysts ranged from $400 to $460 a week in March 1978 in most regions. Computer programmers averaged $262 to $326, and operators earned $181 to $233. Electronic technicians accounted for less than 1 percent of the workers and earned $250 to $300. Office clerical employees account for 32 percent of employment. With the exception of some of the accounting clerks and messengers, they are virtually all women. Two-fifths of them are key-entry operators earning $150 to $205 (Class A) or $135 to $175 (Class B). Personal secretaries are not numerous, but they are highly paid in comparison with other clerical workers. In the highest category they earn between $195 and $230.

The study of wages in this industry suggests that high-tech employment, like employment in the United States generally, is two-tiered. The growth of high-tech service-sector employment has meant an increase in professional, technical, and managerial jobs at the top, but it has also meant an increase in clerical, sales, and nonprofessional service jobs at the bottom.

It's not news that most jobs in high-tech manufacturing industries are not high-tech jobs, but it may be surprising to learn that many are not even very good jobs. BLS surveyed the semiconductor industry, which currently employs 242,600 workers.[7] Of the workers employed in this industry, approximately 58 percent are production (plant) workers, and 14 percent are office (nonplant) workers. The remaining 28 percent are administrative, executive, professional, and technical employees who are "used as a separate work force on the firm's own properties." Six production occupations are included in the study: assemblers (class A, B, or C); crystal processors (crystal coaters, cutters, finishers, growers); inspectors and testers (class A, B, or C); maintenance (electricians, machinists, general, pipefitters); janitors, porters, and cleaners; laborers, material handlers. More than 60 percent of the plant workers are in the first three occupations, most of them women. Two office occupations were included in the survey — computer operators and engineering technicians classes 1 through 5 — most of whom are male. These account for 40 percent of the office employees; the others are employed as general office clerks and secretaries.

Table 1–3. Production and Office Workers in the Semiconductor Industry.

Occupation	Percentage Female	Average Hourly Earnings	Occupational Distribution (percentage)
Assemblers	92.0	$4.08	45.1
Crystal processors	73.2	4.18	2.5
Inspector and testers	88.1	4.84	7.0
Maintenance	0.0	6.50–8.48	2.0
Janitors, porters, and cleaners	13.6	4.34	0.9
Laborers, material handling	18.7	4.14	0.5
Computer operators	49.6	5.97	0.4
Engineering technicians	12.3	6.80	6.8
Class V	0.0	8.41	2.4

Source: Bureau of Labor Statistics, *Industry Wage Survey: Semiconductors*, Bulletin 2020 (September 1977).

Percentage of females and average hourly earnings for each occupation studied are summarized in Table 1-3. (Data are for 1977, when the study was done.) Average hourly earnings of plant workers ranged from $3.38 for crystal coaters (90 percent female) to $7.94 for maintenance pipefitters (100 percent male).

A wage below $6.00 an hour placed a U.S. worker in the bottom third of the income distribution in 1977, while a wage above $9.50 placed that person in the top third. On that criterion, 28 percent of the jobs in this industry were good jobs at the top of the distribution, 9.2 percent were in the middle, while 62.8 percent were low-paying jobs. Low-wage production jobs in the industry are poor in other respects as well: They are tedious and they expose workers to dangerous occupational health hazards.

If these two industries — one in goods production and one in services — prove to be at all representative, then it seems evident that the new high-tech industries will not provide alternative employment opportunities in the 1980s for male blue-collar workers displaced from the older industries. Apart from the limited number of aggregate jobs produced by the high-tech sector, skill requirements in industries in this sector do not correspond to the skills of the displaced workers. Thus, most of the jobs held by male workers in the computer and data processing services industry require two to four years of technical training. In semiconductors the fact that male plant workers (skilled and unskilled) make up less than 5 percent of the work force creates a problem. Moreover, male workers with middle-level skills are not represented in this industry at all.

What is striking about the motor vehicles and parts, basic iron and steel, and iron and steel foundries industries is the large number of occupations in every skill category among plant jobs. The significance of having a wide variety of jobs available is the wide variety of skills and skill levels that can be accommodated in employment in these industries. In addition, most of the plant occupations do not require formal schooling beyond high school, and the skilled trades can often be learned through apprenticeship or other training programs. This contrasts markedly with the two high-tech industries for which data on occupations and wages are available.

A comparison of the current occupational profile of U.S. robot manufacturers with the occupational structure of the motor vehicle and equipment industry and with all manufacturing (presented in Table 1–4) provides further confirmation of structural dislocation. In robot manufacturing, two-thirds of the jobs are for professional or technical workers, administrators, salespersons, and clerical workers, while in motor vehicles about four-fifths of the jobs are for craft workers, operators, and laborers.

Changes in technology combined with the shift to service-sector employment are eroding the middle of the job distribution, making the labor market more starkly two-tiered with good jobs at the top, poor jobs at the bottom, and shrinking opportunity in the middle. The best jobs and the poorest jobs are both expanding in number. It is the young people who complete high school and then enter the world of work who will find it difficult to find worthwhile jobs in this emerging work environment. Well-paid, stable employment in basic manufacturing industry for men and traditional clerical employment for women filled the middle of the occupational distributions for male and female high school graduates, respectively. The contraction of the middle of the opportunity structure is a treacherous problem whose dimensions will become clear by the end of this decade.

Table 1–4. Current U.S. Occupational Profiles: Robot Manufacturing, Motor Vehicles and Equipment, All Manufacturing, and All Industries.

Occupation	Employment Distribution (percentage)			
	Robot Manufacturing	Motor Vehicles and Equipment	All Manufacturing	All Industries
Engineers	23.7	2.3	2.8	1.2
Engineering technicians	15.7	1.2	2.2	1.4
All other professional and technical workers	4.2	2.4	4.0	13.5
Managers, officials, proprietors	6.8	3.3	5.9	8.1
Sales workers	3.4	0.5	2.2	6.3
Clerical workers	13.9	6.2	11.3	19.9
Skilled craft and related workers	8.4	20.8	18.5	11.8
Semiskilled metal-working operatives	4.2	15.8	7.2	1.7
Assemblers and all other operatives	19.0	38.6	36.2	13.1
Service workers	0.0	2.8	2.0	15.8
Laborers	0.7	6.1	7.7	6.0
Farmers and farm workers	0.0	0.0	0.0	1.0
Total	100.0	100.0	100.0	100.0

Source: Hunt and Hunt, *Human Resource Implications of Robotics*, Table 4–2. Based on data from 1980 OES survey provided by the Office of Economic Growth and Employment Projections, Bureau of Labor Statistics, U.S. Department of Labor, Washington, D.C. Columns may not add to total due to rounding.

POLICY IMPLICATIONS

Public and private programs to upgrade training and education and to provide for retraining are an essential and welcome means of reducing the severity of this problem. There is evidence to suggest that an active labor-market policy—providing job search, employment counseling, and relocation services and establishing retraining programs for workers displaced from jobs in the primary labor-market segment, as well as training for unemployed workers in the secondary labor-market segment—can be effective in reducing structural employment. But such programs are inadequate, by themselves, to eliminate the emerging structural employment problems. To solve the structural problems, programs to improve the education and training of workers will have to be linked to programs to transform the characteristics of poor jobs and to new initiatives in macroeconomic employment policy. The sex-stereotyping of jobs, which is deeply embedded in both labor-market structures and popular culture, increases the difficulty of adjustment to the changing industrial base. It will have to be overcome through the intense application of antidiscrimination policies. Faith in the job-creating potential of high-tech to solve the emerging employment problems—higher rates of unemployment and job growth in low-wage industries—appears to be unwarranted.

NOTES

1. The Department of Commerce reports that fixed investment increased from 9.5 percent of GNP in 1950 and 1960 to 10.5 percent in 1970 and 11.3 percent in 1980.
2. Automobile employment in 1978 from *Employment and Earnings* (1982); projections to 1990 and 1995 from Personick (1983: Table 5).
3. Except where noted, all data in this section are from *Employment and Earnings* (1971, 1981, 1983; Tables B-2, B-3).
4. A less compelling argument advanced by economists is that exchange-rate adjustments will be able to resolve the problems described above in the text. The objection can be summarized as follows: To the extent that a pessimistic outlook hinges on a loss of comparative advantage in durable goods manufacturing, freely floating exchange rates and the resulting appropriate depreciation of the dollar will restore the trade balance by making some U.S. goods sufficiently cheap abroad that

other countries' imports of them will increase. This is not a fruitful line of reasoning. First, this scenario depends on the highly questionable assumption that the monetary authorities will allow a sharp devaluation of the dollar, an assumption not supported by past experience. Moreover, it would require an about-face on domestic monetary policy, since the high U.S. interest rates support the value of the dollar in international exchange. Still another consideration is the effect that a sharp devaluation of the dollar would have on oil prices and/or oil exports in view of the fact that OPEC oil exports are denominated in dollars. Dollar devaluation would reduce the price of OPEC oil in the rest of the world while leaving it unchanged in the United States, thus reducing the relative cost of producing output in energy-intensive industries outside the United States and worsening the competitive position of American industries in world markets. Of course, a sharply lower real price for oil in terms of international purchasing power is likely to lead the OPEC countries to attempt to increase the dollar price of oil. If successful, this would jolt the U.S. economy with yet another energy shock. Finally, a dollar devaluation, even if it increases total U.S. exports, will not resolve problems caused by the United States' loss of competitive advantage in a number of key industries. Magaziner and Reich discuss this point at length (1983: chs. 5–16).

5. The thirty-six industries that fit this definition of high tech, identified by SIC code, are: 2831, 2833, 2834, 3572, 3573, 3574, 3576, 3579, 3661, 3662, 3671, 3672, 3673, 3674, 3675, 3676, 3677, 3678, 3679, 3721, 3724, 3728, 3761, 3764, 3769, 3811, 3822, 3823, 3824, 3825, 3829, 3832, 7372, 7374, 7379, 7391.

6. Administrative, executive, and supervisory personnel (including working supervisors) are excluded from the survey. All data are from U.S. Department of Labor, Bureau of Labor Statistics (1978).

7. Current employment is given in *Employment and Earnings* (1982: Table B–2). All other data are from U.S. Department of Labor, Bureau of Labor Statistics (1978).

REFERENCES

American Iron and Steel Institute, *Annual Statistical Report* (Philadelphia: American Iron and Steel Institute, 1970 (Table 1A), 1982 (Tables 1A, 7).

American Metal Market, *1981 Metal Statistics* (New York: American Metal Market, 1981), pp. 169, 171.

"America Rushes to High Tech for Growth," *Business Week* (March 28, 1983): 85.

Berndt, Ernst R., "Energy Price Increases and the Productivity Slowdown in United States Manufacturing," *The Decline in Productivity Growth* (Boston: Federal Reserve Bank of Boston, June 1980), pp. 60–89.

Crandall, Robert W., "The Economics of the Current Steel Crisis in OECD Member Countries," *Steel in the 80s* (Paris: Organization for Economic Cooperation and Development, 1980).

Hearings before the House Committee on Energy and Commerce, *Capital Formation and Industrial Policy,* 97th Cong., 1st Sess. (July 1981), p. 302.

Hunt, H. Allan, and Timothy L. Hunt, *Human Resource Implications of Robotics* (Kalamazoo, Mich.: W.E. Upjohn Institute for Employment Research, 1983), Tables 2–10, 3–1, 4–4.

Japanese Government, *Economic Survey of Japan 1979–1980* (Tokyo: Japan Times, Ltd., 1980), Tables II–1–2, II–1–6.

———, *Economic Survey of Japan 1977–1978* (Tokyo: Japan Times, Ltd., 1978), Table 4–2–12.

———, *Economic Survey of Japan 1976–1977* (Tokyo: Japan Times, Ltd., 1977), Table II–2–6.

———, *Economic Survey of Japan 1969–1970* (Tokyo: Japan Times, Ltd., 1970), Tables 74, 76, 77.

Magaziner, Ira C., and Robert B. Reich, *Minding America's Business* (New York: Vintage Books, 1983).

Mandle, Jay R., *The Roots of Black Poverty* (Durham, N.C.: Duke University Press, 1978).

MITI, *Business Analysis of World Enterprises,* cited in Japanese Government, Economic Planning Agency, *Economic Survey of Japan 1979–1980* (Tokyo: Japan Times, Ltd., 1980), Table II–1–7.

New York Times, December 2, 1981. Clyde H. Farnsworth, "Key U.S. Report Details Woes of Auto Industry," page D1, column 1.

Personick, Valerie A., "The Job Outlook through 1995: Industry Output and Employment," *Monthly Labor Review* 106 (November 1983): 33, Table 5.

Rones, Philip L., "Moving to the Sun: Regional Job Growth, 1968 to 1978," *Monthly Labor Review* 103 (March 1980): 12–19.

Thurow, Lester, "Death by a Thousand Cuts," *New York Review of Books* 28 (December 17, 1981): 3–4.

Tippett, W. Paul, "Put Heat on Japan" *New York Times,* March 10, 1983, Page A27, Col. 2.

Tomaskovic-Devey, Donald, and S.M. Miller, "Can High-Tech Provide the Jobs?," *Challenge* (May/June 1983): 60.

United Nations, *Demographic Yearbook 1981* (New York: Statistical Office of the United Nations, 1981), Table 9.

———, *Demographic Yearbook 1978* (New York: Statistical Office of the United Nations, 1978), pp. 286–89.

————, *Yearbook of Industrial Statistics 1979* (New York: Department of Social and Economic Affairs and Statistical Office of the United Nations, 1979).

————, *Yearbook of Industrial Statistics 1978* (New York: Department of Social and Economic Affairs and Statistical Office of the United Nations, 1978).

U.S. Congress, Joint Committee on Taxation, *Analysis of Proposals for Depreciation and Investment Tax Credit Revisions,* pt. 1 (Washington, D.C., May 1981), p. 17.

U.S. Department of Labor, Bureau of Labor Statistics, *Annual Earnings and Employment Patterns of Private Nonagricultural Employees, 1973–1975,* bulletin 2031 (Washington, D.C.: U.S. Government Printing Office, 1979).

————, *Employment and Earnings* (Washington, D.C.: U.S. Government Printing Office, various years).

————, *Handbook of Labor Statistics,* bulletin 2070 (Washington, D.C.: U.S. Government Printing Office, December 1980), Table 166.

————, *Industry Wage Survey: Computers and Data Processing Services,* bulletin 2028 (Washington, D.C.: U.S. Government Printing Office, March 1978).

————, *Industry Wage Survey: Semiconductors,* bulletin 2020 (Washington, D.C.: U.S. Government Printing Office, September 1977).

————, *Middle Atlantic Region News Release* (December 8, 1982).

————, *Profiles of Occupational Pay,* bulletin 2037 (Washington, D.C.: U.S. Government Printing Office, 1979).

2 AUTOMATION AND ITS EFFECT ON EMPLOYMENT AND INCOME

Faye Duchin

The Agricultural Revolution of the tenth millennium B.C.
and the Industrial Revolution of the eighteenth century A.D.
...created deep breaches in the continuity of the historical
process. With each one of these two Revolutions, a 'new
story' begins, a new story dramatically and completely alien
to the previous one.

C.M. Cipolla

[The revolution based on the computer] is going to be the
biggest technological revolution men have ever known, far
more intimately affecting men's daily lives, and, of course,
far quicker, than either the agricultural transformation in
Neolithic times or the early industrial revolution which made
the present shape of the United States.... There was some
excuse for our ancestors' not foreseeing the effects of the
first industrial revolution. There is no excuse this time....
[I]t is their duty [of the Congress and of Parliament] not
to be supine, not to be just carried along dumbly by the
technological tide.

C.P. Snow

Millions of home computers are in use in the world today, as well as
hundreds of thousands of large and small business computers and
several dozen so-called supercomputers capable of executing hundreds
of millions of operations a second. Originally conceived to carry out

This chapter draws in part on results of work supported by the National Science Foundation
research award number PRA80–12844. Any opinions, findings, conclusions, or recommendations expressed in this chapter are those of the author and do not necessarily reflect the views of
New York University or the National Science Foundation.

49

more quickly and accurately computations that would otherwise be done by hand, today's electronic computers—provided with specialized hardware accessories (like robots), software, and databases—can run machine tool factories nearly unmanned, are central to numerous medical diagnostic and information systems, and are used to teach principles of physics to very young children.

While computers had been anticipated by Babbage early in the nineteenth century and even by Pascal, modern, digital, electronic computing dates only from the mid-1940s and can with certainty be said to be in its infancy. As its power and versatility are extended and its real price continues to fall, the computer in its large and growing number of configurations will have a profound effect on our working and nonworking lives through the automation of human physical and mental labor and the changes that this automation will in turn bring about.

The outcome of the proliferation of computers within our society is a story that will be told by future generations. Yet the computer itself provides us now with the computational capability required for a concrete and systematic inquiry into some of its consequences over the next few decades. This chapter conducts such an inquiry into the potential effects of computer-based automation on employment and outlines the issues that need to be addressed in formulating present and future government policy on employment and income.

Computer-based automation has the potential to directly affect every type of work in every sector of the economy, in each case in a manner that is specific to the operations being performed. The prospects for employment and income will be different for workers in the machine tool industry than for those who deliver health care, different for clerical workers than for machinists. Both the specific and also the global effects of automation can be assessed analytically only through a detailed representation of the structure of production in each sector and of the relations among sectors. The perspective provided by a detailed, integrated analytic framework extends the frontier beyond which analysis of questions about the future must yield to pure speculation.

The first section of this chapter describes a model of the national economy in which it is possible to represent specific hypothetical instances of future technological change and compute the effects of such changes on the size and occupational composition of employment and on earnings of the labor force. This framework is then used in the next section to explore the likely range of consequences of technological change. Several aspects of the experience of recent decades are analyzed in the following two sections. An initial assessment of the future impacts of computer-based automation on employment is presented in the next-to-last section, and policy implications associated with different possible future outcomes are described in the final section.

THE CONCEPTUAL FRAMEWORK: A DYNAMIC INPUT/OUTPUT MODEL OF THE U.S. ECONOMY

At any given point in time, the U.S. economy can be described as a set of interrelated sectors producing goods and services, and each sector can be characterized by an average process of production and a common principal output. The plants, mills, and other business establishments, at which production in each sector takes place, employ a specific mix of machines, tools, and human labor to transform a particular combination of purchased inputs (produced by the other sectors) into its characteristic output.

At any given time several distinct technologies or production processes are typically in use at different establishments within a sector or even at a single plant. The average combination of inputs that characterizes the sector corresponds to the different input requirements of alternative technologies and the weight with which each alternative operates in the national economy. Technological change involves a change in these weights, where typically the newest technologies are progressively phased in (increased weight) and the oldest eliminated (decreased weight). Of course, technological change also involves the emergence of new alternatives that were not previously available. Portions of each sector's stock of plant and equipment are periodically replaced, and any net additions to each sector's capital stock make it possible to increase output in the future. The technological requirements for the replacement of existing capital (in order to maintain current production capacity) are in large part dictated by the mix of investment goods already in place and to this extent reflect the technologies already in use. Some modernization also takes place; this involves the incorporation of newly available technologies into existing plant. However, the new technologies are typically reflected first in the newly produced capital goods that are installed expressly for the expansion of existing capacity and then in the occupational composition of the labor force that works with the new capital equipment and in the composition of the other inputs to production. At each point in time, the unit price of each sector's output covers the cost of all its inputs, including but not limited to the wage bill and the cost of capital as well as profits and rents, per unit of output. In addition, total national income (that is, wages plus property-type income) must cover national expenditures for personal and government consumption and new investment.

The national economy is described in terms of these interrelationships by the two matrix equations of the standard dynamic input/output model set out in Leontief (1970),[1] with extensions described in Duchin and Szyld (1984)[2] and a third equation formulated here to represent the relations between wages and profits on the one hand and consumption and investment on the other. The parameters and variables of the three equations and the equations themselves have a concrete interpretation that is described in nontechnical terms below. The basic model in its simplest mathematical form is presented in Table 2–1. The first matrix equation consists of n individual equations.

Table 2–1. Parameters, Variables, and Equations of the Dynamic Input/Output Model.

Parameters of the Model

A_t	$n \times n$	inputs on current account per unit of output
B_t	$n \times n$	capital stock requirements per unit increase of output
L_t	$m \times n$	labor requirements per unit of output
r_t	scalar	money rate of interest (cost of capital)
w_t	$m \times 1$	wage rates (by occupation)
π_t	$n \times 1$	rates of profit

Variables of the Model

x_t	$n \times 1$	sector outputs
y_t	$n \times 1$	final consumption (excluding investment)
e_t	$m \times 1$	employed labor force
p_t	$n \times 1$	sectoral prices

Equations of the Model

(1) $x_t = A_t x_t + B_{t+1}(x_{t+1} - x_t) + y_t$

(1') $e_t = L_t x_t$

(2) $p_t = A_t' p_t + [(1 + r_{t-1})B_t' p_{t-1} - B_{t+1}' p_t] + L_t' w_t + \pi_t$

(3) $w_t' L_t x_t + r_{t-1} p_{t-1}' B_t x_t + \pi_t x_t = p_t' y_t + (p_t' B_{t+1} x_{t+1} - p_{t-1}' B_t x_t)$

They are called physical balance equations because each describes the distribution of a particular sector's output among all the sectors of the national economy that use this output. The physical balance equation for each sector states that output produced by that sector in the current time period is absorbed in one or more of three ways: as intermediate inputs required by that or other sectors for their own production, as investment in additional productive capacity that will be used in that or other sectors in the following period, and as final consumption.

Given the initial conditions of the economy, the deliveries of goods and services that must be made to final consumers in the first and subsequent time periods, and the technologies that will be used to produce those goods and services, these balance equations can be solved simultaneously for the level of output that each sector will need to produce in each subsequent period. The model can also be solved for the total (direct and indirect) labor requirements by occupation for the national economy in subsequent time periods.

The second matrix equation consists of n individual price equations, each of which describes the price of a unit of output of the corresponding sector in terms of the costs of its inputs. The individual cost components include the cost of intermediate inputs required per unit of output, the cost of capital required per unit increase in output, and the costs of other inputs contributing to value added, which in this basic statement of the model are limited to the wage bill per unit of output and the rate of profit. The wage bill per unit of output is calculated by multiplying the labor requirements to produce a unit of output (per year), for each individual occupation, by the average annual wage for that occupation. The cost of fixed capital for each sector, during a given time period, is computed as if the entire capacity required by that sector to produce its current output is purchased at the end of the preceding period and sold off at the end of the current period, having been revalued in terms of replacement technology and prices. A rate of interest, which can also be interpreted as the opportunity cost of the capital stock, is charged on the value of the stock.

The final equation of the model is a balance equation that states that the wage bill, the interest on capital, and profits will necessarily cover outlays for consumption and for increases in the stock of capital. This is a single equation (not a matrix equation) because the equality of value added and final demand must hold for the economy as a whole but not in general on a sectoral basis. (For example, wages earned by auto workers will not be spent exclusively on automobiles, and part of the wages paid out in other sectors will be used to purchase automobiles.) The analytic usefulness of this equation in conjunction with the matrix equations of the dynamic input/output model will become apparent in the next section.

To examine the future impacts of automation, the model can be used over a time horizon, conveniently measured in years, that begins in the past or present and that extends to the future, let us say from 1980 through 2000. Year by year over the specified time horizon, the changing prevalence of existing technologies and the phasing in of newly available technologies are represented by changing the values of the parameters or technical coefficients of the model. These technical coefficients are the individual entries in the matrices appearing in the equations of the model. They govern

1. The inputs of intermediate products required per unit of each sector's output (A matrix);
2. Requirements of each type of capital good used by a sector per unit increase in the sector's output (B matrix); and
3. Requirements of each type of labor employed by a sector per unit of its output (L matrix).

Table 2–2 illustrates the way in which presumed future technological changes are directly reflected in the technical coefficients. The first column of Table 2–2 identifies specific hypothetical changes in the process for producing automobiles in 1990 compared to 1980, and the second column describes the corresponding changes in technical coefficients.

Specialized sector studies based on the technical literature and direct survey are required to estimate the actual magnitudes of coefficient changes for emerging technologies and the rates at which they will displace existing technologies in future years.[3] Within the framework of the economywide model, the output required to deliver a specific quantity of the automobiles to final demand in a given year will reflect not only the technological changes experienced directly in the automobile sector (suggested in the table) but also the analogous changes in all other sectors that directly or indirectly provide inputs to the automobile sector.

Table 2–2.   Schematic Input/Output Representation of Technological Change in the Automobile Industry.

Nature of Hypothetical Technological Change between 1980 and 1990	Corresponding Changes in Technical Coefficients[a]
Use of new materials	Increase in coefficients governing the use of certain intermediate inputs (e.g., plastics), decline in others
Increased use of robots for painting	Increase in capital coefficient governing the use of robots Decline in labor coefficient governing the use of painters Decline in intermediate coefficient governing the use of paint (assuming more efficient use of paint)
Increased use of computers for design	Increase in capital coefficient governing the use of computers Decline in labor coefficient governing the use of draftsmen Increase in labor coefficient governing the use of computer programmers

[a] The technical coefficients appear in the A, B, and L matrices of the model. Inputs and outputs are assumed to be measured in physical units like tons per car or in fixed base-year prices. Thus, changes in coefficients measure changes in usage. (Only indirectly do they reflect any changes in relative prices.)

Projections about the future obtained with this or any other model can be based only on analysis and imagination. The typical procedure is to identify the phenomena of interest and to postulate a set of relationships among them, these relationships sometimes having themselves been suggested by a study of data describing completed events. The parameters of the theory are quantified, and it is then iteratively tested and refined, using data describing the past. If the postulated relationships appear to survive this process, they become the basis for projecting future events. Since it is obvious that the values of parameters and independent variables that will obtain in the future are unknown, these projections often take the form of alternative scenarios about the future.

The relationships among technological change, employment, and the distribution of income have been studied at length by economists. My intention in closing this section is to contrast briefly some of the characteristic features of the present model with other approaches.

The building blocks for any model are the parameters that relate one phenomenon to another, through structural relationships that presumably change relatively slowly and whose variations from one period to another are systematic (that is, "stable"). An early aggregate econometric growth model of the U.S. economy, which charted the direction for a great deal of subsequent work (Klein and Kosobud 1961), used five "great ratios of economics" as the fundamental parameters for its seven equations: the savings-to-income ratio, the capital-to-output ratio, labor's share of income, velocity of circulation, and the capital-to-labor ratio. The authors proposed the labor force participation rate as a potential sixth great ratio that, they reported, fluctuated about 55 percent with practically no trend over the period 1900–52. The stability of the capital-to-output ratio and labor's share of income — actually their lack of stability — will be examined in detail below. By the time the article was published, the proposed sixth ratio had already begun its historic climb due to the massive, unprecedented, and unforeseen entry into the labor force of white women of childbearing age. By 1980 the overall participation rate stood at 64 percent.

Other well-known and widely used formulations have, through a host of "elasticity" parameters, constrained the capital- and labor-saving characteristics of technological change that could be investigated by fixing the responses of various physical variables to changes in prices. In these formulations, the values of parameters are either assumed or else estimated by (statistical) inference — that is, formally extrapolated from correlations that held in the past.

By contrast an enormous amount of highly structured information describing techniques of production is required to compute the fundamental parameters of the empirical dynamic input/output model, and most of these parameters describe technical relationships that are "netted out" in other formulations. The input/output parameters are not extrapolated on the basis of past trends. Rather they quantify specific technological assumptions as opposed to the parameters that are so complex that a host of factors will affect their future values.

Each sector's choices among alternative technologies and the rates at which newly available technologies are adopted will in fact be based on corresponding costs of production and will both affect and be affected by changing relative prices and other considerations. No simple automatic relationship (based, for example, on speculations about "ealsticities of substitution" of capital for labor) can describe the complex processes of innovation and its adoption. The model that has been described in this chapter is based, instead, on plausible external assumptions about technological change.

USING THE MODEL FRAMEWORK OF THE DYNAMIC INPUT/OUTPUT MODEL TO EXPLORE THE CONSEQUENCES OF TECHNOLOGICAL CHANGE

To illustrate the use of this analytic framework, let us imagine that over a given period of time technological change in the economy is such that all input requirements (that is, all technical coefficients describing requirements for intermediate inputs, capital goods, and different categories of labor) decline 1 percent a year. Then in each year following the initiation of these changes, a given final bill of goods can be satisfied with less overall production than in the absence of these technological changes. Alternatively, the level of production of the initial year could, in subsequent years, support increased consumption or increased investment resulting in a larger capacity for future production. With the reduction in labor requirements per unit of output, the size of the employed labor force will obviously fall unless overall output (for increased consumption or investment) rises by at least a compensating amount.

Of course the changes in the technical coefficients will not follow any such neat pattern as a uniform 1 percent reduction per year, and in any realistic experiment about the future some technical coefficients will rise and others will fall to reflect specific changes in each projection in each sector. The physical balance equations of the model allow us to compute the effects on employment of specific combinations of technological changes (that is, changes in the coefficients governing intermediate inputs, investment in capital goods, and labor requirements), sector by sector and occupation by occupation, and to quantify the results of each experiment. For example, one can compute how much the level of consumption (and sectoral production) would have to increase year by year between 1983 and 2000, assuming a specific pattern of technological change between now and then and a given composition of consumption, in order to absorb a certain level of aggregate employment (say, "full employment" of the projected labor force) by 2000.

Since factor payments in the economy as a whole are by definition equal to the value of aggregate final demand, the wage bill, interest, and profits will cover the cost of consumption plus expansion investment; this is shown by the income balance equation that is solved using the outputs computed in the physical balance equations and the prices computed in the price equations. If the wage bill happened to just equal the cost of consumption, then the cost of expansion could be covered by individual and corporate property-type income. Some savings out of labor income would be available for investment if labor income exceeded consumption. Alternatively, labor income will need to be supplemented by consumption spending out of property-type income if labor income alone is not adequate to cover consumption.

The plausibility of each of these three alternative outcomes depends on the relative changes in wage and profit rates and their impacts on other prices. If, for example, we make the hypothetical assumption that future wage and profit rates (and the exogenously fixed money rate of interest) remain unchanged in nominal terms and that technological change by and large economizes on inputs, then the price equations show that prices of goods and services will fall resulting in an increase in both the real wage bill and real profits per unit of output. Whether or not the resulting total wage bill will cover total consumption depends on the specific magnitudes of all the parameters involved and can be assessed by evaluating the terms in the income balance equation.

About all we can say in the abstract is that increases in real wages will be sought by those dependent on labor income, while downward pressure on real wages will result from the pursuit of higher rates of profit, price competition among firms including competition with foreign producers, and the threat of further reductions in labor requirements through increased investment in automation on the part of the producers. The dynamic input/output model can be used to compute the consequences of alternative numerical assumptions about the movements in wage and profit rates combined with alternative assumptions about technological change.

The physical balance equations of the dynamic input/output model have already been implemented and are the basis of the preliminary results reported in this chapter. This work required projecting the future values of the technical parameters, in particular those governing the future use of capital and labor inputs. The next section describes the experience of recent decades with respect to the changing use in the past of capital and labor inputs and spells out the diversity that lies behind the aggregate ratios of capital to output and labor to output. The eventual implementation of the price equations will require projections about future wage and profit rates. The fourth section takes a brief look at the experience of past decades with respect to the distribution between labor income and property-type income.

THE EXPERIENCE OF PAST DECADES: CAPITAL AND LABOR REQUIREMENTS

This section contains data illustrating some historical relationships between average capital and labor inputs and output. For a discussion of data issues related to these series, the reader is referred, for example, to the methodological sections of U.S. Department of Commerce (1975) and U.S. Department of Labor (1979, 1981a).

The process of industrialization, in particular the recent wave of computer-based automation, appears to be marked in virtually all stages and all sectors by increasing use of physical capital (measured in base-year dollars) per unit of labor and declining labor requirements, of changing occupational composition, per unit of output. These observations characterize the most advanced technologies: Relations involving the *average* stocks and labor inputs clearly move in this direction only with considerable inertia, especially in the case of fixed capital stocks.

New types of equipment are generally involved in the introduction of new techniques: In some cases more and in some cases less "aggregate" capital will be required to produce a unit of output than in the case of the former techniques. As known processes are improved and the improvements more widely adopted, aggregate capital requirements per unit of sectoral output can be expected to decline, but less steeply than aggregate labor requirements.

The first column of Table 2-3 is a measure of the stock of capital (the aggregate value in 1929 prices, including residential capital) per

Table 2–3. Capital Stock Per Unit of Output for Selected Sectors, 1870–1960.

	(1) Gross Capital Stock Net of Retirements to Net National Product	(2) Capital to Output, All Manufacturing	(3) Capital to Product for Mining Industries		(4) Reproducible Farm Capital to Average Gross Farm Income	(5) Capital to Product in Regulated Industries		
			Metals[a]	Petroleum and Natural Gas[b]		Steam Railroads[a]	Electric Light and Power[b]	Telephones[c]
1870	4.6	—	1.29	1.75	2.56	—	—	—
1880	3.3	0.55	2.30	2.06	2.46	15.95	—	—
1890	4.5	0.73	2.73	3.78	2.45	9.84	12.06	4.99
1900	4.5	0.80	—	—	2.14	6.43	12.48	4.12
1910	5.0	0.97	2.50	5.05	2.40 2.26	4.35	10.47	2.54
1920	5.0	1.02	2.16	5.86	2.57 2.40	3.17	4.51	1.58
1930	5.7	0.89	1.71	3.58	1.93	4.23	3.64	1.88
1940	3.8	0.74	1.24	2.25	1.60	4.10	2.39	1.84
1950	3.6	0.61	1.16	1.56	1.63	2.66	1.30	1.85

Notes: All data are valued at 1929 prices unless otherwise noted and are taken from Domar (1961), which should be consulted for the origi-nal sources and discussion of the data. Capital is typically measured net of depreciation except for column 1. Below are the tables in Domar's article from which columns 1–5 of the present table are constituted:

Column 1: Table 5, column 4. These ratios are presented not for single years but as estimates for decadal periods starting around the year indicated to the left: For example, the first entry, 4.6, is reported for the period 1869–1878.

Column 2: Table 7, column 2. Some liberty has been taken to adapt the data to the dates used in this table. (The original dates after 1910 are 1919, 1929, 1939, 1948, and 1953).

Column 3: Table 10, rows 2 and 9. "Capital" is here explicitly defined as depreciated net value of structures and equipment plus inventories, cash, and receivables. "Product" appears to mean total output (not just value-added). As in column 2 of this table, the data are adapted to the dates reported here.

Column 4: Table 11, column 3. In 1910–14 prices. The overlapping series correspond to alternative sources for farm income.

Column 5: Table 13, columns 3–5.

Source: Domar (1961).

unit of output (also measured in 1929 prices) in the economy as a whole, which is shown to rise from the late nineteenth century through the 1930s and to decline thereafter. According to column 2, capital in place per unit of output in manufacturing peaks somewhat earlier, around 1920, and then also declines. The next column shows capital to output ratios for the mining of metals (3a) and of petroleum and natural gas (3b). Both display the characteristic pattern, with the former peaking before 1910 and the latter around 1920.

Capital (excluding land) per unit of output in agriculture, as measured in column 4, is relatively constant between 1870 and 1920, when it begins to decline. In the last three sectors — steam railroads, electric utilities, and telephones — the ratio declines steeply (especially for the first two) throughout the period.

The historical data presented in Table 2–3 suggest considerable sectoral diversity in capital-to-output ratios but might lead one to the conclusion that capital requirements per unit of output, after having reached a maximum early in the twentieth century, have been in secular decline in the U.S. The more recent data discussed below suggest an even more complicated picture.

Turning now to detailed data describing more recent periods (which enter with minor modifications into the database used in the computations reported in the next-to-last section, I have computed (but do not show here) capital-to-labor, labor-to-output, and capital-to-output ratios, respectively, in 1972 and 1963 for eighty-five sectors comprising the private economy. All values are in 1972 prices except employment, which is measured in person-years; the sector classification is given in Appendix Table 2A–1. Data are based on U.S. Department of Commerce (1969, 1979, 1981a, 1981b, 1982) and U.S. Department of Labor (1979, 1981b).

In almost seventy of the eighty-five sectors, each employee worked with less than $25,000 (in 1972 prices) of fixed capital, on the average, in 1963; and only in petroleum and gas extraction (sector number 8) and utilities (70) did this amount exceed $100,000. The capital-to-labor ratio increased for all but four sectors by 1972, and the number of sectors with $100,000 or more of fixed capital per employee grew to include additional mining sectors (5 and 6), petroleum refining (30), and telephone communications (68).

Most labor-to-output ratios declined between 1963 and 1972, by which time only a handful of sectors still required more than fifty employees to make a million dollars worth of output. While most of the so-called service sectors (69–85) experienced a decline in labor coefficients, they also account for most of the eleven sectors whose labor coefficients appear to have *increased* over the period. This apparent increase is probably explained in most cases by the systematic overestimation of price deflators for services.

The amount of fixed capital required to produce a dollar's worth of output in 1963 ranged from ten to fifteen cents on the low end (in 1972 prices) in the tobacco (14), construction (11), and apparel (17) sectors to about four dollars in petroleum and gas extraction (8) and utilities (70). Capital in place per unit of output declined over the period for only about one-third of the sectors. While the amount of capital required to mine a ton of metal declined over the first half of this century according to Table 2–3, it apparently increased sharply for five of the six mining sectors (5–10 except 8) between 1963 and 1972.

Finally, Table 2–4 shows the occupational composition of the labor force of selected sectors in 1960 and 1978. Individual sectors are characterized by very particular occupational patterns. (This remains true at much greater levels of occupational and sectoral disaggregation than is shown here.) For example, almost half of those employed in producing medical and educational services are categorized as professionals in the classification scheme of Table 2–4; over half the finance and insurance work force are clerical workers; about 40 percent of those employed in the manufacture of durables, and 45 percent in the case of nondurables, are semiskilled operatives. The last column shows that the national labor force has experienced a significant increase in the number and proportion who are professionals and clerical workers between 1960 and 1978 and a dramatic decline in agricultural workers over this period.[4]

THE EXPERIENCE OF RECENT DECADES:
EARNINGS OF CAPITAL AND LABOR

Prospects for the future material standard of living will depend on the availability of jobs, real wages, and the distribution of total product between consumption and investment. Analysis of the relationship between labor income and outlays for consumption will eventually need to be carried out at a level of detail distinguishing many different types of households (analogous to the distinctions among the sectors of the economy producing different goods and services). This is not yet possible, and the discussion in this section is of the aggregate earnings of labor and of capital and their disposition between 1929 and 1979 based on data from U.S. Department of Commerce (1981a, 1982). For a discussion of definitions and measurement techniques, the reader is referred, for example, to Kravis (1959) and U.S. Department of Commerce (1976).

Labor income has grown substantially over the past several decades, rising steadily from less than 60 percent of national income in 1929 to about 70 percent by the mid-1950s, a percentage that has been sustained until the present time. In the preceding computation labor income is defined to include earnings of government employees and employee payments to social security and excludes all entrepreneurial income, while business income includes employer payments to social security. Other definitions of labor income also exhibit the same increasing trend, as Kravis (1959) found for the period 1900–57. However, if the *entire* entrepreneurial income is counted as employee compensation, as in Klein and Kosobud (1961), by this definition labor's share falls from about 80 percent since the 1930s to about 75 percent in recent years.

Personal disposable income per employee nearly doubled in real terms between 1929 and 1979, and the rate of increase on a per capita basis was even greater due to the steady increase in the overall rate of labor-force participation. The net effect of income taxes and transfers has been to reduce labor income by several percentage points, and only with the scarcity of consumer goods during World War II has labor income alone (either before or after taxes and transfers) been approximately adequate to cover personal outlays. However, when personal property-type income is included, about 6 percent of total personal income has for several decades been left for net savings of households.

As these numbers indicate, the real average standard of living in the United States has improved over the last half century (and longer). The expanding labor force and increasing real wage rates have been the result of many interacting factors, including new technological possibilities, all of which are changing. Any projections about the future standard of living will have to be based on explicit assumptions about the specific determining factors.

Table 2–4. Occupational Composition of Employment for Selected Sectors, 1960 and 1978 (percentage).

		1960						
		Manufacturing				Medical and		
	Agriculture	Durables	Nondurables	Trade	Finance and Insurance	Educational Services	Business Services	National Economy
Professionals	1.01	9.70	5.57	1.92	3.27	54.08	36.84	11.21
Managers	0.54	5.72	6.78	24.18	19.81	3.36	12.82	10.60
Clerical workers	0.57	12.46	12.26	13.98	54.36	13.44	29.32	14.67
Sales workers	0.15	1.85	5.01	23.10	18.01	0.19	2.46	6.60
Craftsmen	0.48	22.49	14.39	6.72	0.82	2.45	5.48	12.84
Operatives	1.78	38.24	48.49	12.72	0.32	2.02	4.97	17.98
Service workers	0.23	1.80	2.05	13.08	3.28	23.63	7.11	12.52
Laborers	2.49	7.74	5.45	4.31	0.14	0.85	1.00	5.50
Farmers and farm workers	92.76	0.0	0.0	0.0	0.0	0.0	0.0	8.09
Total employment	100.0	100.0	100.0	100.0	100.0	100.0	100.0	100.0
Total employment (thousands)	5816.0	9749.0	7558.0	13365.0	2172.0	7301.0	1661.0	66681.0

1978

	Agriculture	Manufacturing		Trade	Finance and Insurance	Medical and Educational Services	Business Services	National Economy
		Durables	Nondurables					
Professionals	3.24	11.09	8.18	2.84	5.72	46.06	37.55	15.09
Managers	0.99	6.77	7.35	18.11	20.95	5.84	8.65	10.71
Clerical workers	1.65	11.98	12.17	18.09	52.85	18.87	29.92	17.91
Sales workers	0.38	1.45	3.82	19.09	17.82	0.17	2.22	6.31
Craftsmen	1.65	21.44	16.92	9.02	0.65	2.12	4.36	13.12
Operatives	1.71	40.14	45.62	9.92	0.24	1.71	3.39	15.28
Service workers	0.32	1.81	1.95	17.12	1.67	24.30	13.13	13.60
Laborers	9.76	5.32	4.00	5.81	0.09	0.92	0.79	5.01
Farmers and farm workers	80.29	0.0	0.0	0.0	0.0	0.0	0.0	2.96
Total employment	100.0	100.0	100.0	100.0	100.0	100.0	100.0	100.0
Total employment (thousands)	3485.0	12348.0	8264.0	20613.0	3753.0	16195.0	4547.0	94373.0

Source: U.S. Department of Labor (1969, 1981a).

IMPACTS OF COMPUTER-BASED AUTOMATION
ON EMPLOYMENT: SOME PRELIMINARY RESULTS

As part of the inquiry addressed in this chapter, it is possible to report some preliminary results about the effects of computer-based automation on employment in the United States through the year 2000. These results have been obtained using the physical-balance equations of the dynamic input/output model and the database described in earlier sections; the other parts of the model have not yet been implemented. (For detailed documentation, see Leontief and Duchin (1984).)

The dynamic input/output model is used to project the sectoral outputs and investment and labor requirements of the U.S. economy, in terms of about ninety producing sectors and over fifty occupations, under alternative assumptions (scenarios) about its changing technological structure. The reference scenario, designated scenario one, assumes no further automation or any other technological change after 1980. Final demand, however, is assumed to continue to grow over a projected path through 2000. This scenario thus makes it possible to assess future employment and other requirements to satisfy plausible final demand in the absence of technological improvements from 1980 on.

Scenario two differs in its technological assumptions (that is, the parameters in the A, B, and L matrices) for years after 1980 and represents the fastest rates at which different sectors of the U.S. economy might be expected to absorb the new technologies. This scenario projects an increasing use of computers in all sectors for specific information processing and machine control tasks and their integration. Computerizing each task also involves changes in other inputs, notably labor inputs. The demand for computers (measured in constant prices per unit of output) is naturally higher in 2000 than in 1990.

The second scenario also represents greater use of two other microprocessor-based devices—robots and computer numerically controlled (CNC) machine tools—for a growing range of specific manufacturing operations. These changes involve the replacement by robots of six categories of production workers in many manufacturing sectors and substitution of CNC for conventional machine tools with corresponding reductions in direct requirements for the metalworking occupations.

The projections assume that computer-based work stations will replace conventional office equipment and that most deliveries after 1985 will be for integrated electronic systems rather than stand-alone devices. Corresponding direct impacts on the demand for managerial, sales, and six categories of clerical workers in different sectors of the economy are represented in detail.

Scenario two assumes the continuation of recent trends in the input structures of the health-care sectors: notably increased use per case of various types of capital equipment for diagnosis and treatment, of drugs and other chemicals, and of plastic disposable items, as well as an expansion of nonphysician medical personnel. The health-care sectors also continue the automation of office-type operations, with the direct consequences described above.

Just as computers are increasingly affecting the conduct of professional and leisure activities, the demand for computer-based education, training, and recreation in schools, on the job, and in homes will also increase. Scenario two assumes a growing number of computer-based courses per student and corresponding increases in teacher training. It also postulates on-the-job training in a variety of sectors for a growing number of occupations.

The analysis that is reported here involved computing the amount of labor of each occupational category required in each sector of the economy year by year until 2000 in order to deliver a projected mix of goods and services for private and public consumption under the two extreme sets of technological assumptions, the baseline scenario and the rapid adoption scenario.[5] The employment projections are summarized by broad occupational category in Table 2–5.

These computations show that computer-based automation will result in sizable reductions in the total labor required to produce a plausible final bill of goods over the next twenty years — 11 million fewer worker-years are required in 1990 under scenario two than under scenario one and 20 million fewer in 2000. By the year 2000, "aggregate labor productivity" (defined here as the value of total deliveries to private and public consumption per worker) is computed to be about 13 percent higher under scenario two than under the baseline scenario.

While the labor savings due to automation are significant, comparing the future labor requirements according to scenario two with present projections of the future labor force suggests that the aspects of automation that have been represented are not likely to displace

Table 2–5. Levels and Composition of Employment[a] in 1978 and Projections for 1990 and 2000 under Alternative Scenarios.[b]

Millions of Worker-Years

Occupation	1978	Scenario One		Scenario Two		Scenario Three	
		1990	2000	1990	2000	1990	2000
Professionals	13.9	19.8	25.6	20.9	31.1	19.6	25.6
Managers	9.5	14.4	19.0	12.4	11.2	11.6	9.2
Sales workers	5.9	9.1	12.4	8.2	10.2	7.7	8.4
Clerical workers	15.9	24.7	32.6	16.7	17.9	15.6	14.7
Craftsmen	11.8	18.0	23.3	17.5	23.4	15.9	18.9
Operatives	14.0	22.0	27.6	21.1	25.8	19.1	20.9
Service workers	11.1	16.7	22.3	16.8	23.0	15.9	19.1
Laborers	4.3	6.6	8.7	6.4	8.7	6.0	7.0
Farmers	2.8	4.2	5.3	4.2	5.4	4.0	4.5
Total	89.2	135.5	176.8	124.1	156.6	115.3	128.2

Percentages

Occupation	1978	Scenario One		Scenario Two		Scenario Three	
		1990	2000	1990	2000	1990	2000
Professionals	15.6	14.6	14.5	16.8	19.8	17.0	19.9
Managers	10.6	10.6	10.8	10.0	7.2	10.0	7.2
Sales workers	6.6	6.7	7.0	6.6	6.5	6.7	6.5
Clerical workers	17.8	18.2	18.4	13.5	11.4	13.5	11.5
Craftsmen	13.3	13.3	13.2	14.1	15.0	13.8	14.7
Operatives	15.7	16.3	15.6	17.0	16.5	16.5	16.3
Service workers	12.4	12.3	12.6	13.5	14.7	13.8	14.9
Laborers	4.9	4.9	4.9	5.2	5.5	5.2	5.5
Farmers	3.2	3.1	3.0	3.3	3.4	3.4	3.5
Total	100.0	100.0	100.0	100.0	100.0	100.0	100.0

[a] Includes all private-sector employment (jobs) plus employment in public education and health. Does not include public administration, armed forces, or household employees (which *are* included in Table 2–4).

[b] Scenario one assumes BLS final demand projections and no technological change after 1980. Scenario two assumes the same final-demand projections as scenario one

labor at such a rapid rate over this period as to necessarily result in unemployment. Sharp reductions in direct labor requirements are offset by the assumption of a moderately increasing standard of living plus the additional labor required to produce and service the automatic equipment.

A third computation, designated scenario three, shows that if the *entire* future projected labor force is employed under the technological assumptions of scenario two, real personal and public per capita consumption can grow at about 2 percent per year in the 1980s and 0.5 to 1 percent a year in the 1990s in the absence of any other changes. Of course, the effect of changes in production other than automation, like higher-yield crops and the use of newly developed materials, as well as aspects of automation that have not been given full consideration like telecommunications, will eventually need to be taken explicitly into account.

The bottom portion of Table 2–5 shows the occupational composition of labor requirements under the three scenarios. These numbers indicate that by the year 2000 automation will involve a sharp decline in the proportion of clerical workers and middle managers and an increasing proportion of professionals, especially computer professionals. The increased percentage of craftsmen and operatives under scenarios two and three relative to the baseline scenario (despite reductions in direct requirements for many subcategories) reflects compensating increases in demand due to their importance in the production of capital goods. Significant occupational shifts also take place *within* each of the broad categories reported in Table 2–5. Both conventional and computer-based educational and training efforts will need to be mobilized to facilitate these shifts in work skills, and the computations include projections of the resources that will be devoted to these efforts.

POLICY IMPLICATIONS

Often the purpose of government policy is to deal with problems that are already acute. Adjusting to changes that have already occurred,

---

Notes to Table 2–5 (Continued)
coupled with the accelerated adoption of computer-based automation. Scenario three uses the same technological assumptions as scenario two, leaves the level of final demand unconstrained, and fixes future aggregate employment at levels consistent with official labor-force projections. Scenarios are described in more detail in the text.

far from being a viable basis for policy, is the high cost of not looking ahead. It is defended by arguments about an appropriately passive role for government and, ultimately, by appealing to the inscrutability of the future. However, realistic objectives for the future and realistic means for attaining them, independent of the political processes by which they are arrived at, require *anticipating* the changes that are emerging. Furthermore, the implications of our preliminary investigation are sufficiently compelling as to confirm the possibility of distinguishing plausible from unlikely outcomes in the future.

Two important conclusions can be drawn from our preliminary findings. First, the occupational composition of the labor force can be expected to shift significantly over the next two decades with the progressive automation of factory and office work. The services of human office workers, especially clerical workers but also middle management, will be the most sharply curtailed. Production workers on the whole will maintain their relative share of the labor force, while the relative demand for computer programmers and analysts and also for most categories of engineers can be expected to grow over this time horizon. Private industry will provide substantial computer-based, on-the-job training in the emerging technologies for many categories of professional and managerial workers. Development of programs for training and retraining others already in the labor force and curricula for teaching new skills to those who will first enter the labor force over the next two decades are bound to entail a growing public commitment. The study provides guidelines as to target occupations for large-scale training programs.

The second major conclusion of the preliminary study has to do with the rate at which labor will be displaced by computers and related equipment. While those technologies are unambiguously labor-saving, over the next two decades the net potential job loss due to computers could be compensated by moderate increases in output and the standard of living. There may of course be continued high rates of unemployment in the United States due to the combination of automation with many other factors not considered here. Our study suggests that automation will be a contributory factor but not in itself responsible for a dramatic contraction in the level of employment opportunities over the next two decades at the rate at which automatic equipment is likely to be absorbed.

While this last finding suggests that personal income will still be largely distributed by the paycheck for the foreseeable future, the effects of computer-based automation on the distribution of income between investment and consumption on the one hand and among different categories of workers on the other have not yet been systematically addressed. From the point of view of policy priorities, extending the research in this direction — using the model developed in the first part of this chapter — will be an important next step.

Table 2A–1. Enumeration of Eighty-five Sectors Comprising the Private Economy.

Section Number	Section Name
1	Livestock and livestock products
2	Other agricultural products
3	Forestry and fishery products
4	Agricultural, forestry, and fishery services
5	Iron and ferroalloy ores mining
6	Nonferrous metal ores mining
7	Coal mining
8	Crude petroleum and natural gas
9	Stone and clay mining and quarrying
10	Chemical and fertilizer mineral mining
11	Construction
12	Ordnance and accessories
13	Food and kindred products
14	Tobacco manufactures
15	Broad and narrow fabrics, yarn and thread mills
16	Miscellaneous textile goods and floor coverings
17	Apparel
18	Miscellaneous fabricated textile products
19	Lumber and wood products, except containers
20	Wood containers
21	Household furniture
22	Other furniture and fixtures
23	Paper and allied products, except containers
24	Paperboard containers and boxes
25	Printing and publishing
26	Chemicals and selected chemical products
27	Plastics and synthetic materials

(Table 2A–1 continues overleaf)

Table 2A–1. (Continued).

Section Number	Section Name
28	Drugs, cleaning and toilet preparations
29	Paints and allied products
30	Petroleum refining and allied industries
31	Rubber and miscellaneous plastic products
32	Leather tanning and finishing
33	Footwear and other leather products
34	Glass and glass products
35	Stone and clay products
36	Primary iron and steel manufacturing
37	Primary nonferrous metals manufacturing
38	Metal containers
39	Heating, plumbing and structural metal products
40	Screw machine products and stampings
41	Other fabricated metal products
42	Engines and turbines
43	Farm and garden machinery
44	Construction and mining machinery
45	Materials handling machinery and equipment
46	Metalworking machinery and equipment
47	Special industry machinery and equipment
48	General industrial machinery and equipment
49	Miscellaneous machinery, except electrical
50	Electronic computing equipment
51	Office, computing, and accounting machines, except electronic computing equipment
52	Service industry machines
53	Electric industrial equipment and apparatus
54	Household appliances
55	Electric lighting and wiring equipment
56	Radio, television, and communications equipment
57	Electron tubes
58	Semiconductors and related devices
59	Electronic components
60	Miscellaneous electrical machinery and supplies
61	Motor vehicles and equipment
62	Aircraft and parts
63	Other transportation equipment
64	Scientific and controlling instruments
65	Optical, ophthalmological, and photographic equipment

Table 2A–1.   (Continued).

Section Number	Section Name
66	Miscellaneous manufacturing
67	Transportation and warehousing
68	Communications, except radio and television
69	Radio and television broadcasting
70	Electric, gas, water, and sanitary services
71	Wholesale trade
72	Retail trade
73	Finance
74	Insurance
75	Real estate and rental
76	Hotels, personal and repair services, excluding automobiles
77	Business services
78	Eating and drinking places
79	Automobile repair services
80	Amusements
81	Hospitals
82	Health services, excluding hospitals
83	Educational services
84	Nonprofit organizations
85	Government enterprises

Note: This classification scheme is a slightly disaggregated version of the two-digit input/output classification of U.S. Department of Commerce (1979).

NOTES

1. While this version is standard in the theoretical literature, it is to be distinguished from the static input/output model that is still used in virtually all empirical work.

2. It is well known that in the standard version of the model described in this section, the economy can proceed into the future only along the knife's edge of a particular balanced growth path: If it deviates from that path, it "blows up." The current version of the model (described in the reference) is considerably more realistic and allows for "unbalanced" growth through over- or underutilization of existing productive capacity. The meanings of the parameters and the basic relationships illustrated in the text by means of equations (1) through (3) below still hold.

3. Sector studies producing input/output coefficients have been carried
    out for education, health care, and the automation of most sectors of
    production and office operations by David Howell, Glenn-Marie Lange,
    and Catherine McDonough and appear as chapters 4–8 of Leontief and
    Duchin (1984).
4. These trends in the United States have been uninterrupted since the
    earliest years for which we have data. In 1900 professionals accounted
    for 4 percent of the labor force, clerical workers only 3 percent, and
    farmers and farm workers, 38 percent.
5. Projected private and public consumption is based on projections in
    U.S. Department of Labor (1982). Scenarios one and two correspond
    to the scenarios called S1 and S3, respectively, in Leontief and Duchin
    (1984). Scenario three discussed below corresponds to S4.

REFERENCES

Cipolla, C.M., *The Economic History of World Population* (Sussex: The
Harvester Press, 1978).

Domar, Evsey D., "The Capital–Output Ratio in the United States: Its Variation and Stability," in F.A. Lutz and D.C. Hague, eds., *The Theory of
Capital,* (New York: St. Martin's Press, 1961), pp. 95–117.

Duchin, F. and D. Szyld, "The Dynamic *IO* Model," chapter 2 in Leontief
and Duchin.

Klein, L.R., and R.F. Kosobud, "Some Econometrics of Growth: Great
Ratios of Economics," *Quarterly Journal of Economics* 75, no. 2 (May
1961), pp. 173–198.

Kravis, Irving B., "Relative Income Shares in Fact and Theory," *American
Economic Review* 49, no. 5 (December 1959), pp. 917–949.

Leontief, W., "The Dynamic Inverse," in A.P. Carter and A. Brody, eds.,
Contributions to Input–Output Analysis (Amsterdam: North–Holland
Publishing Company, 1970), pp. 17–46. Also appears in W. Leontief,
Essays in Economics: Theories, Facts, and Policies (White Plains, N.Y.:
M.E. Sharpe, 1977), pp. 50–77.

Leontief, W., and F. Duchin (principal investigators), *The Impacts of
Automation on Employment, 1963–2000* (prepared for the National Science Foundation, #PRA-8012844, Final Report, 1984).

Snow, C.P., "Government, Science and Public Policy," *Science* 151 (February 11, 1966): 650–53.

U.S. Department of Commerce, Bureau of Economic Analysis, *Input–
Output Structure of the U.S. Economy: 1963,* vols. I, II, and III (Washington, D.C., 1969).

———, *A Study of Fixed Capital Requirements of the U.S. Business Economy, 1971–1980* (Washington, D.C., December 1975).

————, *Readings in Concepts and Methods of National Income Statistics* (Washington, D.C., 1976).

————, *The Detailed Input–Output Structure of the U.S. Economy: 1972.* Vols. I and II (Washington, D.C., 1979).

————, *The National Income and Product Accounts of the United States, 1929–76, Statistical Tables* (Washington, D.C., 1981a).

————, *Employment and Employee Compensation in the 1972 Input–Output Study,* BEA Staff Paper no. 38 (Washington, D.C., October 1981b).

————, "Revised Estimates of the National Income and Product Accounts," *Survey of Current Business* 62, no. 7 (July 1982).

U.S. Department of Labor, Bureau of Labor Statistics, "Percentage Distribution of Industry Employment by Occupation, 1960 and Projected 1975," in *Tomorrow's Manpower Needs,* Bulletin 1606, vol. 4, app. G (Washington, D.C., 1969).

————, *Capital Stock Estimates for Input–Output Industries: Methods and Data,* Bulletin 2034 (Washington, D.C., 1979).

————, *The National Industry–Occupation Employment Matrix, 1970, 1978, and Projected 1990,* Bulletin 2086, vols. 1 and 2 (Washington, D.C., 1981a).

————, *Time Series Data for Input–Output Industries: Output, Price, and Employment,* unpublished update on computer tape DATA, SIC 72, received July 1981b.

————, *Economic Growth Model System Used for Projections to 1990,* Bulletin 2112 (Washington, D.C., April 1982).

3 TECHNICAL ADVANCE AND OTHER SOURCES OF EMPLOYMENT CHANGE IN BASIC INDUSTRY

Robert A. Levy, Marianne Bowes, and James M. Jondrow

Although technical change leads to the development of new and better-quality products and new and more efficient production techniques, it can create hardships for those who use outdated or inefficient production methods or make products that are no longer wanted. Consequently, the net effect of technical change on workers is hard to predict a priori. Workers in a particular industry benefit from technical change if the change permits competitive gains against producers of similar products. As consumers, workers benefit from productivity gains that are translated into lower-priced consumption goods. But some workers end up as net losers—namely, those who cannot adapt to new production methods and lose their sources of livelihood as a result.

The prospect of direct substitution of machines for labor has been the focus of most concern about technical change. It was expressed in the fears of the Luddites in the early 1800s, and those fears continue today about programmable robots and other emerging technologies.

This chapter draws in part from results of work supported by the National Science Foundation Grant No. PRA78-20297. Any opinions, findings, conclusions, or recommendations expressed in this chapter are those of the authors and do not necessarily reflect the views of the Center for Naval Analyses or the National Science Foundation.

77

Yet it is not clear that technical change is actually an important source of worker displacement. In many cases other factors — such as rising wages, increased energy prices, import competition, changing consumer preferences, and the business cycle — may have more to do with worker displacement than the introduction of advanced technology.

This chapter presents estimates of how labor demand was affected by the introduction of new production technology in five basic American industries during the 1960s and 1970s. The five industries — steel, automobiles, aluminum, coal, and iron ore — are often mentioned in public discussions as the sort of old-line American industry that has been subjected to stiff competition by foreign producers who are technologically more advanced. Steel and automobiles are two of the largest and most important U.S. manufacturing industries, both in terms of output and employment. The aluminum industry, though substantially smaller, competes with the steel industry in many markets, including those supplying the automobile industry. The iron ore and coal mining industries produce inputs used in the steel industry. Metallurgical coal is made into coke, which is used in blast furnaces to produce iron. Iron, in turn, is refined into steel. These interrelationships define a set of industries fundamental to the American economy.

In recent decades, all five industries have experienced technological innovation — for example, the adoption of the basic oxygen furnace and continuous casting in the steel industry, the pelletizing of iron ore, and the use of transfer machines in the automobile industry (see the second part below). However, the pattern of employment changes in these industries has been varied. Employment grew in the automobile and aluminum industries for most of the 1960s and 1970s but was stagnant or declining in the other three industries. This mixed pattern makes it difficult to distinguish the effect that technical change had on employment from the effect of other changes that occurred at the same time. For example, technical change might have decreased employment in a particular industry by reducing labor required per unit of output in that industry, or it might have contributed to increased employment by helping to keep the industry's product competitive in world markets. On the other hand, during the same time period, increased wage rates may have encouraged a shift to less labor-intensive production at a given level of technology.

An econometric model expressing these interrelationships is needed to sort out the different effects that technical change can have on employment and to untangle the influence of technical change from the influence of other variables. Our modeling and analysis involved estimating the direct effects of technical change on the demand for labor in each industry, estimating the indirect effects of technical change that occur as costs fall and output and employment rise, and comparing the combined direct and indirect effects to the quit rate in each industry.

The first two parts of this chapter set out the concepts that were the starting point of our analysis and summarize the structure and results of the model we developed to estimate the direct effects of technical change on employment. The next two parts summarize the model and the results for the indirect effects of technical change and present a comparison of the combined direct and indirect effects of technical change on employment to the quit rate in each industry. Key findings are summarized in the final part.

UNDERLYING CONCEPTS

The primary objective of our work has been to measure the relationships between technical change and the demand for labor. However, the demand for labor in an industry can shift for reasons other than technical change, either because relative input prices change leading to substitution between inputs or because the level of industry output changes. To isolate and measure the effects of technical change, these other determinants of the demand for labor must be taken into account.

In addition, any procedure for estimating the effects of change must recognize the different ways that technical change can influence labor demand. The direct effects of technical change work in two ways. First, technical change can increase overall productivity for all factors of production used in an industry—that is, reduce the total bundle of inputs needed to produce a given level of output in that industry. This overall rate of reduction in input use is called the rate of technical change. Second, technical change can shift demand away from one input and toward another. This is the bias in technical change.

The combined effect on labor demand of the overall rate and bias in technical change can be measured by the percentage change in labor demand when technology increases by one unit (see the discussion of measures of technical change below). The combined effect is a partial effect in the sense that other variables that might also influence employment (that is, input prices and the level of output) are being held constant.

Technical change in an industry can also affect labor demand indirectly by lowering the price of industry output, causing the quantity of output sold to rise, and thus increasing the demand for all industry inputs including labor. This indirect effect on labor demand is what we call the output-enhancement effect of technical change. The net effect of technical change on labor demand depends on which effect, the direct effect or the indirect effect, is greater.

THE DIRECT EFFECT OF TECHNICAL CHANGE

Modeling the Direct Effect

While it is straightforward to define a labor-demand function with parameters that allow the calculation of the direct effect of technical change, estimation of the parameters themselves is not so simple. The estimation must be based on a model that is flexible enough to consider the demand for a number of different factors of production. Using recent econometric breakthroughs, we have estimated a model of industry behavior from which the demand for labor can be derived. In this model, firms are assumed in competitive equilibrium to minimize cost, given input prices, the level of output, and the level of technology.

The model we developed for the steel, automobile, and aluminum industries included five inputs—production labor, nonproduction labor, capital, energy, and materials—in the firm's cost function and imposed no restrictions on how the inputs could be substituted for each other at a given level of technology. The manufacturing industries were defined at the four-digit Standard Industrial Classification (SIC) level, a more detailed level of disaggregation than that used in most industry studies. For example, the four-digit industry classification for basic steel is 3312, which includes the largely integrated producers of carbon steel but excludes stainless or specialized alloy steel and firms specializing in one stage of production, such as rolling. For coal and iron ore, data were not available for the full set of inputs. We therefore estimated a simpler labor-demand equation directly.

The equations in the econometric system that we estimated for each of the manufacturing industries included the cost function as well as equations for the share of total cost represented by each input. The share equation for each input expresses that input's share in total cost as a function of input prices, the level of output, and the level of technology. The share equations describe how input/output coefficients (that is, input per unit of output for each input, also measured as the cost for the input relative to total cost) move over time. Changes in input/output coefficients are explained in terms of (1) the adoption of new technology, (2) changes in input prices, and (3) changes in the level of output.

The share equation for labor in particular describes how changes in the ratio of payroll cost to total cost are determined by changes in the wage rate, other input prices, output, and the level of technology. Effects of changes in these variables on labor's share were estimated using multiple regression analysis. For example, the bias of technical change is described as labor-saving, labor-using, or neutral if the estimated parameter for the level of technology is negative, positive, or zero. Accordingly, labor-saving technical change means that as the level of technology increases, the share of payroll cost in total cost decreases (all other exogenous variables held constant). The combined effect of the bias and overall rate of technical change was, in turn, used to derive the effect of technical change on the amount of labor used.

Multiple regression analysis was used to distinguish between input substitution at a given level of technology and input substitution due to an increase in technology. In other words, we wanted to investigate the extent to which firms might respond to higher wage rates by substituting new production techniques that conserve on labor rather than simply increasing the use of capital or other inputs, at a given level of technology.

The regression analysis also permitted us to distinguish between productivity growth due to output growth (when there are economies of scale) and productivity growth due to technical change. Earlier industry studies have frequently assumed constant returns to scale — that is, when industry output changes, the use of each input changes in the same proportion as output, all else equal. However, the assumption of constant returns to scale turns out to be inappropriate in many time-series applications. Because the stock of some inputs (such as capital) cannot be changed quickly, their use may seem to be fixed in the short run, even when output is changing. As a result, measured returns to scale turn out to be increasing, rather than constant as is often assumed, and an increase in output leads to an increase in measured productivity. But if constant returns to scale are assumed, then the increase in productivity due to increased scale will seem to be due to technical change, and the effect of technical change will be overstated.

To avoid overstating the effects of technical change, we did not assume constant returns to scale. Instead, we empirically estimated the extent of scale economies in each industry and the degree to which input stocks might be fixed in the short run. Our investigation showed that all three manufacturing industries have capital stocks that are relativly fixed in the short run. Because this is especially a problem for the aluminum industry (which is very capital-intensive), we extended our econometric model for aluminum to allow for a slowly adjusting production input.

Measuring the Level of Technology

In addition to allowing measurement of productivity growth and its components, our econometric model allowed us to investigate the way technical change unfolds in an industry. In earlier studies of technical change, the level of technology has generally been represented by a simple time trend. The time-trend measure of technical change is accurate if changes in technology unfold gradually and at a constant rate. The time-trend measure is inaccurate if new production processes are introduced rapidly and erratically. It is important to determine which pattern prevails because sudden or unexpected shifts in production processes and labor demand can make adjustment to technical change difficult for an industry's work force, whereas gradual change can be more readily accommodated.

To investigate which pattern prevails, we constructed both a time-trend measure and a direct measure of the level of technology in an industry. Our strategy for developing the direct measure for each industry was to estimate the extent of adoption of well-publicized advances in technology for that industry, if such occurred during our period of study. If no such advances occurred during our period of study, as was the case in the aluminum industry, we constructed only a time-trend measure.

In developing a direct measure for the steel industry, we focused on three new technologies: the basic-oxygen furnace (BOF) and oxygen lancing in open-hearth furnaces, both of which are important advances in the steelmaking process, and the pelletization of iron ore in the mining sector, which reduces the subsequent costs of transforming ore to steel. We combined data on the adoption of these innovations into a single index, weighted by the percentage that each was expected to reduce costs in the steel industry.

In the automobile industry, technical change since World War II has involved the substitution of machines for workers in production processes such as welding. To quantify the concept of automation in the automobile sector, we measured the stock of transfer machines, the basic unit of what has come to be known as "Detroit automation." A transfer machine performs several different operations, each of which would otherwise be performed at different work stations on the production line. We constructed an index of the number of transfer machines (adjusted to take account of the complexity and size of the individual machines) expressed as a fraction of the industry's total capital stock.

For the iron ore industry, we experimented with a number of different measures of technical change. The measure we ultimately used was the one that turned out to have a significant effect on the demand for labor—the fraction of tonnage taken from open-pit mines as opposed to underground mines.

There are two basic methods of coal mining: underground mining and surface mining. We constructed a separate measure of technology for each method. In underground mining, the important steps are cutting, loading, and hauling away the coal. Technical change has been concentrated in cutting and loading. We measured the level of technology in underground mining as the fraction of total coal production carried out by the newer methods: continuous, shortwall, and longwall mining.

Surface mining involves cutting, loading, and hauling and the removal and replacement of overburden, the material covering the coal. The main form of technical change in surface mining has been increased equipment capacity at all stages of the mining process. We measured the level of technology in surface mining by the percentage of industry power shovels and dragline excavators with a bucket capacity of six cubic yards or more.

Applying the Model

In applying our model to determine the direct effect of technical change on labor demand, we estimated the following: the bias of technical change in each industry, the separate contributions of technical change and scale economies to productivity growth in that industry, and the separate influence of technical change and other variables on labor demand. Results for each set of estimates are given below.

Results: The Bias in Technical Change

In the three manufacturing industries — steel, automobiles, and aluminum — we generally find strong evidence of labor-saving technical change.[1] In these industries, the share of payroll costs in total costs has been decreasing throughout our period of study to a greater extent than can be explained by changes in wages and other input prices. At the same time, the share of capital costs has been rising, evidence of capital-using technical change.[2] In this same time period, we find little evidence of substitution between labor and capital at a given level of technology in response to changing input prices.

One interpretation of these findings is that an increase in the price of labor relative to that of capital causes little short-term substitution of capital for labor but that over the long term it encourages advanced technologies that allow production to be less labor intensive. Thus, we hypothesize induced innovation biased away from labor and toward new capital. This induced innovation has not yet been identified empirically, but generalizations of our model may help quantify the link between new technologies and their determinants.

Results: Sources of Productivity Growth

Table 3-1 illustrates for the steel and automobile industries how we decomposed industry productivity growth into growth attributable to technical change and growth attributable to economies of scale. The decomposition is based on regression estimates that use a time trend to represent the level of technology.[3]

Table 3–1. Contributions to Productivity Growth in Steel and Automobiles (percentage).

Time Period	Average Rate of Productivity Growth		Scale Effect		Rate of Technical Change	
	Steel	Automobiles	Steel	Automobiles	Steel	Automobiles
1960–80	0.44	2.07	0.32	0.14	0.12	1.93
1960–65	1.67	3.17	1.45	0.78	0.22	2.39
1966–73	0.34	2.62	0.26	0.56	0.08	2.06
1974–80	−0.48	0.46	−0.57	−0.91	0.09	1.37

In the steel industry, the estimated productivity growth for the 1960–80 period is made up primarily of the scale component; the contribution of technical change (which is also the rate of technical change) is only slightly greater than zero on average. When the decomposition is done for separate subperiods, both the scale-related increase in productivity and the rate of technical change are lower for the later periods. Indeed, over the 1974–80 time period, there was a decline in productivity growth, to an average of about −0.5 percent per year.

The pattern in the automobile industry is somewhat different. The rate of productivity growth averaged just over 2 percent a year for the entire period. Growth was rapid in the earlier period and then fell in the last two periods. On average, the scale component was a minor contributor to productivity growth, primarily as a result of the decrease in output growth during the last period. The contribution of technical change was much higher than in the steel industry, though it also decreased over time.

Results: Changes in Labor Demand

Just as we were able to decompose productivity changes into scale and technology effects, we were able to decompose historical changes in production worker employment into the effects of changes in input prices, output, and technology.[4] Results for all five industries are presented in Table 3–2. For steel, automobiles, and coal, there are two sets of results, one for the time-trend measure of technology and one for the direct measure. For aluminum, technology was represented by a time trend (as noted above, we did not construct a direct measure). For iron ore, only the direct measure of technology was used.

Generally, the patterns are consistent across industries, regardless of the measure of technology. In every industry, advances in technology, holding constant output and input prices, reduced the demand for production labor. The estimated reduction ranged from an average 1 percent each year in iron ore to over 5 percent in aluminum.[5] The effect on employment of changes in production labor's own wage (holding constant other input prices, output, and technology) was also always negative and, at least in the three manufacturing industries, often larger than the effect of changes in technology.

Table 3-2. Components of Employment Change[a] for All Industries (percentage).

Industry (Measure of Technology)	Price of							
	Production Labor	Non-production Labor	Capital	Fuel	Materials	Output	Technology	Total
Steel (time trend)	-2.03	0.74	0.07	-0.20	0.59	0.48	-1.24	-1.58
Steel (direct measure)	-1.82	1.12	0.05	-0.46	0.50	0.64	-1.31	-1.28
Automobiles (time trend)	-2.19	0.98	0.15	0.08	0.70	3.12	-3.10	-0.26
Automobiles (direct measure)	-3.35	1.39	0.26	0.001	0.76	1.81	-1.08	-0.21
Aluminum (time trend)	-4.59	1.34	—[b]	0.29	3.80	8.17	-5.62	3.40
Coal (time trend)	-0.19	—	—	—	—	1.65	-3.40	-1.94
Coal (direct measure)	-0.11	—	—	—	—	1.62	-4.21	-2.70
Iron ore (direct measure)	-0.68	—	—	—	—	-1.00	-1.00	-2.68

[a] For steel and automobiles, the time period is 1960–80; for aluminum, 1959–77; coal, 1950–78; iron ore, 1956 (when pelletization first appeared) to 1980.

[b] Since we assumed that the capital stock in aluminum was fixed in the short run, a change in the price of capital would have no effect on labor demand.

In contrast to the negative effects of increases in technology and wages, increases in output almost always increased labor demand. Demand for production labor also increased in response to increases in the wages of nonproduction labor (since production and nonproduction labor are substitutes in production). Increases in the price of capital, fuel, and materials taken individually affected employment very little. Taken together, increases in the three input prices usually increased the demand for production labor (indicating substitutability between labor and these inputs).

In the mining industries, where labor-demand equations were estimated directly, changes in technology had a negative effect on production labor, particularly in coal mining. The effect was somewhat higher when technology was measured directly, but generally the results for coal were the same regardless of the measure of technology: Increases in output had a positive effect, and increases in the wage rate had a small negative effect. Overall, the total change in labor demand was negative, the major factor being changes in technology. The same was true in iron ore (except for output), although the magnitudes of individual effects differed in each case.

The findings presented in Table 3–2 are averages over the entire period. In Table 3–3, we break up the period and compare two "bad" years (1979–80) with the rest of the period, focusing only on the steel and auto industries and using the time-trend measure of technology. To simplify the table, we have grouped together all changes in labor demand arising from changes in other input prices.

Table 3–3. Components of Employment Change for Steel and Automobiles (percentage).

Industry	Price of Production Labor	Price of Other Inputs	Output	Technology	Total
Steel					
1960–78	−1.88	1.09	1.39	−1.24	−.64
1979–80	−3.45	2.32	−8.15	−1.20	−10.48
Automobiles					
1960–78	−1.98	1.70	5.13	−3.20	1.65
1979–80	−4.22	3.85	−15.95	−2.12	−18.44

From 1960 to 1978, automobile employment grew and steel employment fell overall at a very slow rate. Changes in output and the prices of other inputs exerted upward pressure on employment, while changes in the wage rate and technology put downward pressure on employment. The direct effect of technical change in the automobile industry was relatively large and would have created an average decline in employment of more than 3 percent per year had no other variables changed.

The pattern changed markedly from 1979 to 1980. Changes in technology still contributed to decreased labor demand, but the average annual effect was smaller in both industries than it had been in the earlier period. The negative effect of increased wages was roughly twice as large in the earlier period. Even more striking was the effect of changes in output. These were terrible years for the steel and automobile industries, and dramatic declines in output put downward pressure on employment of about -8 and -16 percent per year, respectively. Though increases in the price of other inputs did lead to some substitution of labor for other inputs, the overall decrease in labor demand was more than 10 percent per year in steel, and 18 percent per year in automobiles.

Summary Result: Direct Effect

On balance, the direct effect of technical change on labor demand has been the substitution of other inputs for labor in all five industries. However, the effect has proceeded gradually at a generally constant or even declining rate, and its impact on employment has often been far smaller than declines due to changes in wage rates and output, particularly in the recession years of 1979 and 1980.

THE OUTPUT-ENHANCEMENT EFFECT

To measure the total effect of technical change on employment demand, we must consider the way in which technical change can lead to employment gains. This is the output-enhancement effect defined above.

Modeling the Output-Enhancement Effect

To measure the output-enhancement effect of technical change, we constructed a simple model of output change elicited by advances in industry technology. In the model, the demand for an industry's product is conditioned on the presence of a competing, though not perfectly substitutable, import. Improvements in the domestic industry's technology are assumed to reduce domestic production cost and selling price, but import prices are treated as not responding. The rate of change in the domestic price turns out to equal the negative of the rate of change in domestic industry productivity, which means that if domestic technology increases, increased productivity leads to a fall in domestic output price, an increase in sales of domestic output, and an increase in domestic employment. In essence, domestic technical change allows domestic producers either to gain sales at the expense of foreign producers who do not innovate or to prevent a loss of sales to foreign producers who do innovate.

Results: Combined Output-Enhancement Effect and Direct Effect

The total effect of technical change on labor (holding input prices constant) is made up of the output-enhancement effect plus the direct effect described in the previous section. Table 3–4 reports average annual values for the output-enhancement, direct, and total effects of technical change (for the same respective periods as in Table 3–3).

For the steel industry, the output-enhancement effect is negligible regardless of whether the time-trend measure or the direct measure of technical change is used. This, of course, is due to the (almost) zero rate of technical change in steel over the period studied (see Table 3–1). The total effect on employment is negative at 1.1 percent a year using the time-trend measure and 1.3 percent a year using the direct measure.

For the automobile industry, the output-enhancement effect is important but differs in magnitude depending on whether the time-trend measure or the direct measure of technical change is used. When the time trend is used, the effect is more than twice as large as when the direct measure is used (as shown in Levy, Bowes, and Jondrow 1983,

Table 3–4.   The Effects of Technical Change on Labor[a]
for All Industries (percentage).

Industry (Measure of Technology)	Output-Enhancement Effect	Direct Effect	Total Effect
Steel (time trend)	0.13	−1.24	−1.11
Steel (direct measure)	0.04	−1.31	−1.27
Automobiles (time trend)	2.27	−3.10	−0.83
Automobiles (direct measure)	1.03	−1.08	−0.05
Aluminum	13.18	−5.62	7.56
Coal (time trend)	3.65	−3.40	0.25
Coal (direct measure)	4.52	−4.21	0.31
Iron ore	3.50	−1.00	2.50

[a] To obtain values of the elasticity of demand, we relied on Jondrow (1978) for steel and Charles River Associates (1975) for autos. We were able to calculate the values of the elasticity as −1.01 and −1.12 in steel and automobiles, respectively. For aluminum, we used a value of −3, a relatively large value for the elasticity (which we derived from information in Charles River Associates (1971)). It implies that price effects will have a large effect on output. Finally, for coal mining, we derived an elasticity of −1.087 (for details, see Bowes (1982)). For iron ore, we used an elasticity of −1, which was chosen to be similar to that for coal.

this is partly a result of a higher rate of technical change). The direct effect, on the other hand, is about three times as large when the time-trend measure is used. The total effect is −0.8 percent using the time-trend measure and about zero using the direct measure.

The output-enhancement effect for the aluminum industry is large, 13.2 percent per year, and outweighs the partial effect of −5.6 percent per year. The total effect on labor demand is 7.6 percent per year. The substantial output-enhancement effect reflects the high (absolute) value for the output demand elasticity. In essence, the domestic aluminum industry faces fierce competition from imports (and secondary aluminum), so that any relative price shift in favor of imports results in a large loss in domestic producers' sales. Consequently, advances in domestic technology allow domestic producers to maintain competitive prices and higher output levels than would have been possible had they not innovated.

Finally, in the two mining industries, the output-enhancement effects of technology are also substantial and outweigh the negative direct effects. In iron ore, the output-enhancement effect is sufficiently large to create a growth in labor demand of 2.5 percent a year. Note, however, that this estimate probably provides an overly optimistic picture because our mining models were, of necessity, simple and assumed that all technical change was cost reducing with no factor bias, as opposed to labor-saving.

THE ROLE OF ATTRITION IN REDUCING DISPLACEMENT DUE TO TECHNICAL CHANGE

There is yet another factor that mitigates the negative effects on employment arising from changing technology—attrition. Whatever the source of the decline in employment, attrition can potentially lessen the amount of involuntary displacement. One measure of attrition is the industry quit rate, presented in Table 3–5 for the five industries studied, as well as for all manufacturing.

The quit rate is a measure of primarily voluntary job separation. Although the industries we studied exhibit quit rates well below the average rate in manufacturing, the rates are still substantially greater than our estimates of the rate of reduction in labor demand caused by technical change.

It is therefore possible that much of the reduction in labor demand due to technical change can be accomplished through attrition. Nevertheless, technical change is still likely to cause layoffs, especially when

Table 3–5. Quit Rate by Industry for All Industries (percentage).

	Average Annual Quit Rate (1976–80)
Steel	4.1
Automobiles	8.1
Aluminum	6.7
Iron ore	8.4
Coal mining	6.5
Manufacturing	21.8

Source: Department of Labor, (various issues from 1978 to 1982).

its effects are concentrated in a particular area, leading, for example, to layoffs in one geographic region and accessions in another. It is also possible that cyclical downturns, added to the effects of technical change, could overwhelm attrition as a means of accommodating technical change.

Still, the fact remains that the rate of attrition has been far above the employment effects of technical change and has cushioned the effects of employment reduction. Even in the steel industry, with the lowest quit rate (4.1 percent) and a negative total effect of technical change on employment, voluntary turnover has been more than adequate to cover employment reduction.

SUMMARY OF KEY FINDINGS

The total effect of technical change on labor demand consists of a direct effect and an indirect output-enhancement effect. Much of our work has dealt with obtaining better estimates of the direct effect — that is, the effect of technical change on labor demand when output, as well as input prices, are held constant. The econometric model we developed explicitly separated out the effects of technical change on productivity growth from the effect of scale economies. Had we not made this separation, the effects of technical change would have been overstated.

Our model also allowed us to compare the effects of technical change and the implications for employment demand when a time-trend measure and a direct measure of technical changes were used. In general, the way in which technology was measured did not affect the results very much; except for automobiles, the conclusions were substantively the same. Although economists frequently represent technical change with a simple time trend, they are often attacked for having oversimplified. Our results suggest that in most cases the simplification is reasonable.

Our estimate of the direct effect of technical change on employment was negative in all industries, regardless of the measure of technology. The direct effect was strongest in aluminum, coal mining, and automobiles (under the time-trend specification of technology) and weakest in iron ore. Steel, with a virtually zero rate of technical change over the period studied, still experienced labor displacement due to shifts in the technique of production, but this apparently was solely the result of the installation of less labor-intensive production processes at a given level of technology.

The degree of direct labor displacement is potentially lessened by the indirect output-enhancement effect of technology — that is, technical advance leads to lower output prices, increases in the quantity of output sold, and increases in employment. Though the output-enhancement effect was insignificant for steel (since the rate of technical change was near zero), for all the other industries it led to employment growth that counterbalanced much of technical change's labor- saving characteristics, and in some cases more than counterbalanced the entire labor-saving effect. Once both the output-enhancement effect and the direct effect are accounted for, any net decline in employment due to technical change was relatively small and did not typically move in great jumps from year to year. Normal labor turnover — retirements and quits — far exceeded the decline in employment caused by improved technology, thereby cushioning the displacement effects of technical change.

NOTES

1. The only exception is the automobile industry when technology is measured directly.
2. The exception, again, is the automobile industry when technology is measured directly.
3. We also did the decomposition using the direct measure of technology and found that using the direct measure hardly changed the pattern or magnitudes of the two components for the steel industry. For the automobile industry, the pattern using the direct measure was different in the early years, in that scale contributed more to productivity growth than did technical change. After 1965 the pattern was very similar to the time-trend results.
4. Specifically, in order to determine the individual partial effects we used the econometric results to obtain a value for the percentage change in labor demand arising from a change in a given exogenous variable (with the other exogenous variables held constant). This was then multiplied by the average actual percentage change in that variable over time.
5. For coal mining and iron ore, industries where labor-demand equations were estimated directly, technical change was assumed to be Hicks-neutral — that is, lacking any bias. The rate of technical change is therefore obtained as the negative of the coefficient on technology in the

estimated labor-demand equation. Though we do not present the equations in this chapter (see Levy, Bowes, and Jondrow 1983), the rate of technical change in coal mining, when a time trend represents technology, can be seen from Table 3–2 to be equal to 3.4 percent.

REFERENCES

Bowes, Marianne, "Coal Mining" (Center for Naval Analyses, Public Research Institute Working Paper 82–10, March 1982).

Charles River Associates, *Cost–Benefit Analysis of the Effects of Trade Policies on Product and Labor Markets in the U.S. Automobile Industry* (report to the Bureau of International Labor Affairs, U.S. Department of Labor, October 1975).

Charles River Associates, *An Economic Analysis of the Aluminum Industry* (report to Property Management and Disposal Service, General Services Administration, Washington, D.C., March 1971).

Jondrow, James M., "Effects of Trade Restrictions on Imports of Steel," *The Impact of International Trade and Investment on Employment* (U.S. Department of Labor, Bureau of International Labor Affairs, Washington, D.C., 1978), pp. 11–25.

Levy, Robert A., Marianne Bowes, and James M. Jondrow, "Adjustment of Employment to Technical Change in Steel, Autos, Aluminum, Coal, and Iron Ore" (Center for Naval Analyses, CRC 487, June 1983).

U.S. Department of Labor, Bureau of Labor Statistics, *Employment and Earnings* (various issues from 1978 to 1982).

4 MODERNIZING THE FEDERAL GOVERNMENT: EFFECT ON ITS EMPLOYEES

Lucretia Dewey Tanner

As the nation's largest employer, with 4.8 million workers,[1] the U.S. government is considered a monolith in its policies and procedures. In practice, however, each major branch of government — executive, legislative, judicial, the military, and the U.S. Postal Service — functions independently in setting pay and working conditions, as well as in its approach to introducing technological change.

This chapter reviews the research conducted into the federal sector's experience with technological change and analyzes the types of responses to its introduction of new machinery and planning for human-resource needs. Changes are now occurring in work settings with and without ongoing collective bargaining; both will be reviewed. Studies have been conducted to examine the long-range conversion to automated systems at the Internal Revenue Service, the government's new management initiatives, its general assessment of new equipment, and the profound technological changes in one of the government's largest agencies, the U.S. Postal Service. Lastly, productivity in the federal sector is discussed — its methodology, results, and comparison with the general economy.

The research conducted thus far raises many questions about the future, although it is abundantly clear that the introduction of new

The views expressed in this chapter are solely those of the author. In no way do they represent the views of the Advisory Committee on Federal Pay.

technology brings with it change for both management and the employee. For example, what happens to people when technology is introduced: Are they displaced? Are new skills required? What responsibility does management have to retrain? Should the introduction of technology in government be more closely coordinated and responsibility be centralized for efficiency, effectiveness, and good personnel management? What role do unions play in planning and developing? Because of government's size and diversity, the discussion is not exhaustive, but examples have been chosen to illustrate some of these problems and the approaches taken.

This chapter presents the federal government as an employer. The first part describes the changing nature of the work force and studies that have evaluated the change. The second and third parts analyze technological adjustments made by the U.S. Postal Service and productivity in other governmental functions. The chapter concludes with a discussion of the future outlook.

A CHANGING WORK FORCE

The federal government performs a great number of functions and employs people in roughly 400 white-collar and 400 blue-collar job categories. In a relatively short period of time, job titles and functions disappear, new ones emerge, and others gain in employment (Table 4–1). In 1968 the government employed 3,700 computer specialists, and by 1978 the number had grown to 27,000; by 1981 the number had increased to 31,000. This occupation now ranks among the top ten white-collar jobs in terms of number of workers employed. The job title "punch card operator" disappeared but was replaced by "data transcriber," and both jobs employ roughly the same number of people, 15,000. A large occupational group, clerk typists, declined by 12 percent during the decade and registered another 7 percent drop between 1978 and 1981. Further, while the title remains the same, duties have changed with the introduction of the word processor machine.

A Case Study: IRS

A detailed study of the disappearance and emergence of jobs as a result of the introduction of new technology in one agency was com-

Table 4-1. Selected Occupations in the Federal White-Collar Work Force, 1968 and 1978.

	1968	1978	1981
Computer specialist	3,672	26,649	30,617
Computer aide and technician	1,862	6,880	7,746
Digital computer systems administrator	91	1,635	1,100
Digital computer systems operator	1,973	—	—
Peripheral computer equipment operator	945	—	—
Data transcriber	—	13,783	12,401
Computer operator	—	11,197	10,241
Clerk typist	78,447	69,525	63,254
Punch-card operator	15,800	—	—

Source: *Occupations of Federal White-Collar Workers,* Office of Personnel Management, 1968, 1978, and 1981 publications.

pleted by the U.S. Department of Labor's Bureau of Labor Statistics (BLS). The Bureau's Division of Technological Studies undertook a review of the Internal Revenue Service's transition from a manual paperwork operation to computer processing (Rothberg 1969: 26–30). Before the planned conversion in the early 1960s, routine income tax return processing was performed in fifty-eight district offices; these functions were to be transferred to seven regional centers linked to the National Computer Center at Martinsburg, West Virginia. The nationwide conversion, planned for a six-year period, actually took close to ten years to complete. Over this period of time, district office employment had been reduced from 12,000 to 1,515 but had been accomplished without any involuntary transfers or separations.

BLS research focused on the IRS Atlanta Region, dating from 1962 and extending to the end of the decade. Included in its review was an investigation into the planning and administration of personnel changes, the characteristics of employees affected and the new ADP positions created, the selection and staffing of computer jobs, training and retraining, and other human-relations problems. In the Atlanta region during a seven-year conversion period, total employment was 1,451 (1,051 initially on the rolls and an additional 400 replacements hired over the period). By the time of the final phaseout, the work force had been reduced to 120. Almost 70 percent of the employees were transferred to other jobs, with the remaining 30 percent either retiring (59 percent), resigning (37 percent), or dying (4 percent). While the reductions were achieved without involuntary separations or transfers, 109 employees accepted downgrades, with pay maintained at their current level for two years.

Viewed by the BLS, the transition was a success largely because of the close communication with employees and employee organizations. Management demonstrated concern for its employees. It planned well in advance and accomplished the changeover with few displacements, demotions, or involuntary transfers. In addition, it provided retraining opportunities to its current work force. Employment, rather than declining, grew after the merging of the manual routine data process work with the computerized center.

Some occupational shifts did occur, and new ADP positions were created. These new occupations, however, although generally skilled, accounted for only 8 percent of the total new employment. Routine and lower-skilled jobs that already existed — sorting, classifying, examining, and statistical record checking — merely increased.

Since this initial changeover the original machines have been judged outdated, and a new system is being installed. The Memphis office began phasing in the newer generation of machines in October 1982, the only one of the ten centers to do so. The main improvement is expected to be faster processing of data and ultimately collection of additional taxes. A new dunning computer-run method makes random telephone calls during which an IRS employee presents the errant taxpayer with information and asks for the taxes due. Monitoring of the changeover, similar to the previous study, would provide insights into the changed personnel requirements.

Studies by the General Accounting Office

The General Accounting Office, an agency responsible for assisting Congress, its committees, and members, has actively studied technology and productivity issues in response to congressional requests. GAO, a keen observer of the bureaucracy, has in fact produced many studies along with recommendations for program improvements.[2] An entire volume could be devoted to lessons gained from its output alone. Rather than attempt a comprehensive review, it may be more appropriate to highlight key findings.

In one of its more recent studies — made in response to a request by the Senate Appropriations Committee — GAO examined the federal government's management of office automation ("Strong Central Management" 1982). Concern was expressed about whether the increased application of automation would be effectively managed and lead to cost savings and/or improve services to the public. GAO focused on four agencies that were planning for or implementing office automation, how they were monitoring and measuring productivity increases, and the extent of technical assistance available to them from central management agencies.[3] Selection of the four agencies was based on their past or expected acquisition of office automation systems — from word processors to main-frame computers designed for use by clerical, professional, and managerial staff. In addition, they examined four private companies that had considerable experience with office automation.

The results of GAO's review were not encouraging. They found that the agencies studied were not adequately managing the development and implementation of office automation. It warned that without a strong central management a great deal of money is and would be spent with little gain in productivity.[4] Absent from the agencies were comprehensive plans for managing the development and implementation of the change. Also missing were agency economic analyses, pre- and postinstallation, to measure the cost and productivity improvements. The lack of in-house technical capability to understand office automation created reliance on consultants, equipment vendors, or internal staff who were not knowledgeable.

In GAO's study and apparently in the agencies as well, very little information is presented concerning retraining needs, job content changes, and employee fears of change. GAO does note the lack of human-resource assistance in ensuring that the new systems were accepted by the employees; that the machines required testing for potential hazards; and that training was needed for the users. In one agency, the automation systems were minimally used because staff members had not been trained to use the equipment.

These findings supported an earlier study that had been confined to word procssors. Word processors, an important component of modern government office equipment, comprise an estimated annual federal expenditure of $300 million. Effective use of word processors can enhance productivity by reducing the work force or increasing volume with the same or greater work load. GAO's evaluation of the introduction and management of various types of this equipment concluded that most agencies' management could not demonstrate that the machines increased productivity or that they were cost effective ("Federal Productivity Suffers" 1979).

One response to this GAO study was the Reagan administration's announcement of a new management effort called Reform 88, which was expected to take six years to complete. Designed to develop a standard accounting and reporting system, its objective is also to integrate the government's computer systems, with capability to exchange data and cut paperwork. Officials noted that the government has 16,000 computer systems and 325 agency accounting systems, all basically incompatible. The government plans to phase in new equipment as the old needs replacing. Joseph Wright, deputy director of the Office of Management and Buget (OMB), said during a news conference to announce the new project that his goal was to make the government operate as efficiently as Exxon (Early 1982). Exxon, one of the four companies in the GAO study, was cited as having successfully avoided major pitfalls by having a long-term organization plan, conducting postinstallation analyses, and gearing work-force understanding to the automated systems.[5] While focusing on the mechanics of an integrated system, the new federal program apparently fails, at least at this point, to develop a human system for reassigning or retraining of displaced workers.

U.S. POSTAL SERVICE

Now undergoing major technological change is the U.S. Postal Service (USPS), a quasi-public private establishment created in 1971.[6] USPS, an enormous service organization with approximately 670,000 employees, provides mail-processing and delivery services to industries and businesses throughout all areas of the country, urban and rural, and handles about 106 billion pieces of mail annually.

The Postal Act reiterates and strengthens the mandate to use new facilities and equipment to improve the conveniences, efficiency, and cost effectiveness of the mail service. Just as the major modes of transportation — railroad, plane, truck, and automatic sorting machines — have been integrated into mail handling, new ways of conveying messages have potentially major impacts. Two major developments — electronic mail and message systems (EMS) and electronic funds transfer (EFT) — will increasingly compete with the traditional postal service market. EMS was first launched in January 1982 when the Postal Service introduced a domestic service called electronic computer-originated mail or E-Com. In this process, USPS accepts letters in electronic form, converts them to hard copy, including printing and enveloping, and then delivers them.

This experiment was short-lived, however. On June 5, 1984 the U.S. Postal Service Board of Governors directed the Postal Service to lease or sell its computerized mail system. Volume was well below expected levels even though the price of the computer-generated letters was less than the actual cost of delivery. The Rate Commission had asked originally for an increase from the current 26 cents to 52 cents per piece, which the Board rejected. When the Commission came back with a lower price hike of 49 cents the Board rejected this also and called for the leasing or selling of the equipment. Critics of the E-Com effort charged that it was doomed to failure from the start because of the Postal Service's inexperience with marketing and printing, and the constraining rules it operates under.

As soon as the divestiture announcement was made, offers were received from a number of private firms. According to Postmaster Bolger, the arrangements contemplated with the company or companies selected would be similar to those for its Mailgram operations (i.e., that the Postal Service would provide hard copy delivery and other services on a reimbursible basis). Thus, while the operations may be "privatized," the actual housing of the equipment and the handling of volume would be within the Postal Service. The entire changeover is expected to be completed by the spring of 1985 (Isikoff 1984; U.S. Postal Service).

In August 1982, soon after the implementation of E-Com at USPS, the Office of Technological Assessment (OTA) attempted to estimate future volume and employment levels of the Postal Service under varying assumptions. Because the Postal Service is expected to operate the electronic equipment for E-Com with its own employees, the OTA projections are still valid. Under any plausible scenario, USPS is still likely to be handling a large volume of conventional mail in the year 2000 (70–110 billion pieces), despite OTA estimates that labor force requirements will remain well below 1980 levels. Not all agree with the OTA projections, however, and some within the USPS believe that employment will actually increase, particularly if private expectations for the E-Com market are realized.

Table 4–2. Structure of the U.S. Postal Service Labor Force, 1980 and 2000.[a]

Employee Group	Numbers of Employees		Percentage Change
	1980	2000	
Headquarters	2,798	2,800	—
Regional and other field units	6,228	6,220	—
Inspection	5,242	5,240	—
Postmasters	28,967	26,900	−7.3
Post Office supervisors and technical personnel	36,481	29,220	−19.9
Post Office clerks and mail handlers	303,560	204,000	−32.9
City delivery carriers and vehicle drivers	193,370	157,000	−19.1
Rural delivery carriers	53,069	47,600	−10.3
Special delivery messengers	2,502	2,130	−14.9
Building and equipment maintenance personnel	29,409	24,400	−17.2
Vehicle maintenance facility personnel	4,837	4,300	−11.1
Total	666,823	509,810	−30.8

Source: Extracted from *Implications of Electronic Mail and Message Systems for the U.S. Postal Service*, Office of Technology Assessment (August 1982).

[a] Assumes high EMS growth, 2 percent mail stream growth, and 1.5 percent labor productivity improvement.

The Postal Service is a highly labor-intensive organization in which labor represents about 85 percent of total costs. Projections of future work-force requirements will be determined by the volume of mail, its level of service, and the introduction of new technology (frequency and type of delivery) and productivity growth. Table 4-2 presents one set of projections of the future personnel needs by the year 2000 as developed by OTA. It assumes a high but plausible growth of EMS (Generation II), a 2 percent underlying mailstream growth, and a 1.5 percent labor productivity improvement. Over the twenty-year period, employment would decline by 31 percent, given this set of assumptions. Productivity during the 1970s, however, grew at a 3 percent annual rate, and if this variable were substituted, the decline in employment would be even steeper—50 percent. Reductions are not likely to be spread evenly, but as the table suggests the hardest-hit group will be the clerks and mail handlers, with losses in the third to one-half range. Clerks and mail handlers represent the single largest postal employee group and now account for about 45 percent of the total USPS force; it will still be the most sizable group but will represent 40 percent of total.

Not all employment reductions would be evenly distributed over the two decades. About one-half of the loss would occur between now and 1995 and then accelerate rapidly during the next five years to eliminate the other half.

Employees of the U.S. Postal Service represent one of the few groups in the government that bargain collectively over wages and working conditions.[7] Four major unions represent employees along craft lines but have traditionally negotiated a coordinated agreement.

Most clerks' starting pay is at the Grade 5 level, $19,663 as of November 14, 1981; however, Postmaster William Bolger has informed Moe Biller, American Postal Workers' Union president, that two new clerk-level positions will be created, a Level 4 mail distributor and a Level 3 mail processor. Pay at these grades is lower, $19,115 and $18,610, respectively. The decision to downgrade positions is tied to the proposed nine-digit zip code or, more specifically, the automated machines purchased to process the longer code, implemented October 1983. While downgrading is expected to be achieved largely through attrition, it is the result of the reduced skill levels inherent in the application of new optical scanner and bar code reader machinery. While no estimates of the number of employees to be affected have been given, Mr. Bolger at one point suggested that full implementation of the nine-digit zip code would save 60,000 man-years (Williams 1982).

Realizing that technological change and productivity improvements have already eliminated 65,000 jobs during the decade of the 1970s, the parties addressed some of the problems in their collective bargaining agreement. In the contract entered into between USPS and APWU and NALC on July 21, 1981, and extending to July 20, 1984, provisions were made for giving advance notice to the unions of pending change, for providing job security for tenured employees, and for setting up a mechanism for resolving disputes. New jobs created by technological changes are to be offered to employees who have the potential ability to perform the job.

Lifetime job protection is provided to all employees who were full- or part-time, regular or part-time flexible workers as of September 15, 1978, the date an arbitration award on this subject was issued by James L. Healy. This same protected status can be achieved after an employee completes six years of continuous service and works in at least twenty pay periods during each of the six years.

The agreement also established a national Joint Labor/Management Technological or Mechanization Changes Committee, whose purpose is to resolve questions on the impact of the proposed change on affected employees. Unresolved problems are referred to arbitration.

The Postal Service has entered into a quality-of-work-life program with three of the four major unions as another way of coping with the transition to more automated operations. Quality circles (QC's), based on management techniques used in Japan, are founded on the concept that productivity improvements come not only from technological change but also from greater employee motivation and involvement. Included in postal circles are about 10 percent of the workers from the same section, including supervisors, who meet to discuss common work problems. QC's are designed to enhance product quality through more effective teamwork and communications and increased efficiency. This is a particularly important practice when change in the work place is or about to take place and channels information, not rumor, through the system. Worker participation benefits management by providing practical ideas for successfully introducing change. The former Senior Assistant Postmaster, General Carl Ulsaker, has stated that it will probably take ten years more before QC's and other types of employee-involvement programs are operating nationwide.

The postal experience demonstrates that employee involvement in the introduction of new systems and machines is important during all phases. This is being accomplished through the collective bargaining process in one of the largest and highly organized federal agencies. Unions, working with management, are trying to minimize disruption of the work force and have taken steps to see that future changes have little or no adverse impact on the current work force. The results of this cooperative effort are evident in the productivity growth record. During the 1967–81 period, postal productivity grew at a rate of 1.3 percent per year compared to the national nonfarm service sector average of 0.8 percent per year. Postmaster Bolger points to the fact that the Postal Service is delivering substantially more mail today with far fewer workers and that this was accomplished by attrition, and not layoffs.

PRODUCTIVITY IN THE FEDERAL SECTOR

The primary reason for introducing new technology is to increase productivity and thereby reduce cost. While very little research has been undertaken into federal productivity, the Bureau of Labor Statistics has nevertheless collected data and developed productivity measures for federal activities since 1971.[8] Its productivity measurement is limited to labor input because of lack of additional information. As with any single-factor productivity measure, the output-per-unit-of-labor measures reflect other factors, including changes in technology, capital stock, and size of operation, as well as labor's contribution. People who turn out the product, the process used, and the product itself are the three ingredients for productivity changes.

Before examining these components and the use made of the data collected, it first might be appropriate to provide a brief description of the federal index design. Currently the BLS survey covers functions of approximately 65 percent of the work force. The maximum coverage possible is placed at 85 percent of the total civilian employment. The remaining 15 percent includes agency functions devoted primarily to basic research or national policy functions, not easily quantifiable. BLS samples include 455 federal organizational units that represent a mix of several levels of government activity, major departments, bureaus, and field operations. Approximately 3,450 output indicators are included, such as the number of completed cases, complaints processed, reports published, and so forth. These are then categorized into twenty-eight functions for which indexes are constructed.[9] The twenty-eight include the following functions:

(1) audit of operations, (2) buildings and grounds, (3) communications, (4) education and training, (5) electric power product distribution, (6) equipment maintenance, (7) finance and accounting, (8) geneneral support services, (9) information services, (10) legal and judicial activities, (11) library services, (12) loans and grants, (13) medical services, (14) military base services, (15) national resources and environmental management, (16) personnel management, (17) personnel investigation, (18) Postal Service, (19) printing and duplication, (20) procurement, (21) records management, (22) regulation compliance and enforcement, (23) regulation or rulemaking and licensing, (24) social services and benefits, (25) specialized manufacturing, (26) supply and inventory control, (27) traffic management, and (28) transportation.

For example, an index is constructed to measure the productivity for the entire Postal Service. This is an exception, since most functions include several organizational units. One function that has few organizational units, besides the Postal Service, is electric power production and distribution. Included in this category for measurement are Alaska, Southeastern and Southwestern Power Administration, and the Tennessee Valley Authority. After indexes are developed for each of the twenty-eight, a composite index is then developed.

Output per employee varies considerably among the twenty-eight functions. The average annual rate of change for communication exceeds all others, gaining 11 percent each year (measured from 1973 to 1981). Electric power and library services were also high performers, with 8.2 and 8.1 percent, respectively, measured from 1977 to 1981. Not all functions performed as well, however, and actual declines were recorded for nine during the 1967–81 fiscal years. The largest drops occurred in supply and inventory control and military base services, declining 4.2 and 4.1 percent, respectively.

BLS places caveats on using productivity comparisons between the private sector and the federal government. If the comparison is confined to the nonfarm business sector, however, as one possibility for narrowing the definition in the private sector, the productivity rate equals that of the federal government. In the 1967–81 period, productivity increased 1.5 percent per year in both sectors. If, however, the federal sector is compared to the service industries in the private sector, its growth rate over the fifteen years is almost double: 1.5 percent per year in the federal sector compared to 0.8 percent per year in the private-sector service industries.

In a publication issued by the Office of Personnel Management, that agency analyzes overall productivity growth and each of the functional categories from 1967 to 1979. In general, it concluded that productivity increases are attributed to changes in the process, that declines are related to people, and thus that skillful management assists increases while poor management impedes productivity growth. Management decisions and actions that inhibit growth include promoting or permitting high rates of staff turnover (including unnecessary and early retirements), not training or recruiting skilled employees, and scheduling workload or production delays outside employee control. Positive factors include management commitment to training, particularly when programs of work methods change. Employee participation, good communication, job enrichment, and incentive awards are also classified as positive elements (*Federal Productivity Measurement* 1981).

The question now can be raised of how the data collected by BLS is used in carrying out the management function — or how it should be used. The Bureau conducted informal discussions with several agencies to determine data use. Apparently some agencies use it in their annual reports to justify their budgets, while a few use it for control or planning purposes or to allocate funds internally.

Based on this anecdotal of the uses of the data, other questions can be asked. First, it appears that the government has not assigned responsibility for determining the extent of the use of the productivity data. Second, as a manager the government has no coordinated policy on how the data should be used to evaluate agency functions and programs. Even more seriously, it appears that there is little interest in even maintaining a federal productivity database at all. While BLS performs the detailed analysis, OPM, with primary responsibility, has merely delegated the data collection. Whether for philosophical or financial considerations, OPM and/or the Office of Management and Budget has indicated an unwillingness to continue the series. This abdication of responsibility for at least monitoring the federal productivity data series appears contrary to current emphasis on relating pay increases to measurable performance and on increasing the efficiency of the government as a whole. From a management perspective, not having measurement techniques in place at a time when large sums of money are being spent on equipment will obviously hinder analysis of any contributions to reducing costs.

CONCLUSION

In this overview of the federal government's attempt to manage technological change it becomes apparent that results are not uniform. In some instances — the BLS study of the IRS, for example — the attempt was carefully planned and human factors considered. The General Accounting Office reports, on the other hand, have pointed to the deficiencies in management, both in introduction of the machines and in personnel planning.

Strong leadership and direction has been lacking from agencies that are responsible for overseeing the purchase of equipment, offering technical guidance, and personnel responsibilities. A new effort, called Project 88, to be completed in 1988, promises to provide that needed guidance, at least on the coordination of purchase and interchangeability of machines. Effective personnel policies may still be missing, however, from the effort to bring modern technology into the government.

Both government and employee representatives have not focused on the problems already created by technological change or those about to surface — and probably for good reason, since other more pressing concerns have occupied their attention. As an employer, the government has been reallocating its work force, shifting from social programs to defense needs, has proposed major fringe-benefit restrictions, and has failed to provide wage increases comparable to the private sector for several years. The unions, needless to say, have been preoccupied in attempts to halt the threatened erosion in benefits, pay, and working conditions and to preserve their status as bargaining representatives.

Experience has demonstrated that long-range planning and joint cooperative efforts by management and employee representatives are necessary for the successful introduction of new technologies. As OPM's study suggests, while new processes enhance productivity, its decline is directly attributable to mismanagement of people. At this point, however, dialogue at both the general and technical levels appears to be halted, and confrontation on all issues prevails.

While not without their disagreements, the Postal Service and its unions have reached an agreement and are jointly dealing with the problem. The postal unions have faced immediate and drastic cutbacks in employment and grade levels. In order to cope with these current and long-range problems, unions have secured virtual lifetime employment for senior workers in bargaining sessions with management. In an offer to smooth the way for change, labor and management have established committees, both local and national in scope, to work out some of their problems cooperatively. Other government workers and unions have not gained collective bargaining rights of that magnitude and are not in a position to secure such benefits. Failing to maintain even existing working conditions and compensation, unions are devoting more than ever of their resources to legislative appeals as a means to attaining their objectives and have abandoned any hope of accommodation, let alone cooperation.[10]

While it is too soon and perhaps too hazardous to draw any general conclusions, it appears thus far that technological change may not upgrade skill levels; it may require less demanding qualifications. In the IRS, only 8 percent of the new jobs required upgraded skills; other jobs created were the routine. The postal experience clearly indicates that whenever new jobs become available they will be at reduced skill levels. Along with these less demanding skills also comes a drop in wages. Neither does it appear that the work force will expand. Total federal employment has remained relatively stable over a long period of time, and yet the work force has taken on increasing numbers of tasks, supported by the continuous gains in productivity.

Despite the shortcomings of planners and managers, government productivity has continued to increase and compares favorably with the private sector. The government, because of its size, may be too severely criticized and come under attack for the programs it administers, not for its success in carrying them out. Functioning on a daily basis, the government is equal to or even outperforming the mythical "efficient" private sector. In order to continue, however, it may have to look to the best models in the private sector, both in managing technology and its work force.

NOTES

1.   Total civilian and military employment in 1982 was 4.8 million: 2.7 million civilian (which includes 1.4 million white-collar workers, 400,000 blue-collar, 600,000 postal, 200,000 in the Veterans Administration's Department of Medicine and Surgery, and 100,000 others, including the Foreign Service, GPO, and TVA); military was 2.1 million. Sources: Office of Personnel Management and Department of Defense.

2. An annotated listing of GAO reports on productivity shows forty-one studies in the private and public sectors during the July 1978 through mid-1981 period, and others have been completed since that time.

3. The four government agencies selected for the study were the U.S. Departments of Labor and the Navy, the National Aeronautics and Space Administration, and the Forest Service of the Department of Agriculture.

4. The responsibilities for administering and managing automatic data processing activities were outlined in a directive from the Executive Office of the President. Four offices were given specific instructions: The Office of Management and Budget (then the Bureau of the Budget) was assigned overall leadership and coordination of ADP; the General Services Administration, achieving cost effectiveness in the selection of the equipment; the Department of Commerce, technical assistance to other executive agencies on the use and design of the system; and the Office of Personnel Management (then the Civil Service Commission), providing the leadership in managing personnel and the equipment.

   The human services to be offered by OPM include formulating position classification and qualification standards; developing recruiting, designing, testing, and selection devices; and stimulating and coordinating training. In addition, it was to anticipate and minimize adverse effects of ADP on people and to prepare for the future personnel effects. It was also to educate executives and other key personnel to achieve greater effectiveness in ADP management. (OMB Circular No. A–71, March 6, 1965.)

5. The four companies selected were Avon Products, the Bank of America, Continental Illinois Bank, and the Exxon Corporation.

6. The U.S. Postal Service was created as an independent establishment of the Executive Branch by section 2 of the Postal Reorganization Act, approved August 12, 1970 (84 Stat. 719; 39 U.S.C. 101 et seq.). It began operations on July 11, 1971.

7. The Postal Service is by far the largest group within the government that bargains collectively over wages, benefits, and working conditions. Approximately twenty groups, representing 643,000 workers, are also covered by bargaining rights. The largest include the Tennessee Valley Authority, with 51,000; the Government Printing Office, 2,940; Department of Treasury's Bureau of Engraving and Printing, 1,900; Department of the Navy's Military Sealift Command, 1,530; Department of Interior's Bureau of Mines, 1,300, and Department of Energy's Bonneville Power Administration, 1,200. Smaller groupings are scattered among several agencies including: Department of Transportation's Alaska Railroad, 540; the Western Area Power Adminis-

tration, 400; the Bureau of Indian Affairs, 230; and the U.S. International Communications Agency, 155. (See "Comparison of Collective Bargained and Administratively Set Pay Rates for Federal Employees" 1982: 21.)

8. While BLS has published measures of labor productivity output per hour for selected industries in the private sector, it began acting as the collection and measurement agency first under the joint sponsorship of the General Accounting Office, the Civil Service Commission (now the Office of Personnel Management), the Office of Management and Budget, and the former National Center for Productivity and Quality of Working Life. OPM, which has the primary management function, has delegated the actual technical aspects to BLS. During 1982–83, OPM indicated that it was no longer interested in federal-sector-productivity data collection or analysis, and the continuation of the effort is in doubt.

9. Sampling has been expanded over the years. In 1971, only seventeen agencies, with 114 organizational units and 94 percent output indicators, were sampled. These covered 54 percent of the total Civil Service employee-years of 2.9 million. 1981's sample includes 64 percent of the 2.8 million total civilian employee-years. Data from 1962 to 1971 is based on available records.

10. Despite a general contentious atmosphere, a number of joint labor/management committees and efforts are scattered among the agencies.

REFERENCES

"Comparison of Collective Bargained and Administratively Set Pay Rates for Federal Employees" (General Accounting Office, GAO/FPCD 82–40, July 27, 1982), p. 21.

Early, Peter, "Management Reform Plan Unveiled," *Washington Post,* September 23, 1982, p. A21, col. 3.

Federal Productivity Measurement (report and analysis of the FY 1979 productivity data), (Washington, D.C.: Office of Personnel Management, Workforce Effectiveness and Development Group, revised February 1981).

"Federal Productivity Suffers Because Work Processing Is Not Well Managed" (General Accounting Office, GAO/DMDO 79–17, April 6, 1979).

Implications of Electronic Mail and Message Systems for the U.S. Postal Service (Washington, D.C.: U.S. Government Printing Office, August 1983).

Isikoff, Michael, "Postal Service Must Sell E-Com," *Washington Post,* June 6, 1984, p. D8, col. 3.

Rothberg, Herman J., "A Study of the Impact of Office Automation in the IRS," *Monthly Labor Review* 92 (October 1969): 26–30.

"Strong Central Management of Office Automation Will Boost Productivity" (General Accounting Office, GAO/AFMD 82–54, September 21, 1982).

Williams, Bob, "9 Digit Zip Imperils Postal Clerks' Future," *Federal Times* August 2, 1982.

U.S. Postal Service, "PMG Sets Record Straight on E-Com," *Newsbreak* (Washington, D.C.: Public and Employees Communications Dept., USPS, undated flyer).

5 EFFECT OF TECHNOLOGY ON THE DISTRIBUTION OF LABOR INCOME

John Vrooman

Our understanding of why some workers are paid more or less than others has often been frustrated by the abstraction of labor-market phenomena into two mutually exclusive categories—one focused on labor supply and the other on labor demand. As used here, labor-supply phenomena are factors that characterize current or prospective workers and labor-demand phenomena are factors that characterize current or prospective jobs. Although it is widely acknowledged that the earnings of an individual worker are determined by the interaction of both phenomena, empirical studies of the distribution of labor income that are based on conventional economic theory have usually concentrated on the supply side, while the critics of conventional theory have spoken mostly of the demand side.

We are only now beginning to develop theories of income distribution that seek to capture the synergistic interaction of the individual characteristics of workers with the earnings potential inherent in different jobs. If personal and job characteristics are interrelated determinants of the distribution of income, and if certain market-demand

This chapter draws in part from results of work supported by the National Science Foundation under Grant No. PRA79–13737. Any opinions, findings, conclusions, or recommendations expressed in this chapter are those of the author and do not necessarily reflect the views of the University of Utah or the National Science Foundation.

characteristics enhance or retard the earnings potential of the attributes of individual workers, then empirical studies based on singular adherence to either one approach or the other are likely to produce biased estimates. As a result policy derivatives could turn out to be ineffective or even counterproductive. In recent years the systematic anomalies encountered in empirical efforts to explain differences in earnings among workers have caused the supply-side school to gradually acknowledge the possible interactive effects of demand-side factors. As a result, the empirical preconditions for integrating the supply-side and demand-side approaches already exist. Moreover, a synthesis of these two competing approaches is required to isolate and fully understand the interactive mechanism of earnings determination and to evaluate the potential effectiveness of alternative labor market policies.

This chapter reports results of a pilot project to develop such a synthesis for empirical test. The first two parts outline major features of the supply-side and demand-side approaches. The next sets out an integrated approach. The final two parts summarize the results of empirical work and draw policy implications.

SUPPLY-SIDE APPROACH

Early versions of human-capital theory (the supply-side approach) attributed the variation in workers' earnings to variation in the amount of institutionally acquired skills among workers. Although differences in the quantity of institutional training were shown to contribute to differences in earnings, a significant amount of the variation remained to be explained. (See Hanoch 1967 and Harrison 1972.) The persistence of unexplained residuals in empirical analysis based on the early version of the human-capital model prompted strict human-capital theorists to reevaluate their arguments in an effort to explain the anomalous residuals. However, their explanations were usually confined to supply-side phenomena or more generally to more detailed descriptions of worker attributes. Becker (1975) and Chiswick (1974) argued that the residuals were the result of unmeasured or unmeasurable forms of human capital such as the quality of schooling and innate intelligence. (See also Griliches and Mason 1972, Gintis 1971, and Vrooman and Greenfield 1978.) Arrow (1972) hypothesized that the unexplained variation in earnings between races that remained even after controlling for other personal characteristics was evidence of overt (demand-side) discrimination against workers of a particular race by employers operating in noncompetitive markets. At this point, economists moved toward the view that the early failures of the schooling model were due primarily to incomplete specification of the complexities of the earnings process.

Perhaps the most important advance was made when Arrow (1962), Becker (1975), and Mincer (1975) each separately suggested that non-institutional forms of human capital, such as postschool job experience, were relevant explanatory components usually omitted from earlier specifications of the human-capital model. Making some additional minor adjustments and adding the effects of postschool investment in human capital to the model did seem to account for much of the residual variation in earnings; but there was still no *theory* to explain the origin of returns to postschool investment or how the postschool mechanism worked. The absence of a theoretical bridge between the abstract categories of labor-supply and labor-demand phenomena impeded empirical investigation of the potential interaction between job characteristics on the demand side and worker characteristics on the supply side as interactive determinants of the distribution of income.

DEMAND-SIDE APPROACH

While investigating low-income segments of the labor market, several manpower practitioners were separately formulating similar hypotheses about why supply-side models did not adequately explain the distribution of income to and within low-income labor markets. An important advance was made when Doeringer (1969), Doeringer and Piore (1971), and Piore (1968), among others (Thurow 1975; Vietorisz 1970), hypothesized that instead of the labor market's being a queued continuum of workers ordered homogeneously in accordance with their individual skills, the "labor market" was in fact dichotomized into primary and secondary segments. Jobs available in the primary market were characterized as jobs that offer high pay and employment stability, whereas jobs available in the secondary market were characterized as structureless and low-paying, the nature of which encouraged rapid turnover in employment.

Realizing that the simplicity of this original dual-market dichotomy was frustrating attempts for rigorous empirical examination, Piore (1975) later refined the model to include three market segments: (1) secondary-market jobs, which are structureless, unskilled, low-paying, unstable, and nonprestigious (workers in such jobs often lie to others about the nature of their work); (2) subordinate or lower-tier primary market jobs, which are highly structured, well-paid, heavily dependent on job-specific skills, and not necessarily prestigious (workers view their jobs as simply a means to obtain other forms of satisfaction); and (3) professional or upper-tier primary-market jobs, which are not necessarily structured or stable but which require skills obtained through formal education and are high-paying and prestigious (workers view their jobs as a source of satisfaction). Piore's refined model made two important advances toward the integrated approach proposed here: Piore's advances improved our understanding of how supply factors might work within each occupational segment and provided an important clue about how job technology and worker attributes interact to determine the distribution of labor income.

INTEGRATED APPROACH

It can be argued that schooling performs a different function for different segments of the labor market. To see this, consider two aspects of the schooling process. First, schooling can impart cognitive skills and the ability for abstract thought. Second, schooling can foster and stabilize noncognitive behaviors, such as regular class attendance and the ability to function within a structured set of rules that may often seem arbitrary.

Whether either or both of these schooling experiences are sought by employers depends on the nature of the job to be filled. The nature of a job in turn derives from the sorts of skills required to perform the job and the learning processes whereby the skills are acquired. Professional jobs in the upper-tier primary market require cognitive skills that are to be applied in a wide variety of circumstances. Workers in the upper tier are expected to have appropriate professional skills when they are hired. In contrast, jobs in the lower-tier primary market require market skills that are specific to a particular firm or industry and that can be learned only on the job. Workers in the lower tier are not expected to have these specific skills when they are hired (the skills will be learned on the job), but they are expected to have discipline, regular work attendance, and the capacity to function in a stable and structured work environment. Finally, jobs in the secondary market require neither cognitive skills nor work discipline. Workers in the secondary market have few skills when their jobs begin and few when their jobs end. The differences in job requirements in the three segments of the labor market suggest the following hypothesis: Schooling performs a cognitive function for workers in the upper-tier primary market, a noncognitive function for workers in the lower-tier primary market, and neither function for workers in the secondary market.

It can also be argued that the technology of jobs plays different roles in different segments of the labor market. Supply-side empiricists have demonstrated that the returns to postschool experience are an important contribution to earnings differences, but they have not offered an explanation as to why. Drawing from Piore's refined model, I suggest that the mysterious source of the returns to experience for workers in the lower-tier primary market is the level of technology that the workers encounter in their work environment. Specifically, the skills of workers in the lower-tier primary market are firm- or industry-specific, and because these skills are nontransferable, firms are willing to provide on-the-job training. Since the skills are firm- or industry-specific, the worth or quality of these skills should be a function of the firm-specific or industry-specific level of technology. In contrast, professional workers in the upper-tier primary market may exhibit increased earnings over their work lives, but because their skills are not tied to a particular firm or industry (that is, their skills are transferable), their earnings should not necessarily be a function of the firm-specific or industry-specific level of technology. Finally, workers in the secondary market would not be expected to collect significant returns to work experience, regardless of the firm or industry they work in, because their jobs are unskilled and occupationally isolated from the effects of technology. Thus, Piore's trichotomous model provides the framework needed to isolate a possible demand-side source of earnings differentials that earlier appeared to reflect simply supply-side differences in accumulations of postschool investments in human capital.

EMPIRICAL INVESTIGATION: THE INTEGRATED APPROACH

To derive testable hypotheses about whether and to what degree job technology influences the return to various worker attributes, I specified a general econometric model in which earnings for a worker in a particular occupational group are a function of the worker's individual characteristics (for example, years of schooling, work experience) and the interaction of these characteristics with the level of technology in the industry in which the worker is employed. I hypothesized that the significance of the various interaction terms would differ for different groups of workers according to the integrated model outlined in the previous section.

These hypotheses were tested in a pilot study that applied multiple regression analysis (Vrooman 1981) to a subset of data from the National Longitudinal Surveys (NLS) of young men and young women (Center for Human Resource Research 1977). NLS data on workers' earnings, occupation, human-capital characteristics, and industry of employment were linked with measures of industry technology to estimate earnings functions for different occupational groups based on human-capital characteristics and technology interaction terms.

Faced with sparse data for constructing measures of technology, I experimented with three general approaches. The three approaches reflect separate phases of innovative activity: (1) research and development (R&D), (2) applied innovation, and (3) productive output. For each approach I tried a number of potential measures, including for the first approach the ratio of R&D to sales and the rate of R&D growth, for the second approach the ratio of new equipment purchases to value added and the rate of growth in new equipment purchases, and for the third approach the amount of value added per production manhour and the rate of growth in output per production manhour. The measures were constructed by industry, with the R&D measures based on data from the National Science Foundation (1976) and the other measures based on data from the U.S. Department of Commerce (1976).

In initial regression runs with the different measures, I concentrated on technology's influence on the returns a worker collects from his or her years of schooling, cognitive skills, and postschool work experience. I did not at this stage run separate regressions for different occupational groups. The initial results provided some evidence to support the theory of interactive technological segmentation—that is, industry-specific technology does influence the potential returns to human capital. The measures of technology that seemed to work best were the two productive-output measures. These are really "ghost" measures, since they do not measure innovation per se but reflect the productivity growth that innovation creates.

To further isolate the effects of the level of technology on the returns to work experience, I disaggregated the pilot sample into three occupational categories roughly corresponding to Piore's upper-tier primary, lower-tier primary, and secondary labor markets. The results were generally consistent with the hypothesis that technology does segment what was previously assumed to be an occupational continuum of worker attributes into at least three distinct and separate markets, each with its own process of earnings determination. Key findings include the following: (1) Returns to a worker's postschool employment experience are virtually nonexistent in the secondary labor market, regardless of the level of technology in the industry in which the worker is employed; (2) in the lower-tier primary market, the returns to a worker's postschool experience are significant, *but only in those industries characterized by high productivity*; and (3) the returns to experience in the upper-tier primary market are significant and *not* related to the level of productivity in the industry in which the worker is employed.

POLICY IMPLICATIONS

The results of this integrated labor-market analysis and pilot study have substantive implications for understanding the determinants of the distribution of labor income, the influence of technology on the returns to human capital in different market segments, and the design of institutional training programs intended to improve employment opportunities for unskilled or unemployed workers. My concluding remarks focus on institutional training.

The implications of this analysis should not be drawn in ignorance of the potential policy effectiveness of institutional training and formal schooling. A minimum level of competence is certainly necessary for on-the-job acquisition of the specific skills required in the lower-tier primary market and for maintenance of a worker's relative position in that market. In addition, formal education is in many instances an exclusive mechanism for obtaining a job in the upper tier.

However, programs to enable the unemployed and the working poor to penetrate the primary market cannot rely on institutional training alone. A worker's aptitude and training must be matched with job opportunities that are in turn defined by industry technology. Consequently, the roles of institutional training are passively derived from job technology, and the potential effectiveness of institutional programs should be viewed accordingly.

If human-capital formation through institutional training is invoked as a unilateral device for improving employment opportunity, we should be clear about the different roles that schooling plays in different market segments. The results of this study suggest that the returns to formal training may be unrealized, especially for the working poor, if a secondary labor market persists in isolating itself from new technology.

REFERENCES

Arrow, K.S., "The Economic Implications of Learning by Doing," *Review of Economic Studies* 29 (June 1962): 155–173.

———, "Models of Job Discrimination," in A. Pascal, ed., *Racial Discrimination in Economic Life* (Santa Monica, Calif.: Rand Corporation, 1972), pp. 83–102.

Becker, Gary, *Human Capital: A Theoretical and Empirical Analysis, with Special Reference to Education,* 2nd ed. (New York: National Bureau of Economic Research, 1975).

Center for Human Resource Research, *The National Longitudinal Surveys Handbook* (Columbus, Ohio: Ohio State University Press, November 1977).

Chiswick, Barry, *Income Inequality: Regional Analyses within a Human Capital Framework* (New York: National Bureau of Economic Research, 1974).

Doeringer, Peter B., "Programs to Employ the Disadvantaged: A Labor Market Perspective," in Peter B. Doeringer, ed., *Programs to Employ the Disadvantaged* (Englewood Cliffs, N.J.: Prentice Hall, 1969).

Doeringer, Peter B., and Michael J. Piore, *Internal Labor Markets and Manpower Analysis* (Lexington, Mass.: D.C. Heath, 1971).

Gintis, Herbert, "Education, Technology and the Characteristics of Worker Productivity," *American Economic Review: Papers and Proceedings* 61, no. 2 (May 1971): 266–279.

Griliches, Zvi, and William Mason, "Education, Income and Ability," *Journal of Political Economy* 80 (June 1972): S72–S103.

Hanoch, Giora, "An Economic Analysis of Earnings and Schooling," *Journal of Human Resources* 2, no. 3 (Summer 1967): 310–329.

Harrison, Bennett, *Education, Training and the Urban Ghetto* (Baltimore: Johns Hopkins Press, 1972).

Mincer, Jacob, *Schooling, Experience and Earnings* (New York: National Bureau of Economic Research, 1974).

National Science Foundation, *Research and Development in Industry: 1975* (Washington, D.C.: U.S. Government Printing Office, 1976).

Piore, Michael J., "Notes for a Theory of Labor Market Stratification," in Richard Edwards, et al., eds., *Labor Market Segmentation* (Lexington, Mass.: D.C. Heath, 1975).

―――, "On-the-Job Training and Adjustment to Technological Change," *Journal of Human Resources* 3, no. 4 (Fall 1968): 435–449.

Thurow, Lester C., *Generating Inequality: Mechanisms of Distribution in the U.S. Economy* (New York: Basic Books, 1975).

U.S. Department of Commerce, *Census of Manufacturers: 1972* (Washington, D.C.: U.S. Government Printing Office, 1976).

Vietorisz, Thomas, and Bennett Harrison, *The Economic Development of Harlem* (New York: Praeger, 1970).

Vrooman, John, "Technology and Labor Market Segmentation" (unpublished paper presented at the American Economic Association annual meeting, Washington, D.C., December 1981).

Vrooman, John, and Stuart Greenfield, "A Missing Link in the Heroic Schooling Model," *Journal of Human Resources* 13, no. 3 (Summer 1978): 422–428.

6 JOB DESIGN WITHIN CHANGING PATTERNS OF TECHNICAL DEVELOPMENT

Peter S. Albin

Job design is the reciprocal process that fits work assignments and technology together by regulating the worker/machine interface and job content. Generally, in U.S. industry — and in U.S. academic writing — job design fits within the domain of the industrial engineer, the (consultant) industrial psychologist, or the management specialist.[1] Although job-design considerations have been given considerable attention by economic historians,[2] the field and its practices are, by and large, ignored in the economic literature pertaining to growth, technical change, and productivity change. This neglect can be seen as the outcome of implicit adherence to one or several of the following analytical conventions:

1. *a presumption of optimized design,* where job design is unspecified but is assumed to be optimally adjusted within a production function or according to some equilibrium relationship between inputs and outputs;

The research that provides the background to this chapter was supported by the National Science Foundation. The author acknowledges helpful comments from his colleagues Charles Bahn, Farokh Hormozi, Stergios Mourgos, and Arthur Weinberg at the Center for Study of System Structure and Industrial Complexity, CUNY. Any opinions, findings, conclusions, or recommendations expressed in this chapter are those of the author and do not necessarily reflect the views of the National Science Foundation or the City University of New York.

125

2. *implicit Taylorism,* where increased specialization is virtually unquestioned as a source of systemwide industrial efficiency;
3. *human-capital "loading,"* where job content, if considered at all, is assumed to be optimally adjusted to human-capital inputs and thereby proxied by measures of these inputs;
4. *residual "loading,"* where job restructuring is subsumed within more-general indices of managerial performance, learning, or other forms of endogenous (disembodied) change;
5. *technical determinism,* where job designs are believed to be exogenously given by the gods of technique and thereby excluded as meaningful subjects for study.

I have inferred these "conventions" indirectly from a variety of textual indications. There is hardly an official or consensus view within the discipline: The matter of job design simply does not receive attention in mainstream theory.[3] Some implications of particular combinations of these conventions are that job design need not be examined directly, since it can be presumed to be optimally adjusted through routines that determine the equilibrium of the firm; that design policy can be implemented through human-capital formation and the labor and skills markets without particular attention to the design process itself; or that job design is incidental to the larger forces that determine industrial technique.

This chapter examines this unexplored area of the economic literature and presents several hypotheses. First, variations in job-design practice can account for significant variations in technical efficiency and appear to be of critical importance in the current wave of innovations relating to control technology. Second, there are strong indications that present U.S. practices are changing in response to the introduction of new technologies but that the changes do not seem likely to realize the efficiency potential of the new techniques at the partial-equilibrium firm level. Third, spontaneous adjustments seem antagonistic to the broader system and social concerns of sustained full employment, general productivity increase, and opportunities for mobility and personal progress. In brief, the argument is that job-design practice constitutes a parameter that can be instrumental in determining which of several potential long-term growth paths (alternative future histories) will be traveled by the economy and that the parameter now set will result in far less than what is attainable and what other countries—particularly Japan—seem to be approximating.[4]

Despite the apparent force of the above claim it must be emphasized that job design is not a single controlling factor: Appropriate job design is one of several necessary conditions that must be met to reach high-level growth and developmental targets. I have focused on the design factor, in part because it has been the previously neglected factor in economic analyses and in part because recent methodological advances make it now possible to analyze work-floor organization and job content with rigor and precision. Better understanding of the interactions of design, capital formation, and worker-skill levels in emerging worldwide industrial patterns will make it possible to bring new insights to policy interventions through differential investment support, human-resources development, training, and explicit productivity programs.

This chapter looks at job design and the role it can play in furthering social and economic goals as new technologies develop. The first two parts provide a set of working assumptions about job design that will be supported later in the text and set out the role of job design in alternative patterns of the technical development. Job design in basic metalworking is analyzed in the third part. Employment prospects and policy implications are discussed in the last two parts.

JOB DESIGN AS AN ECONOMIC FACTOR

To develop the claims mentioned above, it is first necessary to establish an analytical perspective in which job design and organizational structure can emerge as endogenous economic phenomena, as phenomena adjustable over a significant range, and as phenomena that are unlikely to be adjusted by prevailing practices to either private or social optima.[5] In place of the implicit conventions mentioned earlier, a revised list of working assumptions is advanced. They will be supported in the subsequent text as giving a superior description of the industrial setting. The working assumptions are:

(a) *Within the firm, job-design decisions are subject to severe bounds to rationality, and systematic deviations from optima are expected.* As an area for management decisionmaking, job design comes closer to satisfying the preconditions for the bounded-rationality paradigm (Simon 1978) than to the equilibrium-of-the-firm paradigm. As we will see, the job-design process involves a rich complex of behavioral, technical, and organizational phenomena, many of which are imperfectly specified.[6]

In addition, the process intrinsically engages complex development dynamics external to the firm and is a prominent feature in the political economy and power relations of the work place: At its simplest, the process can be represented only by a deep multiattribute decision function. Under these conditions it would not be surprising to find that rule-of-thumb, general policy, established practices, and traditions dominate. One might wish to presume that such practices give a hit-or-miss approximation to optimality. Perhaps this was the case for the production regime in which the prevailing practices evolved—the late nineteenth and early twentieth century factory systems and systems of industrial relations (with some human-relations modifications). They cannot be presumed to continue to give good approximations to optimality in the production regimes that are currently emerging. The evidence in comparative studies of industrial organization suggests that these approximations have in the United States deviated systematically from the best approach to design. It is sufficient for present purposes to treat the area as one in which problems of both specification and calculation make suspect the presumption of optimal adjustment.

(b) Existing systems of work organization inhibit adaptive response to altered economies of computation. Changes in the economics of calculation that reduce the cost of all computations—and especially those for decentralized control, communication, and decision-making—undercut one presumptive advantage of hierarchic organization and specialization according to Taylor's principles.[7] If changes in management designs lag altered-cost relationships or if designs are inflexible rules as in assumption *(a)*, there is a significant possibility of discrepancies between actual designs and optimal designs. Put another way, Taylor's scientism, as a general operating principle, had in the past been the source of reasonably effective management adaptations to changing technique and reasonably effective adjustments of technique to managerial modifications. Taylor's methods can still prompt an outwardly successful program for reducing labor cost within a technology once installed—that is, it will find economies enough to justify its use. However, the present question is whether a general Taylorist program can lead to alternative industrial designs that realize the larger cost, human, and social advantages of decentralized computation. The working assumption here is that discrepancies between actual and potential efficiency can be far higher now than during earlier phases of applying Taylorist methodology to industrial development.

(c) Human capital mechanisms provide partial adaptation in structural changes. In place of assuming that the adjustment of human skills to job requirements is optimally mediated by labor markets, educational institutions, and training facilities (both within the firm and external to

it), it is suggested instead that there may be several qualitatively distinct equilibrium patterns of technique, job assignments, and human-resource development available to the economy. Each of these patterns may be feasible and sustainable, but markets and signaling mechanisms are only locally effective — that is, they may match job requirements and skills for an established pattern but do not necessarily allocate resources to effect transitions between patterns. The concept of discrete, multiple, growth paths or alternate future histories is a familiar one in the literature of development and comparative growth. Here it means that the apparent matching of job-related skills to job requirements does not necessarily connote the selection of the correct development path.[8]

(d) Job restructuring may be a source of "catastrophic" disembodied technical change. Assumptions (a)–(c) could hold, and yet for purposes of analysis the design factor might still be adequately subsumed within explanations of the general nationwide average of disembodied productivity change — that is, change that goes beyond physical improvement of capital goods themselves. The revised working assumption has two components: (1) the general technical relationship between inputs and outputs may be bifurcated, meaning that identical input combinations could associate with two or more distinct equilibrium output levels;[9] and (2) the reorganization of labor and capital at a bifurcation point can be effected through a virtually costless alteration in job-design practices. The point here is to focus attention on, for example, a U.S. production pattern versus a Japanese pattern, where both patterns build on similar inputs of tools and skill mixes, where both patterns are sustainable, and both associate with apparent local dynamic equilibria. The contention is that traverses or transitions from one regime to the other may not be practicable through fine adjustment and instrumental guidance working on and through the ordinary surface variables relating to operating costs and the productivity of specific facilities. However, the shift could occur through either spontaneous or policy-impelled adjustment of structural variables such as those associating with principles for organizing production and designing jobs.

(e) There exists significant scope for job redesign and reshaping techniques. All of the above discussion would come to naught in the policy domain if technology were immutable and exogenously determined.[10]

For our purposes it suffices that constellations of these conventions hold for some critical industries; no broader institutional claim is required. On the basis of direct observations and a variety of indirect references it appears that job-design ossification is most prevalent within the older basic-production industries, while organizational flexibility is greatest within the newer communications and computation hardware and software industries — although the symptomology is not altogether absent there.

PATTERNS OF TECHNICAL DEVELOPMENT

A *gedanken* concept helps to generalize the analytical viewpoint taken here — "adjustment to changing patterns of technical development." A pattern of technical development can be thought of as an ensemble of parameters and qualitative relationships that together subsume input/output properties of technique, properties of the worker/machine interface and decision mechanisms, characteristic interactions, characteristic communication systems, characteristic systems for management and control, and characteristic problems of system performance. The term "pattern" is used to stress that the analysis focuses on features of similar appearance and common properties, on their interconnection in characteristic ways, and on their replicability. The term "development" is used to stress the dynamic character of the analysis that considers the diffusion of a pattern and its adaptive transformation under the influence of economic incentives. As such, the pattern concept is essentially a historian's construct with evolutionary overtones superimposed on analytical categories in the disciplines of managerial science, business economics, industrial engineering, and job design.[11]

It may be conjectured that much of U.S. basic production is organized according to the historic pattern of industrialization and specialization that has been the foundation of North Atlantic economic development since the mid-nineteenth century. However, a new pattern appears to be emerging. This pattern enables the decentralization of highly complex (in a formal sense to be explained subsequently) control and developmental decisions. The pattern associates with efficient utilization of the intrinsic power of the newer control technology. Surface manifestations of this adaptation include dramatic reductions in work-in-progress inventories, economic lot sizes, and the average period of production. Deeper manifestations are an acceleration in the rates at which highly skilled and educated workers are called into employment and a concomitant reversal of deskilling tendencies prevalent under the Tayloristic principles that were fundamental to the older pattern.

However, as suggested above, U.S. adjustment may be lagging behind Japan's.[12] In addition, there is widespread concern in the United States that if present structural relationships continue into the future, labor will become less important, more jobs will be done by machines, and unemployment will become endemic. Projective studies that take comprehensive account of the emerging control technologies (Leontief and Duchin, 1984) posit offsetting employment effects deriving mainly from elevated demands for the hardware and software needed to install the new manufacturing technologies and from input-output-linked demands for other intermediate goods. The scenarios they project show that there is no necessary inconsistency between material standards of living increasing at the long-run historical rate and high full employment — provided that there is reasonably flexible adaptation to shifting sectoral workforce requirements and provided that the investment demands are supplied by production in the *domestic* capital-goods industries. The last point is critical. The favorable projection ultimately rests on the prospects for sustained employment of machine operatives (the classic mass-production category under the old pattern) but in a complex of industries in which the new pattern is asserting itself strongly elsewhere. If the new pattern does turn out to be dominant in practice the critical industries would be undercut in international trade.

Informal projections based upon interview data pertaining to industrial-planning strategies in Japan present a strongly contrasting description of prospects.[13] The standard projection is for sustained high employment relative to the United States: extinction of the operative categories, increasing demand for skills (in both hardware and software production compartments), and high and increasing educational and human-capital levels. The posited worker-technician will participate actively in highly adaptive work involving the same basic physical technology assumed for the U.S. projections but with far faster machine set-ups and production turnaround, minimal work-in-progress inventories (the *Kanban* system), continuous "learning-by-doing" (the *quality-control circle*), and continuous managerial search for higher value-added opportunities. The industries producing computerized numerically controlled machine tools are taken as paradigmatic in this regard and have already become the leaders in the international market. Sources of domestic aggregate demand to support this projection are not derived formally within a rigorous comprehensive model but are, in effect, assumed to stem in large part from the higher incomes which accompany the posited productivity-generating mechanisms.

Of course, this is not the whole story: Birth and immigration demographics enter as sources of disparity and both projections share a number of expected social dislocations—particularly regarding needs to alter uses of leisure time and adjust to the remaining demeaning work.[14] However the gravamen is clear. In one projection, a moderately increasing material product with rapidly increasing technical coefficients (output/worker, output/machine) implies a potential drop in employment opportunities and some decay in indices of the quality of work. In the other projection, roughly equivalent technical coefficients are tied to a projection of constant employment and improving indices of the quality of work to imply substantial material improvement.

In this light, the pattern concept can be interpreted as a way to tie together technical factors with institutional characteristics and control and guidance properties to describe a putative dynamic equilibrium. The projection for Japan thus represents an internally consistent and self-reinforcing pattern with several desirable properties. The projection for the United States represents the extrapolation of institutional and guidance properties appropriate to past industrial technology but incompatible with those emerging.[15] Specifically, the working assumptions proposed earlier represent conditions under which control and guidance mechanisms—well-adapted to smoothing the everyday functioning of an established pattern—inhibit adjustment to a new set of technical circumstances.

JOB DESIGN ADAPTATIONS TO CHANGING CONTROL TECHNOLOGY IN METALWORKING

This section examines the details of pattern change within a basic production technology. We first examine properties of a reference technology—the family of manually controlled metalworking machines that have been found in machine shops and tool shops for more than a century.[16] Worker/machine interfaces in this technology exhibit a characteristic succession of complexity types that define job content and worker skill categories. After a brief discussion of the measurement and classification of such complexities, we turn to an examination of job-design variations within the technology and recent technological changes that substitute mechanical and numerical control for human controls. It is at this point that the prospect of a pattern shift arises and that we find striking dynamic distinctions attaching to different ways of using physically identical capital goods to put together a workshop.

The Classic Machine Shop

Figure 6–1 gives schematic diagrams for the logical organization of control and decision elements at the worker/machine interface in classic metalworking or machining. Certain characteristic tasks and functional combinations of tasks are shape-coded, as described in the key. [17] As indicated by the boxed instructions, these job components can be put into correspondence with both cognitive demands on the worker and properties of virtual computing devices. The top row of the figure shows a sequence in order of increasing complexity content of jobs within classic manual-controlled machine-tool technology (which originated in the mid-nineteenth century and which is still in active use). The case on the left pictures the control and logical content of operating a simple machine such as a drill press. As shown by parallel analysis, the cognitive content of this job is equivalent to that in different technologies of simple process control or standard assembly in a line built on Taylor's principles. The job is typically filled by entry-level, low-skilled, or unchallenged workers. Set-up, the translation of blueprint or job-order specifications into machine settings, involves slightly more extensive logical choices and is a step toward journeyman or semiskilled status. As indicated in the diagram, the logical content of the set-up operator's job is subsumed within that of the journeyman machinist who operates and performs basic set-ups for simple-cut lathes, restricted milling machines, routers, and similar devices. This job also includes more elaborate feedback functions relating to tool and feed speeds, tool wear, and materials variations.

In turn, the journeyman's job is a "subjob" of the master machinist who operates a multiple-purpose machine such as a turret lathe. The analog control system of the technology permits the experienced machinist scope for physical virtuosity or athleticism. The set-up of the machine is intrinsically rich in formal terms: An optimization over a class of branched routines (the imbedded rectangles) is implicit within it. As we shall see, the level of decision complexity implied is

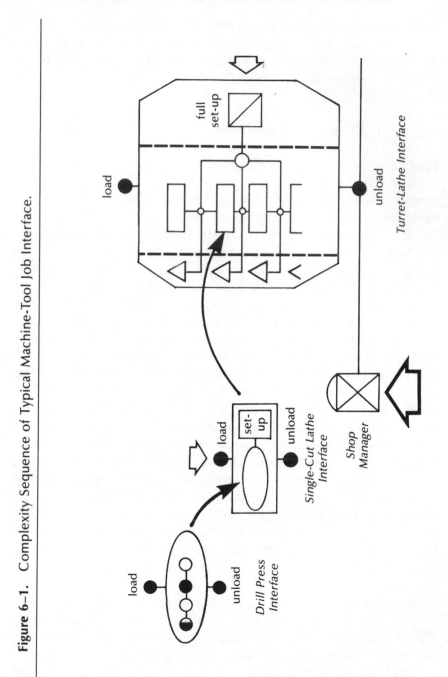

Figure 6–1. Complexity Sequence of Typical Machine-Tool Job Interface.

Figure 6–1. (Continued).

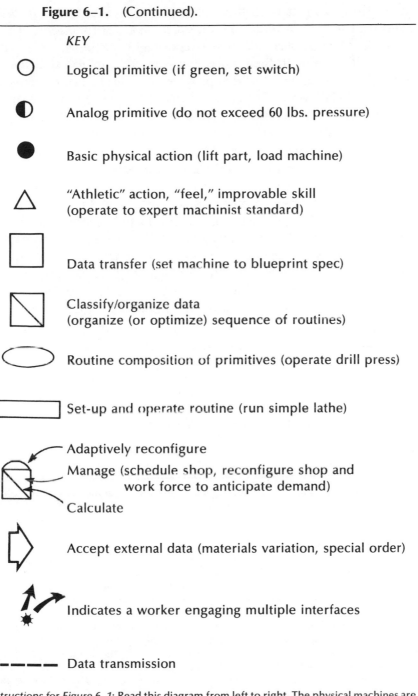

KEY

Logical primitive (if green, set switch)

Analog primitive (do not exceed 60 lbs. pressure)

Basic physical action (lift part, load machine)

"Athletic" action, "feel," improvable skill
(operate to expert machinist standard)

Data transfer (set machine to blueprint spec)

Classify/organize data
(organize (or optimize) sequence of routines)

Routine composition of primitives (operate drill press)

Set-up and operate routine (run simple lathe)

Adaptively reconfigure

Manage (schedule shop, reconfigure shop and
            work force to anticipate demand)

Calculate

Accept external data (materials variation, special order)

Indicates a worker engaging multiple interfaces

– – – – – Data transmission

Instructions for Figure 6–1: Read this diagram from left to right. The physical machines are
not illustrated; instead the logical content and structure of the interface determined by

qualitatively distinct from that in the preceding jobs and is formally equivalent to that in many significant managerial functions: It is so recognized by observers and is self-reported by machinists themselves as a fulfilling value in their work.[18] It is interesting also that the full sequence of machine interfaces provides a natural learning sequence of physical skills and a nested hierarchy of logical routines. Training through work is a significant externality within this technique.

The illustrated sequence of interfaces can be found intact within many machine shops and factories; it constitutes a significant feature of what has been the standard pattern for production technology. Of course the actual distribution of machine types within a specific work-shop reflects a number of other considerations, including run length and the technical requirements of the product. The search for higher productivity and/or reduced cost within this pattern takes on a number of characteristic forms, including (1) product redesign to utilize substitute materials or alternate technologies such as stamping or casting; (2) machine and tool improvement to shorten particular work cycles; (3) multiple-shift operation and improved control over scheduling, maintenance, buffering, and so forth; and (4) job "rationalization" and shop reconfiguring on classical Taylorist lines. The intent in (4) is to increase partial process automation, reduce complexity and content of the worker/machine interface, and substitute lower-paid

---

Instructions for Figure 6–1 (Continued)
the machine and the job design appears in schematic form between the "load" and "unload" points.

The drill-press job is a rigid sequence of simple decisions and actions (equivalent to a checklist or an elevator switching circuit). This routine is, in turn, a "subjob" of the single-cut lathe interface, which also includes a data-transfer set-up (equivalent to a fuel-injection control circuit). This composite job is, in turn, a "subjob" of the turret-lathe interface, which, as indicated in the division to the left, provides scope for "athleticism." The full set-up, to the right, involves, at a minimum, the rigid sequencing of composite jobs and routines (equivalent to a television-game microprocessor controller). Optimizing the subjob sequence according to the operator's own skills, materials variation, special specifications, external standards, cost incentives, and so forth, is more nearly an open-ended problem (equivalent to one that requires a mainframe computer for solution).

The computer equivalents suggest a lexicographic ordering of job complexities—with the final level suggesting significant "rich" human cognition. Note that the drill-press job can be learned by a beginner in a few minutes, and the simple-lathe job is typically learned after a few weeks of shop discipline. Elements of the turret-lathe job can be learned independently (see Figure 6–2), but reasonable competence typically requires several years of experience and technical training. Beyond this point experience and knowledge can accumulate (leading to tool making, set-up machining, design, materials specialization, shop management, and so forth), enabling functions logically equivalent to those assigned to the manager.

workers for journeymen and master machinists. We will examine implications of these efficiency tactics shortly. First, an examination of the concept of job complexity should be useful.

Job Content and Measurable Complexity

In much contemporary usage, "complexity" is undefined yet featured as a critical attribute within the system of discourse. The reader is assumed to understand exactly what is meant by the term even though it variously connotes a cognitive property or an environmental state or serves as a metaphor for confusion. In principle, however, the main features of a technological pattern (for example, the "complexity of the technical interface," the "content" of decisions, the "complexity" of the communications network, "complex control requirements") are all amenable to rigorous classification and measurement.

In brief, the formal theory of organized complex machines (following von Neumann 1966) can be reconstituted so as to apply to technical systems in their economic and social settings. Simon (1960, second edition 1981) has developed one such line that leads to the theory of decisionmaking under real-time computational and organizational constraints. A complementary line focuses on resource-dimensioned measures (for example, equivalent to hardware and time requirements on standardized computers classified as to inherent properties) for human/technology interfaces and for functional components of institutions (for example, data-processing requirements, information content, interaction networks and constraints, control mechanisms).[19] The use of units of measurement with resource dimensions is critical here since it means that system features and structural attributes can be priced, substituted for, or viewed as subject to selection under economic guidance.

The concept of *complexity tradeoff* integrates the systems perspective with economic calculation. Within the domain of computers the same function can be performed by elaborately structured hardware, by simple hardware and simple programs working for a longer time, and other combinations and variations. There is thus the potential for "trading off" one form of complexity for another (for example, intricate machine hardware for software). If one associates hardware with "capital" and software with "labor" and has costs or cost projections for the resource categories, the technical tradeoff relations then become bases for economic design decisions. This is the appropriate setting for study of a wide variety of technological changes. Taking numerical control for an example, favorable cost projections for integrated circuitry (capital) trigger substitution away from a variety of direct labor uses and from certain indirect uses (the "labor" embedded in software development). The economist would also identify output effects associating with the overall reduction in cost for a class of functional complexities. In the macrodynamic setting, unbalanced-growth price, output, and employment effects become highly significant where there are "live human" activities that adjoin the more dynamic machine activities (for example, human auditors of machine-based systems become extremely expensive, as do certain "creative" activities).[20]

In the case of the machine sequence in metalworking, the critical structural factor was the succession of job-content complexities from the most-specialized machine to the general-purpose lathe. This succession, its associated learning and training requirements, and the institutionalized worker skill categories that accompany it reflect, one might infer, an established job-design solution under particular technical and economic constraints. We treat this family of machine designs and content complexities as our reference case and go on to consider organizational changes and technical changes as complexity tradeoffs and substitutions that modify this position.

Hierarchic Reorganization within Classic Metalworking

Part (a) of Figure 6–2 illustrates one standard way to reorganize jobs on the multiple-cut lathe. A specialist set-up machinist translates product specifications into benchmarks, tool selections, and sequences.

Instructions for Figure 6–2: Diagram (a) shows a job-design decomposition of the turret-lathe interface of Figure 6–1. The master machinist provides bench marks, tool choices, and settings to set up several lathes for individual operators with a range of skills—a combined technical and managerial decision. The "athletic" content of the job is distributable, but the scope for operator autonomy is restricted.

Diagram (b) shows a decomposition wherein the operator-control function is automated, leaving only a simple routine at the operator/machine(s) interface(s). The machine set-up may be reproducible, hence the indicated replication factor.

Overleaf: Diagram (c) shows numerical controls devised by a programmer-engineer and transmitted to closed-gate (or "locked-gate") automatic machines with trivial operator interfaces.

Diagram (d) shows an open-gate system where operators have full machinist and programming capabilities.

Figure 6–2.   Organization of Control Systems.

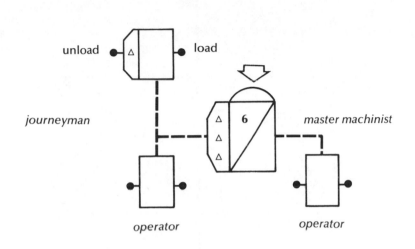

(a) BATTERY OPERATION OF TURRET LATHES

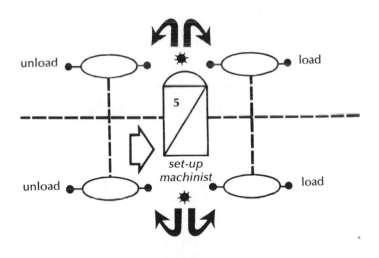

(b) MULTIPLE INTERFACES

Figure 6–2. (Continued).

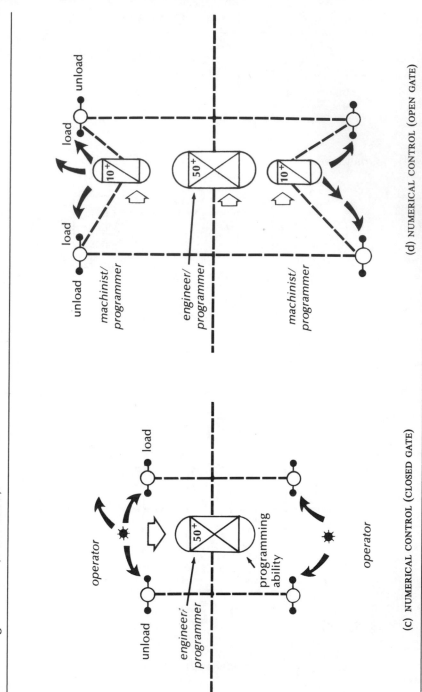

(c) NUMERICAL CONTROL (CLOSED GATE)

(d) NUMERICAL CONTROL (OPEN GATE)

These parameters are then followed by journeymen operators for a production run. The cost justifications for this scheme are straightforward. In place of m lathes run by master machinists who each perform individualized set-ups and runs, the firm employs a small number of high-wage master machinists who do set-ups exclusively, and a larger number, n, of lathes staffed by lower-wage operators. Provided that the wage differential is great enough, the set-up frequency is low enough (this organization design works best for long product runs), and the productivity of journeyman operators is not too far below that of master machinists, the job redesign will pay off.

In terms of complexity the reorganization has several effects: (1) a shift from jobs that are relatively homogeneous in high-level content;[21] (2) an increased level of organizational complexity (represented by the logistic and administrative decision functions implied by the increased hierarchy) with a concomitant reduction in operator decision responsibility and autonomy; and (3) a rupture in the learning sequence. As noted above, these complexity tradeoffs may appear to be warranted for their effects in reducing the short-term wage bill; however, there are other implications to consider. The first organizational design associates with relatively high degrees of adaptability, run flexibility, superior quality, positive worker attitudes, plus the learning externality.[22] All yield productivity effects that presumably enter the systemwide index of "disembodied"[23] technical change (for example, the (BLS) multifactor measure).

In concrete terms, the master machinist acting as set-up operator is capable of adjusting to material and tool-wear variations, debugging and refining an initial workable set-up, and personalizing an initial set-up for the athletic phase of the run. The effects of overelaboration of the hierarchic design intervention are thus conjectured to be (1) the loss of adaptive flexibility resulting from the substitution of specialized machinery for general purpose machinery; (2) analogous adaptive decay resulting from the substitution of low-skilled workers for the legendary autonomous machinist; (3) centralized control over a more-complex shop floor where the cost of control defects is registered in requirements for bigger inventories between work stations and longer completion times; and (4) fracturing of the natural learning sequence discussed earlier, a consequence of which is the anomalous "machinists" shortage. All of these conjectured effects impact negatively on the potential for technical change of the disembodied type. It should also be noted that much of the potential for efficiency changes embodied in the machinery itself may have already been achieved during the generations since the basic designs for machine tools were fixed and their use broadly extended.

Partial Technical Automation

Let us now look at a technological miscarriage. Part (b) of Figure 6–2 illustrates interface complexities for a general-purpose machine tool under mechanical control—in effect, "music-box" automation. The technique fails in practice because of extremely poor feedback response, but its noteworthy property is the extent to which it specializes the set-up machinist versus operator rationalization pictured in Figure 6–2(a). The machine can be loaded and set in operation by an entry-level worker who is literally "locked away" from contact with any controls but the start switch and the panic button. The complexity tradeoff described above is further exaggerated in this technology. Although the music-box approach is by-and-large a failure in machine shops, it can be thought of as a bridge example that describes the salient characteristics of specialized metalworking in mass-production industries (prior to the introduction of numerical control). Our consideration of employment conditions in these industries will draw on this model of technique.

Closed-Gate Numerical Control

The organization of work in the music-box machine shop is mirrored in the far more successful "locked-gate" numerical-control device pictured in Figure 6–2(c). The locked-gate device, which typifies the mainstream U.S. approach to automated technology, can be viewed as the penultimate rationalization under the old pattern. The set-up is performed by a white-collar, engineer/programmer who translates product specifications into data that serve as input for a microprocessor controller. The complexity of the operator interface is virtually zero and is staffed accordingly. In effect, the complex control processes faced by the classical autonomous machinist have been substituted for by highly effective electronic sensing, computational, and control devices. The configuration works fast, is mechanically efficient, and yields a product of high quality. Set-ups are storable and instantly accessible (note the replication efficiency index), and the age-old battle for control over work-floor pacing is won by management as represented by the engineer/programmer. In brief, the technology enables a complex machine to replace complex workers, and the conditions of choice—a complexity tradeoff—are perfectly represented in standard form as the substitution of capital for expensive labor. In this case the disjunction between operator and set-up specialist is nearly complete, and the learning sequence dismantled. The parallel economic tradeoff sets reduced instantaneous labor cost against the potential for disembodied technical change. As we shall see, the decision to favor the former has far-reaching social and systemic implications.

Open-Gate Numerical Control

The story, however, does not end here. An emerging Japanese pattern involves use of the same basic machine and programming facility but under an open-gate arrangement whereby the floor operators are already master machinists who are trained in programming and who are given entry to the control facility (gate) for on-the-spot interventions and program suggestions to be acted on by quality control circles or other floor organizations. The approach focuses on expediting learning-by-doing improvements in the program and facilitating adaptive reconfiguration of the work floor. It also represents a restoration of control and authority to the work floor—a quality-of-work-life initiative, and a humane activity that can, in part, check alienation. The sum of these effects may also be expected to enhance long-term productivity.[24] In brief, the properties of the open-gate approach suggest that the antinomy between it and closed-gate organization can be paradigmatic for future industrial development.

Static Choices of Industrial Technique

Why do closed-gate designs with concomitant diminution of job content on the floor develop in one industrial society and not in another? A definitive answer is not really possible at this time: It is not yet clear that the question definitively represents the empirical situation nor what dimensions are appropriately included in an answer. There are, however, a few points of potential importance that derive from viewing the choice as determined by an economic tradeoff representing costs and values of the underlying complexity tradeoff. We consider, in turn, (1) substitution effects associated with falling costs of computation, (2) training effects and other externalities, and (3) special institutional conditions.

(1) Substitution Effects. It is not entirely unreasonable to view centrally controlled hierarchic organization and Tayloristic specialization as past adaptations to high costs of calculation. Once the locus of computation and control had been established in a central directorate, subsequent drops in relative costs of calculation could be perceived as cheapening the cost of extending the scope and scale of that directorate. The directorate can afford more-comprehensive central calculation — and can extend access to parts of the system to minor executives with personal computers. It may be difficult for the directorate to comprehend that the dramatic cost trends in computation have undercut the initial rationale for centralization itself. The further that job-design rationalization had gone in eliminating content at the blue-collar extremes of the organizational hierarchy, the more remote the economic justifications for restored decision autonomy would appear to be: The closed-gate arrangement with programming control located in the directorate follows as a natural consequence. (A full exploration of this point requires the dynamic approach introduced in the next section ("Employment Dynamics") to encompass labor-market conditions, employment trends, and the relative cost of human-capital development.)

(2) Externalities. Since development of the open-gate model requires skill enhancement, it will be fully attractive to firms only if its costs are assumed externally (that is, by the worker or by society through subsidized education and training) or if its benefits can be held within the firm. Clearly, Japanese industrial relations, which feature the reciprocal attachment of worker to firm and a de facto guarantee of lifetime work, favor cultivation of the open-gate approach. In this regard, it should be noted that analysis of responsibilities for providing employment continuity can be approached via the "externality" framework — if a firm pursues internal policies that reduce its work force, it is, in effect, sluffing responsibility for job creation onto other firms or society.[25] One can carry the matter of exter-

nalities one step further to the question of the impact of job-design practices on the "dead-end" work component of structural poverty. This question will be touched on in the sections dealing with dynamics and policy intervention.

(3) Institutional Factors. As already intimated, the broad choice of production technique is influenced by such institutional factors as the mobility/tenure norm within industrial relations. Other institutional conditions that appear to tip U.S. choices away from the open-gate path include the following: business school training and socialization that enshrine hierarchic control, downgrading of hands-on production experience in the development of managers, low priority given historically to quality-of-work-life concerns in collective bargaining, the lack of strong academic and public institutions with a job-design or quality-of-work-life orientation. Finally, we should note that the standard management techniques and decision apparatus for review of business practices and design of interventions are poorly adapted to handling the kinds of structural phenomena that we have been considering. Neither incremental adjustments to established equilibria nor minor modifications in standard operating procedures will suffice.

EMPLOYMENT DYNAMICS

The antinomy between the closed-gate and open-gate designs is suggestive as to developing tensions in U.S. industry. However, we have still some analytical distance to go before these tensions can be translated into systemwide projections for employment and components of growth. This section considers, in turn, the extrapolation of job-design practices into sectoral growth and employment projections, general macroeconomic and developmental conditions that can sustain a broad industrial pattern, and the problem of comparative patterns or alternate paths.

To arrive at employment and general productivity effects it is necessary to work with a multisector model of the background economy, and here an unbalanced-growth (Baumol 1967) system — modified by the author (Albin 1978) later — offers a number of analytical conveniences.

We partition the economy according to activities with high (progressive) or low (stagnant) rates of productivity change and according to high or low educational requirements for the activity.[26] This leads to a four-compartment economy:

The first compartment combines progressive technology with a highly skilled and educated work force. This is a natural description of the high-technology activities that both produce and use control technologies.

The second compartment (progressive technology and lower educational requirements) associates with basic production. In terms of the proposed research it is the "swing sector," since under open-gate organization its characteristics can move toward those of the first compartment, whereas under closed-gate organization its employment demands can shrink both in absolute terms and for higher-skill categories.

The third compartment (stagnant technology and low educational requirements) associates with dualistic or structural poverty. It is the potential resting place for those displaced from the second compartment.

The fourth compartment (stagnant technology and high educational levels) associates with live performance, education, and other public services. It is subject to cost pressures under the unbalanced growth mechanism.

The description of this type of background economy is usually completed with assumptions that permit labor-market segmentation and barriers to human-capital development.[27] Our concern will be that of determining conditions that can sustain the extreme forms of work organization.

Full formal analysis can become extremely complex. As a short cut, Table 6–1 compares sustained open- and closed-gate systems according to preliminary projections of their implications at three levels of analysis: *(A)* short-run effects at the (partial-equilibrium) level of individual activities; *(B)* progressive-sector industrial development; *(C)* contribution to expansion of high-level activities. Of course, each table entry could separately be the subject of a major research project; but it nevertheless seems useful to work on the scheme as a whole — putting together bits and pieces of the mosaic. There is hardly a limit to the number and variety of comparative development paths consistent with a dynamic model of this sort, so it is best to concentrate on a few themes of policy significance and immediacy.

Past U.S. survival of dramatic technical changes encourages the myth that new jobs will emerge in the face of the control-technology driving force in (1) the industry itself, (2) related transformed activities such as programming, (3) capital-goods industries feeding the development, and (4) other services and basic industries fueled by general growth. However, preliminary projections for the closed-gate extreme suggest that output effects (Table 6-1, entry 12) on employment will be minimal and that the fall in floor jobs per unit produced (entry 1) may not be offset by sectoral expansion. Furthermore, the tendency to move toward simplification of the lowest-level production jobs will, if anything, exacerbate tendencies to shift production offshore (entries 8, 14). At the other end of the production spectrum, the comparative qualitative disadvantage (entry 6) in producing capital goods (entry 16) will worsen (entry 12), thus undercutting the strength of what heretofore had been a leading sector.[28]

The adverse extreme prognosis is best capsulized in the projections for variables affecting the human resource. Unbalanced-growth cost pressure on education, public-sector services, and (possibly) R&D as a "live" activity continues with some slight abatement (entry 13); but the lack of demand for all but the highest skills suggests continued decline in production-oriented human-capital development — in keeping with deteriorating expected returns (entries 7, 11). With the disappearance of traditional avenues for blue-collar mobility (entries 9, 10), there is a very real prognosis for hardening of dualistic divisions. The final entries in section C of Table 6-1 reinforce this image of retrograde development.

To summarize, at the broadest level of generalization there are two ways in which a society can raise its overall rate of growth: by raising the productivity of individual activities within the progressive sector or by expanding the relative size of the progressive sector within the overall economy. Clearly, the highest potential for growth associates with combined effects in which developmental expansion of progressive activities as a whole and favorable technical changes for individual activities within the progressive sector feed one another. Conversely, the lowest growth potential associates with shrinkage of progressive-sector employment and interactively induced declines in the rate of technical advance for individual activities. In all cases, cyclical factors can force realized growth short of potential. The "worst of the worst" is thus a situation in which realized growth is significantly below a growth potential that is itself depressed because uniformly

Table 6–1. Qualitative Effects of Introducing Modern Control Technology under "Open-Gate" and "Closed-Gate" Job-Design Principles (for representative manufacturing industries previously operating with a mix of control technology vintages).

A. Effects for Production Level Fixed

Effect	Open Gate	Closed Gate
(1) Number of floor jobs	Fewer	Fewer
(2) Content level of floor jobs	Transformed high content or higher content	Significantly decreased content
(3) Number of first-level technical jobs	Constant or higher	Constant or higher
(4) Administrative employment	Lower	Constant or higher
(5) Effects on instantaneous unit-labor cost	Somewhat lower	Significantly lower

B. Potential Impact on Industry Development

Effect	Open Gate	Closed Gate
(6) Production adaptability	Significantly higher	Marginally higher
(7) Projected disembodied technical change	High	Low
(8) Plant site mobility	Low in short- and long-run	Low in short-run; high in long-run
(9) Worker skill development	Intensified	Significantly reduced
(10) Complexity learning sequence	Retained but transformed	Significantly reduced

(11) Constraints in skilled labor markets, sources of technical knowledge	Likely strong constraint without parallel educational expansion	Relatively unconstrained: excess labor supply in most market segments excepting state-of-the-arts techniques

C. *Incremental Impact on Expansions of Progressive Sector as a Whole*

Effect	Open Gate	Closed Gate
(12) Instantaneous effects on aggregate demand	Mildly contractionary (some reduced production employment)	Strongly contractionary
(13) Effects on educational development	Strong demand for skills can offset unbalanced-growth cost pressure	Reduced incentives for human capital accumulation (despite moderate unbalanced-growth cost pressure)
(14) Response to conventional expansionary stimulus	Strong developmental response	Loss of foot-loose industries
(15) Minimal conditions for sectoral expansion	Moderate macroeconomic stimulus Accommodating infrastructure and educational support Moderately expanding international markets	Strong macroeconomic stimulus Strong developmental stimulus Strongly expanding international markets—particularly for capital-goods exports
(16) Prognosis for capital goods industries	Strong expansion, improving international competitive position; effects (6), (7) dominate	Weakened international competitive position
(17) Prognosis for eliminating stagnant activities and/or poverty dualism	Continued expansion of progressive-sector employment	Relapse to hardened dualistic structure

unfavorable expectations regarding cyclical, structural, and technical factors have their predictable (and self-fulfilling) effects on capital formation, R&D, and human-capital development.

The categorization of growth configurations in the previous paragraph focused on the production side. Its analytical dual is a description focused on the human resource: income prospects, the distribution of employment opportunities, the potential for skill development, and the upgrading of opportunities. The compartmentalized production prospect associates with sharp labor-market segmentation maintained by an educational barrier that limits the expansion of employment opportunities within the mass production blue-collar compartment. In particular, this description associates with the phenomena of "hard-core," "structural," and "intergenerational" poverty—the target of the 1960s' antipoverty effort.

The human-factor dual in an expanding progressive sector is a situation in which the skill and education levels of the population are increasing (either in response to economic pressures or through policy intent) and appropriate job opportunities increase *pari passu*. The payoff to education comes in the form of higher initial salaries, superior income prospects, and greater job stability in the expanding progressive-production component. This story describes the long period of parallel industrial and educational expansion that extended from the 1870s to the 1950s. One notes, however, that the educational expansion of the 1960s to the mid-1970s was unmatched by a parallel expansion of employment in the progressive sectors: Public-service employment and superior macroeconomic efficiency (on average) took up some of the slack. In other words, the policy of this period improved the cyclical performance of the progressive sector, increased the number who through education had achieved prerequisites for progressive-sector employment, but did not lead to significant (proportionate) expansion of progressive-sector productive activities.

This situation suggests an unfortunate, but possibly informative, test case. From the late 1970s to the foreseeable future, support has dried up for public-sector employment, for the full-employment goal, for education (as a conduit to improved opportunity and as an employer of the educated), and for R&D (as a growth generating factor and as an employer of the high-level work force). The test centers on whether the progressive sector will on its own create employment opportunities to fill the gap; on this issue, the job-design factor may be critical.

POLICY

The foregoing discussion generates a number of necessary conditions for reversal of the stagnation trap brought about by incomplete accommodation to the potentialities of emerging control technologies. My list of such conditions is hardly unfamiliar. Support for education, R&D, and skill development is a broad requirement, and industrial policy and reconstruction finance aimed at key industries and technologies are essential as well. Yet it should be clear that interventions in these directions — even massive ones — may not be sufficient to reverse the decay tendencies implicit in the way production attributes are organized. If the economy does fit together in the ways described in Table 6-1, then ordinary stimuli and growth incentives simply reinforce the structure without transforming it.

Interventions affecting the design of technique and the way work is done are rarely discussed, yet it is hard to escape their inevitability if the production economy is to be effectively restructured. Perhaps the least controversial avenue of approach is through the educational system: funding of production engineering, humanistic industrial engineering, and industrial research with a focus on work systems and in-plant skill development. This can point the industrial horse toward water, but the problems of leading it there and cultivating its thirst remain. A first step in that direction might be taken through redirection of the large but largely uncoordinated collection of agencies, authorities, institutes, commissions, and information bureaus that individually perform functions in technology assessment, skill development, manpower, and employment. These institutions form the building blocks for a national manpower policy, but they are not coherently assembled to do much more than predict technological trends and translate them into medium-term manpower advisories. This was perhaps sufficient "planning" for an economy in which the prospect was for continuous expansion of progressive-sector production activities and the need was to assemble manpower skills and coordinate infrastructure development. It is grossly inadequate when the "spontaneous" path of industry as a whole (on the organizational principles in force) is to shrink itself and employment prospects well below potential capacity and sustainable expansion paths.

Although it runs against the spirit of this chapter to look to bureaucracy, hierarchy, and centralization for solutions, it would appear that a strong case can be made for a "super-bureau" planning approach that shifts the orientation of existing agencies and institutions from a passive manpower approach toward active encouragement of technologies, industrial practices, and organizational designs that will meet societal employment and human-development goals. In effect, the existing apparatus is oriented toward taking projected production levels and the technical coefficients that translate production into manpower needs as data. The problem is to reverse the process: to take the potential manpower and skill-level supply as data, seek a degree of control over the technical coefficients (for example, by influencing work organization), and then support a level of aggregate demand that can sustain the target employment. How this large first step might come about politically is a matter for speculation. If one instead seeks smaller first steps, some proximate changes could evolve locally and within existing agencies — or develop through ad hoc legislative initiatives.

A minimum goal is to attach principles of skill development, job continuity, and social control over technique to existing manpower agencies and to supply them with the resources and expertise needed to effect simple plant-floor restructuring. Suppose, for example, a community-based training facility were able to alter its stance from a passive attitude of "We will train workers to meet the job specifications and requirements you dictate or those traditional in the industry" to an attitude of "We will assist you in setting job assignments, in laying out the plant floor, even in selecting technology, and we will train workers to meet these assignments and place them with you. Furthermore, we will assist you and consult with you continuously and enlarge our training operations in order to meet the dual objectives of improving your competitive productivity position and improving the quality of the work experience for those we place with you. You should consider this type of service as essential in the present economic environment of unforgiving markets for your product and dramatic alterations of the automation/robotization types in the way work is evolving."

This type of approach is not all that unreasonable: The business clientele for a wide range of established public and not-for-profit manpower institutions consists of smaller firms that tend themselves to be passive consumers of technology without the internal expertise to do much more than install the minimal soon-to-be-automated job design. It is in just the areas of small-line parts fabrication and assembly, custom fabrication, short-run metalworking, and so forth that the process of simplifying down to low-content work requiring only entry-level employees leads to a unprogressive facility that can, in effect, be transplanted intact overseas as a turnkey operation to take advantage of lower labor cost. The implied alternative is to reorganize production facilities in the direction of manpower development, job content and the learning and adaptability dimension.

For the larger employers who operate with their own internal expertise oriented to traditional Taylorism and within an elaborate framework of industrial relations, the problem is quite different. On the positive side there is the widely reported degree of interest in Japanese approaches and a degree of dissatisfaction with the older Harvard MBA curriculum. However, this is offset by the enormous relative attention given by management to activities other than nuts-and-bolts production and to the essentially combatative and confrontational spirit that pervades much of large-firm industrial relations and that has directed union interest to "work rules rather than work reorganization." Even so, recent attention given to bargaining on de facto job guarantees opens the door slightly to codetermination of factory-floor conditions.

The prospects here appear unstable — and potentially volatile. The job redesign factor does amount to a relatively costless reorganization of existing resources and facilities, and the reorganization potential is latent within the industrial system. The matter for active policy is to find means to activate the potential.

If it is recalled that numerical control was originally invented by the air force, it does not seem improper to suggest that job design and skill development criteria be imbedded within procurement guidelines. Similar guideline interventions could be instituted over a range of activities where the objective is to generate experience with alternate production organization.

Again, these are small steps aimed at creating a basis for spontaneous reorganization. The steps can be lengthened slightly by a few strategically placed expenditures — for example, to machine-tool makers for pilot hardware and job-design systems for both the United States and Third World economies. However, the problem of structural reorganization is not amenable to the application of magic-wand instruments in the form of conventional incentives or subsidies. Lacking a major superagency initiative, the hope lies in the smaller steps buttressed by macroeconomic stimulation and reconstruction finance.

NOTES

1. For an informative study of U.S. practice and a review of the literature see Hackman and Oldham (1980).
2. Factory organization and "scientific management" before and after Taylor have received serious attention from the major historians of technology and the industrial era, including Landes (1969), Rosenberg (1972, 1976, 1982); David (1975) (see references to individual studies therein). Job design has also been the focus of work by a number of historians who have examined the design process as a concrete manifestation of relations of production. See Clawson (1980) for this perspective regarding the endogeneity of technique and Noble (1977, 1979) for this perspective applied to scientific management and detailed analyses of developments in metalworking.
3. It is difficult to cite definitively the nonappearance of a concept, but my search has been of some duration. It should be reiterated that the lacunae deplored here are in a literature that promises a comprehensive view of growth processes, technical change, and employment potential. In this regard, the implied gap in a study such as Dennison (1979) is characteristic. One should perhaps note that job structure was one of the factors subsumed in Viner's "real costs," a perspective that was displaced with the broad acceptance of "opportunity-cost" reasoning. See Viner (1937).
4. The comparative material is based in part on the author's observations in Japan, Holland, France, and Germany. In the foreign literatures, job-design factors are strongly emphasized in partial-equilibrium contexts and in institutional studies. They are not formally incorporated in the most general productivity studies but are encompassed in industrial planning, educational planning, and manpower models at a fairly comprehensive level. For references to the European literature see Hackman and Oldham (1980). Institutional background can be obtained from a number of sources, but in particular see Clark (1979). A highly recommended perspective on the human factor in Japanese technology appears in the institutional advertisement "Japanese Technology Today" (Abegglen and Etori 1982) — to be discussed at a later point in the text.
5. The reader should recognize that this argument is directed to the professional economist who may require assurance that (1) a putative "neglected factor" has not already been subsumed in the relevant models; and (2) no violence is done to the theoretical core of economic analysis by bringing the factor into play. The working assumptions in the text should satisfy all but a few on these theological matters. See Reder (1982).

6. A crucial point here is that there has been no rigorous quantification of job content, the critical variable in job design. See the discussion below and Albin and Weinberg (1983).

7. Consider, for example, a tree graph as the model for a hierarchic organization. High communication costs would dictate that communications to and from the extreme branches of the system should be kept to the minimum. A system that can function with only an occasional flow of simple rules and orders from the trunk to the twigs and even less frequent flows of feedback data from twigs to trunk ideally satisfies this cost requirement. To prevent surprises to calculators in the trunk, the scope for decisions at the twig positions should be reduced to the barest minimum — for example, Taylorist specialization. Clearly, a cheapening in communications and information-processing costs can eliminate the economic rationale for the tree structure as the basic organizational model.

8. For example, in the United States, enrollment in computer-science courses suggests that there is matching of skill development and requirements in the expanding software-oriented industries, while a decline in training for production jobs seems consistent with the "sunset" of several basic industries. Several questions arise: Is the implied mix of products and services one that could sustain full employment? Could the United States revitalize basic production using highly skilled workers for specialty and customized products? If so, would present human-resources development and training provide the foundation for such industries?

9. The mathematics for this point are developed elsewhere (Albin and Hormozi 1983). In essence, standard neoclassical production theory cannot exclude catastrophic jumps from one equilibrium production regime to another regime that has equivalent equilibrium or steady-state properties. It is reasonable to propose that certain potential catastrophic jumps associate with production reorganization. "Theoretical possibility," of course, does not imply "pragmatic necessity."

10. Closed-form technology certainly does exist — for example, a "turnkey" rayon mill ordered by a LDC "off the shelf" of a West German machine manufacturer. The plant comes complete with an organizational chart, training resources, and start-up plan, all of which must be strictly adhered to or the rayon will not flow when the key is turned. In advanced countries that are themselves technology creators, "soft-technical determinism" (in Heilbroner's words) seems closer to reality. With "soft-technical determinism" installed technique limits managerial choice, but the parameters of the machine at the design stage are determined in part by current cost relationships and in part by an inherited history of past design solutions, some of which must embody "relations of production" in Marx's sense.

Table 6–2. Cost Advantage Held by Japanese Automakers over U.S. Automakers for Producing Subcompact Automobiles (dollars per automobile).

Advantage	Cost Advantage
Superior technology	$ 73
Better management systems	
Quality control	320[a]
Just-in-time production techniques	550[a]
Materials handling engineering	41
Other (quality circles, job classification)	487[a]
Total, better management systems	1,398
Union/management relations	
Less absenteeism	81[a]
More flexible relief systems and allowances	89[a]
Union representation	12
Total, union/management relations	182
Lower wages and fringe benefits	550
Total cost advantage to Japanese	$2,203
Less shipping costs	485
Net cost advantage to Japanese	$1,718

[a] See Note 12.

11. The construct associates closely with Drucker's focus on work as the critical nexus of technology and is an underlying theme in much modern research following volume 4 of Oxford's *A History of Technology* (Singer, Holmyard, Hall and Williams 1958).
12. The data in Table 6–2 assign only a small fraction of the Japanese cost advantage in producing subcompact cars to the physical input/output superiority of machines. Instead, the bulk of the differential is attributed to organizational and managerial factors — many of which associate directly with the design of work (denoted by [a]).
13. These projections are abstracted from "Japanese Technology Today" a *Scientific American* institutional advertisement (October 1982). See also the successor document "Japanese Technology Today" of November 1983.
14. A full comparison would include data on saving rates, rates of exit from agriculture and extractive industries, trade protection and subsidization, and so forth. It should be clear that the text does not pretend to give a full explanation: For example, an alternate explanation

for the two patterns might be found in Japan's success in sustaining domestic employment through export expansion.

15.   One might wish to evoke Kahn's (1959) distinction between "golden-age" and "leaden-age" growth for an analogy drawn from capital-theoretic reasoning. However, the complex of distinct factors involved in a broadly defined pattern would appear to make the present case significantly richer and require much more in the way of ad hoc analysis.

16.   For many years metalworking technology retained essentially similar technical characteristics in the sense that a drill, milling machine, or lathe of a late-nineteenth century vintage can be easily mastered by a contemporary machinist, while it is a fair conjecture that a machinst from the earlier era would find recent machines to be familiar and usable after a relatively painless period of adjustment.

17.   The diagrams are composites deriving from observational data (Nepco forged products, Mitsubishi heavy industries, Phillips electronics, IBM, and others) and data in a large number of technical reports, machine specifications, and handbooks. In several studies emulating "computer models" of the machine, interfaces using methods described in Albin, Hormozi, and Mourgos (1984) are employed.

18.   Results from an interview study of forgers and machinists (operating jobs coded as in Albin, Hormozi, and Mourgos 1984) are reported in Albin, Bahn, Hormozi, Mourgos, and Weinberg (1982).

19.   The propagation of the personal computer has transformed complexity measurements and comparisons into familiar occurrences. Now familiar are descriptions of machines as compositions of discrete components (for example, an Apple II + 64K add-on memory + disc operating system + 2 disc memories + ...). It is understood that each of these components has measurable capacity indices (in the jargon, 64K RAM, 16K ROM, 32-bit words, and so forth); that these capacity indices relate to both local and global limits of the machine; and that these limits determine whether more complex or less complex problems can be solved with the machine. Thus, there is, at least at an intuitive or metaphorical level, an association between complexity of a problem or operation and the design, organization, and complexity indices of a machine that can solve the problem or perform the operation. One can thus suggest that there is a presumption of legitimacy in a definition of complexity phrased in terms of attributes and capacities of components, circuits, and computers.

Still at a metaphorical level, it should be noted that pure technological change can alter the economic costs of particular facets of system complexity (for example, memory as opposed to interconnectivity); that the scheme admits categories resembling fixed capital and variable labor (such as hardware versus software solutions); that qualitative organizational patterns are well described through architectural schemes and circuit designs; and that certain artificial computational schemes mimic or emulate human cognitive processes (short of creative thought). Given the above, it is reasonable (still within the metaphor) to specify "an economic function embodying a particular level of complexity" as, literally, one of a family of designs for a computing device that satisfies the complexity requirement. The choice of design under economic criteria, the modification of an established design to meet new requirements, the adding on of components, and so forth, complete the metaphor. In practice, particularly where the empirical referent is in part a technical system, the metaphor can be realized.

20.   It should be stressed that the objective in this type of exercise is *not* to measure or value "global system complexity." Rarely, if ever, will such a measure be calculable, and if calculable, informative. Instead, the natural focus is on microorganization, the identification and classification of complexities (emulating devices) associating variously with separable functions of control, communications, decision content, scheduling, and so forth. One typically asks, for example, if the abstract machine modeling a worker's function with job X is imbedded within the machine's modeling the putatively "richer" job Y, not whether a factory is more or less complex than a workshop or the world more complex since yesterday.

21.   Master machinists who set up their own production runs place high value on the "athleticism" involved in optimizing the physical movements required for the run (Albin, Bahn, Hormozi, Mourgos, and Weinberg 1982). Set-up specialists lose this "satisfier," and since their set-ups are usually designed to be impersonal and "idiot-proof," they afford the journeyman operator little scope for such activity.

22.   Since the machinist's skills are transferable from job to job, the firm is not encouraged to incur costs to develop skills that can not be captured for the firm's exclusive benefit. The accumulation of such worker skills is a benefit generally to society, but the benefit is *external* to the individual firm's profit calculation.

23.   Technical change can be embodied in a machine design or disembodied if it represents organization, learning, and efficiency factors that can be separated from the installation of the machine itself. The two characteristics are generally thought of as interactive. Thus, installation of a new machine can yield an immediately realizable productivity increase (the embodied component) plus a refreshed potential for disembodied change (Hahn and Mathews 1968; Arrow 1962).

24.   Aside from the present comment, the text will ignore indirect human-relations effects that build productivity by working on worker's morale or satisfaction — terms that can mean as little or as much as "absence of revolutionary alienation." The economic analysis can be brought to a conclusion with consideration of direct productivity effects only.

Put another way, what counts most for a comparative analysis is the content of the job on the factory floor, not the content of the company song sung outside. If substantial content is itself a "satisfier" that enhances performance, the argument and policy suggestions presented here receive even stronger support.

25. There is a legitimate controversy on how responsibility for maintaining employment should be shared between specific employers and society in general. Clearly, rigid employment guarantees can restrict the efficiency associated with labor and capital mobility. A case to consider involves job-design practice in the mass manufacture of personal computers. The tendency has been to follow Tayloristic prescriptions to reduce the content of basic manufacturing jobs to the point that production and assembly are carried out in what amounts to turnkey facilities that can be staffed with unskilled workers anywhere in the world. To no one's surprise, jobs in this "sunrise" industry appear in the East — in Pacific Basin export platforms specifically.

26. The scheme is adapted from Albin (1978). The job-design and pattern shifts of interest here were only sketched in a rudimentary fashion in this work. The reasons for elaborating the macroeconomic dynamic setting go back to the chapter's earlier discussions of "working assumptions." The argument — that individual firms have a discretionary range of choice over technique and that the effective choices for aggregates of firms are relatively free from market constraints — implies a macroeconomic setting in which strong qualitative sectoral divisions can exist. Labor-market segmentation according to skill and educational level is one such institutional component, another is division according to activities in which the potential for managerial discretion is high. The model of this section lumps together these institutional conditions in a way that permits job-design factors to appear as systematic tendencies rather than as aberrations or imperfections in an otherwise well-functioning economy.

27. Albin (1978) suggests that the proportion educated and skilled and the proportion of employment opportunities generated by progressive activities are critical parameters in the economy. Models of this type are highly complex and exhaustive analysis is rarely desirable. Instead, the focus is on processes that resemble equilibrium and critical paths or alternative futures. In this model the reference equilibrium-like process is one in which the educational proportion and employment within the progressive sectors remain constant over several generations despite growth successes within the progressive sector. The critical factor turns out to be the barrier of direct educational cost, which hardens since rising salaries in (technically stagnant) educational activities are not offset by productivity gains. This is the now-familiar unbalanced growth cost mechanism first presented by Baumol (1967).

28. Anecdotes abound. Equivalent automatic machining centers from U.S., West European, and Japanese sources are reported to have delivery times of six months, less than two months, and less than one month, respectively, and to cost $120K, $100K, and $85K, respectively. It is interesting to note as well that U.S. machine tool manufacturers are currently operating at a fraction of (production line) capacity and that the Japanese manufacturers build machines to order on advanced generalized numerically controlled machine tools using the open-gate principle and top-grade machinists.

REFERENCES

Abegglen, James C., and Akio Etori, "Japanese Technology Today," supplement in *Scientific American* 249 (November 1983): J1–J41.

———, "Japanese Technology Today," supplement in *Scientific American* 247 (October 1982): 85–116.

Albin, P.S., *Progress without Poverty* (New York: Basic, 1978).

Albin, P.S., F. Hormozi, and S. Mourgos, "An Information System Approach to the Analysis of Job Design," in H. Chang, ed., *Information Systems and Productivity* (New York: Plenum, 1984).

Albin, P.S., C. Bahn, F. Hormozi, S. Mourgos, and A. Weinberg, "Worker Perceptions of Job Content," Working Paper #22, Center for the Study of Systems Structure and Industrial Complexity (City University of New York, 1982).

Albin, P.S., and F. Hormozi, "Theoretical Reconciliation of Equilibrium and Structural Approaches," *Mathematical Social Sciences* 6 (November 1983).

Albin, P.S., and A. Weinberg, "Work Complexity in Structured Job Designs," *Human Systems Management* 4, no. 2 (1983): 69–81.

Arrow, K.J., "The Economic Implications of Learning by Doing," *Review of Economic Studies* 29 (June 1962): 155–173.

Baumol, William F., "Macroeconomics of Unbalanced Growth," *American Economic Review* 57 (June 1967): 415–426.

Clark, Rodney, *The Japanese Company* (New Haven, Conn.: Yale University Press, 1979).

Clawson, Dan, *Bureaucracy and the Labor Process* (New York: Monthly Review Press, 1980).

David, Paul A., *Technical Change, Innovating and Economic Growth* (New York: Cambridge University Press, 1975).

Dennison, Edward F., *Accounting for Slower Economic Growth* (Washington, D.C.: Brookings Institution, 1979).

Drucker, P., *Technology, Management and Science* (New York: Harper & Row, 1970).

Hackman, J.R., and G.R. Oldham, *Work Redesign* (Reading, Mass.: Addison Wesley, 1980).

Hahn, F.H., and R.C.O. Mathews, "The Theory of Economic Growth: A Survey," in American Economic Association and Royal Economic Society, ed., *Surveys of Economic Theory,* vol. 2 (London: MacMillan, 1968): 1–124.

Kahn, R.F., "Exercises in the Analysis of Growth," *Oxford Economic Papers* 11 (1959).

Landes, David S., *The Unbound Prometheus* (Cambridge: Cambridge University Press, 1969).

Leontief, W., and F. Duchin, principal investigators, *The Impacts of Automation on Employment, 1963-2000,* #PRA–8012844 (Washington, D.C.: National Science Foundation Report, 1984).

Noble, David F., "Before the Fact: Social Choice in Machine Design," in Andrew Zimbalist, ed., *Case Studies in the Labor Process* (New York: Monthly Review Press, 1979)

———, *America by Design: Science Technology and the Rise of Corporate Capitalism* (New York: Alfred A. Knopf, 1977).

Reder, Melvin W., "Chicago Economics: Permanence and Change," *Journal of Economic Literature* 20 (March 1982): 1–38.

Rosenberg, Nathan, *Inside the Black Box: Technology and Economics* (New York: Cambridge University Press, 1982).

———, *Perspectives on Technology* (Cambridge: Cambridge University Press, 1976).

———, *Technology and American Economic Growth* (New York: Harper & Row, 1972).

Simon, H., "Rationality as Process and Product of Thought," *American Economic Review* 68 (May 1978): 1–16.

———, *The Sciences of the Artificial* (Cambridge, Mass.: MIT Press, 1960).

Singer, Charles, E.J. Holmyard, A.R. Hall, and Trevor I. Williams, eds., *A History of Technology,* vol. 4 (New York: Oxford University Press, 1958).

Viner, Jacob, *Studies in the Theory of International Trade* (New York: Harper & Row, 1937).

von Neumann, J., *Theory of Self-Reproducing Automata* (Urbana: University of Illinois, 1966).

7 INDUSTRY PERSPECTIVES ON ADJUSTMENT TO ECONOMIC CHANGE

Kenneth McLennan

The long-run success of business organizations in all industries is determined by their ability to adapt to and take advantage of continuous economic change. All organizations must make both short-run adjustments to cyclical economic change as well as more gradual adjustments to the changing structure of the economy. This chapter discusses some of the public and business policy issues that concern industry as the economy experiences structural change. While there is probably considerable agreement among all industry groups on what constitutes the important issues, there is certainly no industry position on the appropriate policies for responding to structural change. For example, there is considerable divergence of interest on specific public policies among capital-intensive and labor-intensive industries, among high-technology firms and firms whose technology is well along the experience curve, and among industries whose markets are confined to the United States and those that participate in worldwide markets.[1] Despite differences among industry views, there is a general consensus on the nature of current structural changes in the economy and the role of public policies in facilitating adjustment to these changes.

The views expressed in this chapter are solely those of the author. In no way do they represent the views of Committee for Economic Development trustees or their organizations.

This chapter presents the business viewpoint of technological change and economic conditions. The first two parts review productivity and its prospect for growth through technical change and examine shifts in employment and the internationalization of manufacturing. The final two parts review the recent recession interest rates and compensation costs and discuss public policy and the structure of collective bargaining.

STIMULATING TECHNOLOGICAL PROGRESS

The poor productivity performance of many U.S. industries has become an increasing concern of U.S. business. In the second half of the 1970s businessmen acknowledged that the decline in productivity growth rates had become a problem, but the general view was that the United States still had a higher level of productivity than all other countries and that U.S. products and services were still highly competitive. Many businesses reexamined their personnel policies and introduced new approaches, such as quality work circles for improving the day-to-day management of the work force and operations. Business groups felt that insufficient investment was a major reason for the slowdown and placed much of the blame on government tax and regulatory policies and the government's failure to control inflation.

In the last few years, however, U.S. business has recognized the importance of comparative productivity performance to the future of U.S. international competitiveness. It is now realized that our productivity growth rates compared to the rates in most industrial countries have been lower—and in some cases significantly lower—for at least twenty years. This has led to a convergence of productivity levels among industrial countries for a wide range of industries, with an increasing number of U.S. jobs threatened by import penetration.

Business response has been to advocate a range of public policies that—at least in a period of noninflationary economic growth—are likely to increase the rate of U.S. innovation. Many businesses appear to have taken steps to improve efficiency—including some "shedding" of employees beyond what would normally occur in a recession, as well as innovative approaches to motivate workers to achieve greater productivity.

Initially, there was a fairly optimistic view that an innovation surge would be led by the introduction of new technologies represented by major breakthroughs in science and technology. The benefits of genetic engineering, robotics, and microprocessors were seen as the new wave of knowledge industries on which the U.S. economy would substantially increase its level of productivity.

The application of new scientific and technological developments does indeed offer considerable potential benefits for the economic and social welfare of society, but achieving these benefits is not costless, and few benefits are likely to be achieved within the next decade.[2] It is now realized within industry that no "silver bullet" is available to stimulate productivity growth to much higher rates of growth than existed in the past. The ultimate solution is undoubtedly more rapid innovation, but it is likely to be many years before new inventions are incorporated into the production process and widely diffused throughout the economy. The rate of diffusion depends on the rate of saving, the cost of capital relative to the rate of return, and the availability of the industrial capacity to produce the new technology. Society will not receive the benefits of new technology without some sacrifice – in social programs or defense and certainly in some current consumption. Business generally believes that the current consumption bias in our tax code should be corrected, as should the consumption bias in public expenditures. Business also believes that its activities are over-regulated, even though some firms continue to look to the government to protect them from competitive market forces.[3]

Business does not believe that an increase in the rate of innovation will result in a new increase in unemployment. On the contrary, it believes that research on the effect of technological change strongly supports the view that innovation generates employment. Business is much more worried about what will happen to employment if the innovation rate is too slow. At the same time, it is realized that some workers will be permanently displaced from their present employers and will suffer permanent income losses. Some employers have negotiated job-security provisions in collective bargaining agreements with labor unions, and some companies have unilaterally adopted personnel policies that attempt to assist permanently displaced workers. All business believes that government should play an important role in adjustment assistance, but most business groups are critical of past federal employment, training, and adjustment policies.

THE MAGNITUDE OF STRUCTURAL SHIFTS
IN THE ECONOMY

During the past two decades important structural shifts have gradually changed the industrial base of the U.S. economy. In most industries and regions, the labor force has adjusted to these changes without any major employment dislocations as workers moved to occupations in which jobs were increasing.[4]

Structural Shifts among Major Sectors of
the Economy

As shown in Table 7-1, the output of service industries now accounts for at least 57 percent of U.S. gross national product. This represents a 1 percentage point increase since 1960, when these same sectors accounted for 56 percent of GNP. If transportation and public utilities are classified as service, the twenty-year change represents an additional 2 percentage point shift toward service industries.

The growth within this rather extensive definition of service followed this pattern: There was a slight growth in the share attributable to business and personal service (1 percentage point); to finance, real estate, and insurance (4 percentage points); to transportation and public utilities (2 percentage points). This increase in the share of output in some service industries is entirely consistent with the growth of income for some population groups. These proportionate increases, however, were at the expense of the government services as well as agriculture, mining, and construction sectors—not manufacturing. Indeed, manufacturing share of GNP was about the same in 1980 (23.7 percent) as in 1960 (23.3 percent). On the basis of this analysis it can be predicted that the relative importance of nonmanufacturing sectors is likely to continue to increase but that manufacturing will continue to be a major component of our industrial base.

Structural shifts in the economy are more extensive when changes in the distribution of employment are used as an indicator of the nation's changing industrial base. Manufacturing employment in absolute terms remained almost constant in the 1970s and is projected to expand slightly in the 1980s. However, manufacturing sector's share of total civilian employment declined from 26.4 percent in 1970

Table 7–1. Real-Value Industry Outputs as Percentage of Real GNP.

Year	Agriculture, Forests, and Fisheries	Mining	Construction	Manufacturing	Transportation and Public Utilities	Wholesale and Retail Trade	Finance, Insurance, and Real Estate	Services	Government
1960	4.4	1.8	6.3	23.3	7.8	15.9	13.9	11.3	14.6
1961	4.2	1.8	6.2	22.7	7.7	15.7	14.2	11.4	14.8
1962	4.0	1.7	6.0	23.3	7.7	15.8	14.2	11.3	14.4
1963	3.9	1.7	6.0	24.3	7.8	15.7	14.0	11.3	14.3
1964	3.6	1.7	6.0	24.7	7.8	15.9	13.9	11.3	14.0
1965	3.5	1.7	5.9	25.5	7.9	15.9	13.8	11.1	13.8
1966	3.2	1.7	5.5	25.9	8.1	15.9	13.6	11.1	13.9
1967	3.2	1.7	5.3	25.1	8.1	15.8	13.8	11.4	14.2
1968	3.0	1.7	5.4	25.3	8.3	16.1	13.8	11.2	14.1
1969	3.0	1.7	5.1	25.5	8.5	16.0	14.1	11.4	14.0
1970	3.2	1.7	4.9	24.1	8.7	16.2	14.4	11.7	14.1
1971	3.2	1.6	5.2	23.8	8.7	16.5	14.5	11.4	13.7
1972	3.0	1.6	5.0	24.7	8.8	16.8	14.3	11.5	13.1
1973	2.8	1.5	4.8	25.9	8.8	16.8	14.1	11.5	12.5
1974	2.9	1.5	4.3	25.0	9.0	16.6	14.8	11.9	12.9
1975	3.0	1.5	3.9	23.5	9.2	17.0	15.2	12.0	13.3
1976	2.8	1.5	4.1	24.4	9.1	16.9	15.0	11.9	12.7
1977	2.7	1.4	4.0	24.7	9.1	16.8	15.2	11.8	12.3
1978	2.6	1.4	4.1	24.8	9.3	16.8	15.2	11.9	12.0
1979	2.7	1.4	3.9	24.8	9.5	16.7	15.3	12.0	11.8
1980	2.7	1.5	3.7	23.7	9.7	16.4	16.0	12.4	11.9

Source: *Economic Report of the President* (February 1982), p. 245.

to about 22.2 percent in 1980 and is projected to decline further by 1990.

Over the same period there was a significant decline in the relative importance of agriculture as a source of employment. The largest increase in employment growth occurred in several service industries (wholesale and retail trade, finance, insurance and real estate, and business and personal services) as their share of civilian employment increased from about 50 percent in 1970 to 55 percent in 1980.

The relative decline in manufacturing employment is attributable to higher productivity growth in manufacturing as well as to gradual changes in demand and a loss of comparative advantage in some parts of the traditional U.S. industrial base. Labor markets readily adjusted to this structural change. The growth of the labor force was absorbed into many expanding industries that probably had a high proportion of what might be loosely described as service jobs.

During the past decade a considerable amount of reallocation of capital and labor occurred in response to market forces. Much of the structural change involved change within sectors as well as among sectors. There is also evidence that this reallocation of resources contributed substantially to the performance of the economy. Without this reallocation the U.S. productivity performance would have been even worse (Gollop 1985).

Changing Trade Patterns

In the United States the growing importance of the service sector is reflected in the changing composition of U.S. trade. Trade in services has become more important in the U.S. balance of payments and provided a positive balance, which partially offset a negative balance in trade in goods during the 1970s. Although our merchandise trade position has weakened seriously since the mid-1970s, the positive balance in services is largely attributable to the earnings from U.S. investments overseas. Indeed, other services have had only a small positive balance since the mid-1970s.

A large positive balance in services is achieved only by adding investment earnings and other services together, despite the fact that most investment earnings are not directly related to the service industry. Indeed, almost 70 percent of investment earnings come from U.S. investment overseas in petroleum and manufacturing. When investment earnings are excluded from the broad definition of services, the contribution of other service exports to a positive U.S. balance of payments is quite modest.

The contribution of all sectors to the U.S. balance of trade is important, but it should be clearly understood that in 1980 exports of goods accounted for about 65 percent of the value of all U.S. exports. This percentage has remained about the same since 1970 (*Productivity and the American Economy* 1982: 629–39 [testimony of Kenneth McLennan]).

Changing trade patterns have increased foreign competition for the U.S. industries that make up the nation's industrial base. Over the past two decades, a small group of newly industrialized countries has become an increasingly important source of manufactured goods, and their production costs have gradually become competitive internationally. U.S. exports as a share of world manufacturing exports have declined from about 17 percent in 1960 to 13 percent, which is now less than West Germany's current share. Japan has doubled its share to over 12 percent. A group of ten newly industrialized countries, including Korea, Taiwan, and Singapore, has rapidly increased its combined share to over 9 percent of world trade in manufactures (OECD 1979).

The United States still maintains a comparative advantage in a number of manufacturing products, including machinery and appliances, plastics, power-generating equipment, chemicals, agricultural machinery, and aircraft. Over the past two decades, however, our comparative advantage has declined in such industries as rubber tires, inorganic chemicals, and motor vehicles (Aho, Bowen, and Pelzman 1980: 2–5).

The trend toward the internationalization of the manufacturing process accelerated in the early 1970s when U.S. manufacturing firms increased the offshore assembly and sourcing of components as a way of expanding production. Offshore manufacturing by U.S. firms is a form of imports that has remained at about 6 percent of all imports since 1978 but in absolute terms has expanded gradually along with the growth of international trade. In the case of offshore assembly in developing nations, the U.S. manufacturer concentrates on its comparative advantage in capital-intensive production and high-skilled labor, while the less developed country utilizes its supply of low-skilled labor in the labor-intensive part of the production process. U.S. offshore assembly in industrialized countries such as West Germany and Japan is undertaken to take advantage of the higher productivity and lower unit costs of production in some industries in these countries.

In many cases this is essential if U.S. final manufactured goods are to compete internationally (U.S. International Trade Commission 1982).

The United States has made a significant structural adjustment as the developing nations have increased their investment in productive facilities and achieved relatively strong economic growth. From 1973–80 U.S. exports of capital goods (in real terms) grew at 11.2 percent per year. At the beginning of the decade 30 percent of our exports in these goods went to developing countries, but by the end of the decade the proportion was 42 percent. U.S. exports of agricultural products have also been particularly strong, with a $25 billion trade surplus by the end of the decade. As part of a complementary trade pattern U.S. imports of consumer goods (nonfood, nonauto) from developing countries also grew rapidly during the 1970s (*OPEC Surplus and U.S.–LDC Trade* 1982: 170–208 [testimony of William H. Branson]).

PRESENT AND FUTURE STRUCTURAL PROBLEMS

During the 1970s several major components of the U.S. industrial base lost their competitive positions and experienced substantial import penetration. Inability of U.S. industry to adapt to the ongoing process of economic change is currently heavily concentrated within the automobile and steel industries. In automobiles the penetration came from a surge of Japanese imports in 1975–76 when Japanese auto sales in the United States increased substantially. This was the result of a significant shift in consumer demand for smaller, more fuel-efficient cars—a demand that U.S. auto companies were ill-equipped to meet. Over the following four years (1977–80) sales of Japanese cars in the United States grew steadily at an average annual rate of about 9.5 percent per annum. Japanese cars now have a share of about 21 percent of the U.S. domestic automobile market and account for about 80 percent of all imports.[5]

During 1981 the sales of *all* auto manufacturers suffered, and by November 1982 almost 252,000 U.S. auto workers in direct manufacturing were on indefinite layoff. The overall unemployment rate for the industry was 23 percent by the end of 1982. This unemployment rate was significantly higher than the rate for manufacturing as a whole, which was 14.8 percent in December 1982.

Part of the decline in demand in the industry has little to do with structural change; the decline in total demand for autos during the recession and the interest-rate cost of automobile financing are cyclical causes of depressed economic conditions. Gasoline prices caused a structural shift in demand in the mid-1970s, but by 1980 these prices were not rising. The major source of the structural changes in the auto industry was the rising cost of producing a U.S. automobile compared to the unit cost of producing a Japanese automobile.[6]

The nature and sources of the problem facing the U.S. steel industry are different from the auto industry, though the problem in both industries has common elements — the persistent threat of import penetration (even in the face of a recession) and rapidly rising unit costs of production since the late-1970s.

The demand for steel is strongly influenced by the demand for automobiles. In December 1982 the unemployment rate for workers in primary metals was 28.6 percent, twice the rate for manufacturing. Steelworkers in basic steel and iron and steel foundries make up a little more than half the employment in primary metals. Given the differences in the demand for primary metal output and basic steel, the unemployment rate among steelworkers was undoubtedly higher than 28.6 percent.

The problem of the changing U.S. industrial base has been heavily influenced by insufficient productivity growth and rapid increases in costs of production in the steel and auto industries. Comparatively low rates of investment in new plant and equipment and excessive increases in labor compensation costs proved to be major culprits.[7]

The problem of declining competitiveness was not confined to a few industries. Prior to 1973 the combination of low rates of compensation increases offset relatively low productivity growth and made most U.S. manufacturing products highly competitive in world trade. However, Table 7-2 shows that since 1973 our relative cost advantage over all countries disappeared. Except for Japan, our average increase in unit labor costs was similar to the increase experienced by all our major trading partners. In Japan, however, unit costs grew much slower than they grew in any other nation. This gave Japan a significant trade advantage throughout the entire 1973–81 period. In the late 1970s the U.S. unit cost position deteriorated seriously compared to Japan and Germany. In 1980, U.S. manufacturing unit labor costs rose over 11 percent but in 1981 moderated to the average level of the post-1973 period. In 1980, and to a lesser extent in 1981, Japan's extremely low growth in unit labor costs in producing manufactured goods gave them a considerable advantage in international markets.

Table 7-2. Average Annual Percentage Increase in Unit Labor Costs in Manufacturing for Major U.S. Trading Partners, 1960–81.

Trading Nations	1960–73		1973–81		1980		1981	
	Country Currency	U.S. $	Country Currency	U.S. $	Country Currency	U.S. $	Country Currency	U.S. $
United States	1.9	1.9	7.7	7.7	11.6	11.6	7.2	7.2
Canada	1.8	1.9	9.5	6.5	12.8	13.0	10.7	8.0
Japan	3.5	4.9	2.7	7.2	-0.2	-3.5	4.0	6.7
France	3.1	2.8	10.0	9.4	14.8	15.7	14.6	-10.5
Federal Republic of Germany	3.7	6.1	4.7	9.1	7.0	8.1	4.7	-15.7
United Kingdom	4.1	2.6	16.6	15.0	22.9	34.6	9.7	-4.5

Source: Adapted from data presented in Capdeveille, Alvarez, and Cooper, (1982: 7, Table 3).

While government regulatory and macroeconomic policies may have produced an environment that made it difficult to reduce costs and moderate compensation increase, both management and labor in some industries must share part of the blame for the erosion of an important segment of the U.S. industrial base.

The weakness of some of the industries in the traditional U.S. industrial base affected the geographic distribution of employment. During the 1970s, employment growth was more pronounced in the west and south as manufacturing employment in the northeast and upper midwest stabilized or declined in some industries. The industrial redistribution of employment was greatest in construction and finance, insurance, and real estate, with employment following the geographic redistribution of the population as many industrial states in the northeast experienced little or no population growth in the 1970s. In local economies that relied heavily on the steel, auto, rubber, and glass industries, the increasing cost disadvantage of these industries accelerated the need for workers to adjust to permanent structural change brought about by the loss of comparative advantage.

Current business concern about structural adjustment problems has not been confined to basic industries. Recently many high-technology industries have become concerned about the potential loss of market share. In the early 1960s the United States had a dominant lead in high-technology products.[8] Many industries in the high-technology sector achieved high-productivity growth rates compared to other sectors of the U.S. economy, and a high degree of competition in these industries frequently kept output prices from rising. This produced significant advantages to the entire U.S. industrial base in the form of lower input costs in production. It also provided the United States with a strong export potential. In 1962 our share of world exports of high-technology products was 32 percent, but it dropped to 27 percent by 1974 and has remained at about that level into the 1980s. The main concern is the potential challenge from one country — Japan — whose share rose from 4 percent in 1962 to 14 percent in 1980 (U.S. Cabinet Council in Commerce and Trade 1983: 9). Our high-technology trade balance has been consistently in surplus and growing with all major nations except Japan, with whom we have had a declining deficit. Many high-technology firms — especially those in electronics, computer hardware, and machine tools — are concerned that Japanese industries, with government assistance, are targeting the U.S. market for future import penetration.

INDUSTRY STRATEGIES ON STRUCTURAL EMPLOYMENT ISSUES

Industry's view of the appropriate employment policies for adjusting to the changing industrial base varies with the cause of the decline and whether or not the industry is affected directly by the ongoing change. The following main components of industry strategies are not mutually exclusive.

Temporary Protection from Imports to Permit Gradual Employment Adjustment

For the industries directly affected by economic change there is often a strong mutuality of interest between industry interests and the interests of the work force. Sometimes the initial strategy is to try to reduce the pace of structural change so that most of the employment adjustment can be achieved through attrition. If the adjustment is caused by a rapid increase in import competition, management may ask the government for protection from unfair competition.

This was the immediate reaction of the U.S. steel industry to increasing import penetration. Some of the adjustment being forced on U.S. firms was the result of dumping of steel by foreign companies who were selling steel in the U.S. market at less than the price in their domestic market. Despite a complicated procedure for avoiding such pricing practices it was quite clear that some countries, specifically Japan and West Germany, had more productive steel industries and that many U.S. firms had simply lost their competitiveness. The industry, with the support of the labor unions, now strongly supports the temporary protection afforded by the voluntary import levels that the U.S. government negotiated with European governments. Most other industries, whose costs of production are affected by the price of steel, do not favor temporary protection as a form of adjustment. If, however, the industry receiving temporary protection initiates policies to lower its unit costs of production, most of industry will not oppose such protection.

Recent economic history provides many illustrations of other industries arguing for temporary government assistance. In some cases specific industries, along with direct participation of labor and the government, have been successful in receiving the protection of Orderly Marketing Arrangements that have proved far from temporary. In the textile industry the multifibre agreement originally negotiated by the industrial nations to temporarily control imports from developing nations has become remarkably permanent. Similarly the voluntary restraint agreement on Japanese automobile imports was implemented in 1981 for a two-year period but has since been extended twice. This agreement expires in April 1985 but labor and to some extent management is already lobbying for an additional extension.

In other cases industries have a legitimate argument for protection from unfair competition based on failure of the U.S. government to apply the appropriate remedies under international trade agreements and failure of our trading partners to provide U.S. business with access to their markets while foreign companies have relatively free access to U.S. markets. What is unique about current industry views of adjustment to economic change is that many of our most successful industries are concerned with unfair practices of other nations. This makes international trade arrangements an important policy area that will determine how well all industrial nations adapt to continuous structural change.

Government Adjustment-Assistance Programs to Assist Permanently Displaced Workers

There does not appear to be any significant support for the existing federal worker-adjustment programs, many of which were designed to assist specific groups of workers that were laid off through economic change. The rationale for those programs was that government policy indirectly initiated the economic change—through such actions as deregulation of an industry, expansion of a national park, a modification of federal health-care policy, or a reduction in tariff barriers—so that society could benefit from greater international trade. Experience both here and abroad has shown that well-intentioned public policies to encourage adjustment to economic change frequently end up protecting existing jobs and the income of a relatively small group of workers but fail to encourage these workers to move to more productive employment.

During the current period of a changing industrial base employers believe that the government can play a role in the retraining and relocation of permanently displaced employees. Government employment and training policies should include funding for retraining experienced workers who have been permanently dislocated. However, decisions on the type of training and the delivery of the training services should be local decisions, since local labor, business, and public institutions are in the best position to assist displaced workers.

There is a growing interest in permitting permanently displaced workers receiving unemployment insurance (UI) benefits to participate in retraining and relocation programs without losing their UI benefits. Some employers favor making receipt of extended UI benefits (beyond twenty-six weeks) conditional on enrolling in retraining. Employers generally favor changes in the unemployment insurance system so that it provides more than income maintenance during a period of job search. Some employers believe that the UI system must do more than process UI benefits; it should help prepare the unemployed to improve their own job search.

On reforming the UI system, however, there is a diversity of views among employers. Many employers do *not* believe that the UI taxes are providing sufficient benefits to either the unemployed or the workers and employers who finance the system. However, employers in industries subject to seasonal changes in demand are apprehensive about changing the UI tax structure, or the waiting period for benefit eligibility, since their employees receive much more in benefits than the taxes they pay into the system. Essentially this group of employers (and their employees) are using the UI system to pay part of the cost of adjusting to temporary and sometimes permanent changes in the demand for labor. The cost of this subsidy is borne by the employers (and their employees) who have relatively stable employment patterns.

Government Policy and the Supply of Skills in a Changing Economy

There is a general consensus within business that as high technology begins to play a greater role in the economy the elementary and secondary educational system must improve the quality of scientific, mathematical, and computer literacy of the current generation of elementary and high school students. Business stresses the importance of these basic skills so that the next generation of workers will be able to adjust to future technological change.

Business has traditionally been concerned about potential skill shortages and its ability to maintain the skills of the work force. Despite the lack of evidence of impending shortages of labor skills, or of insufficient business investment in retraining existing workers, some groups within the business community are urging government to provide industry with special incentives for retraining current employees. While many in industry are convinced that retraining our work force and a major increase in research and development are essential for adapting to future economic change, this is not a top priority among most business executives.

Compensation Flexibility as an Employment-Adjustment Mechanism

There is a strong consensus within business that the government has the major responsibility for ensuring a noninflationary economic environment and negotiating a trading system in which all nations gradually reduce restrictions to imports and refrain from subsidizing domestic industries for the purpose of achieving an "unfair" advantage in foreign markets. Business feels that such an environment is essential for producing strong economic growth, which is by far the most important policy to facilitate adjustment to economic change.

Most groups in business are opposed, in principle, to government microlevel interventions in markets to rescue industries, firms, or plants facing adjustment difficulties. Most, however, recognize (and in some cases request) that microlevel interventions are inevitable. The majority opinion in business is opposed to any organized form of government strategy to determine when and how adjustment to change should occur. If firms lose their competitive positions, then inefficient plants must be either modernized or closed. Capital and labor must move to their most productive use if business and society is to benefit from economic change.

This view of the government's role explains why business is opposed to plant-closing legislation and legislated severance rights for permanently displaced employees. Business strongly opposes interventions that have traditionally been the domain of collective bargaining. Management and labor should be free to modify the content and the structure of collective bargaining to meet the employment problems created by economic change.

Recently, management and labor have initiated innovations in some collective agreements that attempt to assist workers adjust to change. Under these contracts both management and labor have included local educational, training, and governmental institutions in the strategy to facilitate employment adjustment.

There also appears to be growing recognition by labor as well as management that while compensation flexibility will not save firms with out-of-date plant and equipment, compensation levels must be more closely related to the efficiency of local operations. If labor costs do not reflect plant-level productivity, the potential for plant closure will inevitably increase.

There is growing evidence that the changing industrial base is likely to encourage management and labor to modify the structure of collective bargaining.[9] In the opinion of all groups representing business organizations, any change in the structure of collective bargaining is the responsibility of the individual bargaining agents under specific collective agreements. No business group will recommend how collective bargaining should be structured in any industry.

The practice of negotiating pattern-setting agreements based on the most efficient producer in the industry may no longer be in the interests of management or workers. In the past, some cross-subsidization of the least efficient plants by the most efficient plants may have been possible when the industry had oligopoly power in the product market.

The structure of bargaining has always been influenced by the scope of markets. John R. Common's theory of the U.S. labor movement accurately explained early unionization strategy in the United States (Tripp 1963: 52–53). As specialization and growth of trade expanded the geographic boundaries of product markets, labor unions sought to negotiate similar wages and conditions of employment among workers in labor markets within a wider geographic area.

The expansion of trade during the past two decades has posed a similar problem for U.S. labor unions. Initially, this increased the U.S. labor movement's concern for labor standards in industrial and developing countries whose products began competing in U.S. markets. It also gave both labor and management in some industries an incentive to seek trade protection from countries with low labor standards or higher levels of productivity.

The gains from increased international trade are widely dispersed throughout all groups in U.S. society as well as in the nations who are our trading partners. Attempts to expand the concept of similar conditions of employment beyond national boundaries have proved impossible. In a period when more markets have worldwide boundaries, the "orbit of coercive comparison" has expanded to include low-unit-cost producers in foreign countries. Pattern-setting bargaining, within and among industries, based on the assumption that U.S. markets are primarily domestic markets, has become detrimental to the goal of improved competitiveness of U.S. industry as a major adjustment mechanism for responding to economic change.

In the future it is likely that the structure of collective bargaining and the specific provisions of collective agreements in some industries will have to adapt to the economic realities facing individual establishments. In the process the traditional role of industry-wide and multi-plant agreements will change significantly.

If compensation levels were more closely related to local labor-market conditions, the need to adjust to structural change would be more gradual. Workers who were potentially vulnerable would have more options. They could consider relocating in an occupation in which their productivity would be higher or accept lower compensation with an incentive to contribute to the productivity improvement of their own plant.

Compared to other countries the United States has a labor force with extremely high occupational mobility. The U.S. labor force has always adjusted to economic change and absorbed very rapid increases of labor-market entrants. This has been achieved with a minimum of government intervention in labor markets. In the view of most groups in business, temporary protection, worker-adjustment programs, and policies for specific industries and firms should be the exception, not the rule. Government should create the public-policy environment that stimulates noninflationary economic growth and more rapid rates of productivity improvement in all sectors of the economy. At the level of the industry and the firm, in the final analysis it is the actions of management and labor that will determine how successfully the nation adjusts to the employment implications of a changing industrial base.

NOTES

1. For a review of the role of several major business groups that attempt to coordinate these diverse views on important legislative issues, see Levitan (1984).
2. For an assessment of the potential of these new technologies, see *Productivity in the American Economy* (1982: pp. 227–37 (testimony of A. David Jackson), 171–93 (testimony of George S. Ansell)).
3. In almost all instances the regulatory process slows down the pace of innovation and diverts resources away from innovative activities, thus retarding productivity growth. This is a major reason why business advocates less regulation. However, regulatory reform changes the status quo, and inevitably some businesses will lose market share. Consequently, while business is in favor of regulatory reform from a public-interest point of view, they may oppose specific reforms on the basis of self-interest.
4. The unemployment rate is a poor indicator of structural changes in the economy. Most unemployed workers are laid off for cyclical changes in economic activity, and between 70 and 80 percent of those laid off return to work with their previous employer. In any year those permanently dislocated from their previous jobs account for less than 1 percent of the labor force. For some workers cyclical unemployment can be just as serious as permanent dislocation. In the severe recession of 1981–82, the average length of unemployment increased substantially to about seventeen weeks, pushing many cyclically unemployed into the long-term unemployed category. See the Committee for Economic Development policy statement (1984).
5. Sources of statistics on the automobile industry include: Nanto and Elwell (1980); Bass (1982); and Nanto (1982).
6. In the period from late-1978 to early-1983 the yen depreciated rapidly against the U.S. dollar, giving Japanese cars an additional price advantage in U.S. markets.
7. In 1970 the average wage premium (the excess over the average hourly wage of manufacturing workers) was 22 percent. By December 1982 the premium was 47 percent. For auto workers the premium rose from 26 percent to 47 percent. Since steel and auto workers have better-than-average fringe benefits, their total *compensation* premium over the average manufacturing worker is greater than the wage premium.
8. High-technology industries include pharmaceuticals, robotics, aircraft, biotechnology, space, fiber optics, computer hardware and software, semiconductors, and machine tools.
9. For a prediction that pattern-setting bargaining will break down, see Freedman and Fuller (1982: 30).

REFERENCES

Aho, Michael C., P. Bowen, and Joseph Pelzman, *Assessing the Changing Structure of World Trade* (Washington, D.C.: U.S. Department of Labor, Bureau of International Labor Affairs, 1980), pp. 2–5.

Bass, Gwendell, *The U.S. Auto Industry: The Situation in the Eighties* (Washington, D.C.: U.S. Library of Congress, Congressional Research Service, 1982) (photocopy).

Capdeville, Patricia, Donato Alvarez, and Brian Cooper, "International Trends in Productivity and Labor Costs," *Monthly Labor Review* 105, no. 12 (December 1982) (Table 3): 7.

Committee for Economic Development, *Strategy for U.S. Industrial Competitiveness* (New York: Committee for Economic Development, 1984).

Economic Report of the President (Washington, D.C.: U.S. Government Printing Office, 1982), p. 245.

Freedman, Audrey, and William E. Fuller, "Last Rites for Pattern Bargaining," *Harvard Business Review* 60, no. 2 (March/April 1982): 30.

Gollop, Frank M., "Evidence for a Sector-Biased or Sector-Neutral Industrial Strategy: Analysis of the Productivity Slowdown," in William J. Baumol and Kenneth McLennan, eds., *Productivity Growth and U.S. Competitiveness* (New York: Oxford University Press, 1985), Chapter 7.

Levitan, Sar A., and Martha R. Cooper, *Business Lobbies: The Public Good and the Bottom Line* (Baltimore, Md.: Johns Hopkins University Press, 1984).

Nanto, Dick K., *Automobiles Imported from Japan* (Washington, D.C.: U.S. Library of Congress, Congressional Research Service, 1982) (photocopy).

Nanto, Dick K., and Craig Elwell, *Imported Automobiles in the United States: Their Rising Market Share and the Macroeconomic Impact of Proposed Import Restriction* (Washington, D.C.: U.S. Library of Congress, Congressional Research Service, 1980) (photocopy).

Organization for Economic Cooperation and Development, *The Impact of the New Industrializing Countries on Production and Trade in Manufactures* (report of the Secretary-General) (Paris: Organization for Economic Cooperation and Development, 1979).

The OPEC Surplus and U.S.-LDC Trade: Hearings before the Joint Economic Committee, 97th Cong., 2d sess., pp. 170–208 (May 26, 1982) (testimony of William H. Branson).

Productivity in the American Economy: Report and Findings: Hearings before the Subcommittee on Employment and Productivity of the Senate Labor and Human Resources Committee, 97th Cong., 2d sess. (1982) (pp. 171–93 (testimony of George S. Ansell on "Impact of Developments in Biotechnology on Productivity"); pp. 227–37 (testimony of A. David

Jackson on "Impact of Developments in Biotechnology on Productivity"); pp. 629–39 (testimony of Kenneth McLennan on "The Future Role of Service-Type Industries in the Economy: Implications for Productivity Policy")).

Tripp, L. Reed, "Collective Bargaining Theory," in Gerald G. Somers, ed., *Labor Management and Social Policy* (Madison: University of Wisconsin Press, 1963), pp. 52–53.

U.S. Cabinet Council on Commerce and Trade, *An Assessment of U.S. Competitiveness in High-Technology Industries* (Washington, D.C.: U.S. Cabinet Council on Commerce and Trade, 1983) (photocopy), p. 9.

U.S. International Trade Commission, *Imports under Items 806.30 and 807.00 of the Tariff Schedules of the United States* (Washington, D.C.: U.S. Government Printing Office, 1982).

8 A LABOR PERSPECTIVE ON TECHNOLOGICAL CHANGE

Markley Roberts

Workers and their unions have a direct and vital interest in technological change. Unions recognize that technology brings potential benefits—new jobs, safer and easier work, higher productivity, higher levels of living, and more leisure. Unions also recognize that changing technology has potentially destructive effects on workers and on society—loss of jobs, loss of earnings and income, downgrading of skills and experience, new threats to the environment and to workers' safety and health, dehumanization of work, polarized income distribution, alienation, and social instability.

There is no logical or inevitable tradeoff to be made between technological progress and the welfare of workers. But if such a choice is forced on American workers, it should come as no surprise that workers and their unions will make every possible effort to humanize technological change, to ensure that people get priority over technology and productivity and efficiency, and to make human values prevail.

The long-run benefits of progress and the long-run necessity of change are easier for workers to accept if the workers know that job security and income security are protected. Workers want to share in the benefits of technological change and technological progress

Any opinions, findings, conclusions, or recommendations expressed in this chapter are the sole responsibility of the author.

183

without bearing an undue or unfair share of the burden of change, progress, and adjustment. And workers want to participate, through their elected union officials, in the decisions that are going to affect their lives. Too often such decisions are made unilaterally by faceless absentee management. More involvement by workers and unions, more joint decisionmaking, more industrial democracy can raise the quality of working life and raise the quality of humane adjustments to new technology.

In addition to progress achieved through labor/management collective bargaining and work-place democracy, American workers and their unions are looking for a more rational and effective way to avoid adverse effects from changing technology and to achieve faster economic progress through deliberate national industrial policy. Persistent high unemployment, low economic growth, international economic competition, and deterioration of the social capital that encourages economic progress have reenforced labor support for conscious national planning to assure a healthy, growing, diversified competitive economy — one that creates enough jobs, raises the quality of life, maximizes beneficial effects and minimizes negative effects of technological change.

Income distribution is another problem that concerns workers and their unions as they look at the employment shift from goods-producing to services-producing industries and at the earnings distribution among and within industries. Unions are concerned about the prospect of a two-tier, high-skill and low-skill work force without a solid middle-skill, middle-income center. The weakening of America's middle-income, middle class presents serious implications for the consumer-buying base of the U.S. economy and for political democracy and social stability in the United States.

The first two parts of this chapter set out the role of collective bargaining and industrial democracy in handling the problems and opportunities created by technical change. The next three parts examine structural shifts in the distribution of labor income and discuss the role of government policy. Conclusions are stated in the final part.

COLLECTIVE BARGAINING

In the short run, workers and their unions look to collective bargaining as their first line of defense. Collective bargaining holds a vitally important role in meeting the challenges, opportunities, and dangers of new technology. There is much to be learned from past experience in collective bargaining. The flexibility of this institution – the American system of labor/management bargaining at the plant, company, and industry level – helps workers negotiate and settle with employers on reasonable and humane protections against the potentially adverse effects of job-destroying technological innovation. Mature collective-bargaining relationships between labor and management provide opportunities and a sound basis for special labor/management committees to deal with adjustment to technological change within the framework of collective bargaining.

Collective bargaining can help democratize labor/management relations and humanize the work place and work itself, including the effect of new technology on workers' jobs and earnings. It can provide a cushion to soften adverse effects on workers by setting up adjustment procedures and programs at the work place. In a full employment economy – linked with adequate employment services, employment and training programs, and unemployment compensation – the disruption of workers' lives and the job displacement resulting from technological change can be minimized.

Historically, unions have responded in a number of ways to the introduction of new technology. In 1960 Slichter, Healy, and Livernash reported that major determinants of union policies toward technological change are:

1. the nature of the union, specifically whether it is a craft or industrial union;
2. the economic condition of the industry or the enterprise, or occupation, whether it is expanding or contracting, whether the industry is highly competitive or not;
3. the nature of the technological change, the effect on jobs and on the bargaining unit, the effect on workers' skills and job responsibilities; and
4. the stage of development of the technological change and the stage of development of union policy toward the change.

The authors distinguished five principal policies that unions adopt when faced with technological change: (1) willing acceptance, (2) opposition, (3) competition, (4) encouragement, and (5) adjustment with an effort to control use of the new technology. Of the five, they found that the most used policy was one of willing acceptance, particularly if the impact did not greatly change job content or the number of jobs. Slichter et al. go on to point out that no national union in recent years has destroyed itself by fighting technological change. Unions have instead sought a greater share of the distribution of gains and have eased displacement by having management find other jobs or to a lesser extent operate with excessive crews.

Using Slichter et al.'s five principal attitudes found toward change, Doris McLaughlin (1979) conducted a survey of union officials, management, and mediators and arbitrators on the effect of labor unions on the rate and direction of technological innovation. The 1979 McLaughlin study found that willing acceptance was the most common response that American labor unions make to the introduction of new technology. The next most common response was initial opposition, but this was followed by adjustment, so that in the long run willing acceptance or adjustment were by far most common. A negative union response was invariably the result of belief that acceptance would have an adverse effect on a large or important segment of the union's membership. If the employer convinced the leaders that their members would not be adversely affected, or that those who were would receive some offsetting benefit, opposition disappeared.

The state of the economy, union leaders' perception of the inevitability or necessity for the change, and the nature of the industry were the three most determining factors of union reaction. McLaughlin noted that depending on the union's perception of these three variables, a fourth became crucial — where decisionmaking power lay. If the international union held the decisionmaking power, a decision on how to react to the new technology would be made only on consideration of the first three variables. However, if decisionmaking power lay with local union leaders, three additional variables became relevant:

1. how local union leaders perceive the effect of the new technology on the bargaining unit;
2. how local union leaders perceive the quid pro quo offered by the employer to the affected union members; and
3. how local union leaders perceive the effect on those union members left in the unit after the new technology is introduced.

Third-party action by mediators, arbitrators, or judges did not seem to affect the outcome, according to the report, but did appear to affect the process by which unions and management reached accommodation to the effects of the new technology. These third-party agents, as outsiders, serve a useful function in deflecting pressure from local union leaders "when otherwise politically delicate decisions need to be made with regard to the introduction of new technology" (McLaughlin 1979: x). Surprisingly, McLaughlin concludes that labor unions are not the major stumbling block to new technology and higher productivity but that "employer representatives, particularly at the middle management level, were often cited as constituting the real barrier to the introduction and effective use of technological innovation" (McLaughlin 1979: x).

In 1964 the Bureau of Labor Statistics reported that some of the major labor/management efforts to protect against the effects of new technology have included

1. guarantees against job or income loss and in some cases against loss of supplementary benefits for varying periods;
2. compensation for employees who lose their jobs;
3. guaranteed income for workers required to take lower-paying jobs;
4. provisions for retraining;
5. provisions for transfer to other plants and payment of relocation expenses; and
6. agreements to provide workers with notice of plant closings or other major changes.

Some agreements have established joint labor/management committees to recommend methods of providing for workers affected by automation. The Bureau report concluded (Bureau of Labor Statistics 1964: 1) that

> These arrangements typically are combined with provisions for retention of workers with greatest seniority, but in a limited number of cases, efforts are made to spread work among larger numbers of employees or to encourage early retirement of workers with relatively high seniority.

In 1966 the National Commission on Technology, Automation, and Economic Progress called attention to the need for private-sector efforts to facilitate adjustment to technological change, including reliance on attrition, an advance-notice early-warning system, job counseling and job-finding assistance, training and retraining. The

Commission noted the rationality of using the seniority principle in the case of layoffs and the seriousness of the need for pension and health benefits to continue during periods of unemployment. It also pointed out that technological improvements can bring more flexibility to work schedules and more leisure to employees through reduced hours of work per day, per week, and per year.

The record of collective bargaining response to technological change offers many examples of both success and failure. The Commission (1966: 65) noted that

> Collective bargaining has proved to be an excellent vehicle for the effective management of change; it permits those directly affected by the change to deal with it firsthand and with a familiarity that takes into account peculiarities and problems peculiar to an enterprise. Especially in recent years, some managements and unions, occasionally but not usually with the help of outsiders, have developed, with varying degrees of ingenuity and success, plans to facilitate change.

But the Commission warned that procedurally, the collective-bargaining process on basic issues tended to stagnate during the life of the agreement and to accelerate frantically in an atmosphere of crisis immediately preceding contract renewal. Fortunately employers and unions in a number of industries are abandoning this pattern in favor of more or less continuous discussion, since these issues require patient, careful, and continuous problem-solving efforts.

In the fifteen years since the Automation Commission's report, with generally slow economic growth and recessions in 1969–70, 1973–75, 1980, and 1981–82, economic conditions have not contributed to easy adjustments to technological change. The effect of new technology has become much more pervasive in the 1980s than it was in the 1960s.

It must be emphasized that it is easier to deal with adverse effects of technological change in a general economic climate of full employment. National economic policies must aim at full employment for a variety of economic, social, and moral reasons. Among those reasons unions recognize the need to facilitate successful and humane adjustments to job-destroying technology in both the private and public sectors.

Much progress has already been achieved through collective bargaining. For example, a 1981 Bureau of Labor Statistics study, updating a similar 1966–67 study, presents a wide range of contract language and statistical summaries of contract language on plant movement, plant transfer, and relocation allowances, many of which relate to the effects of technological change. Agreements limiting plant movement rose from 22 percent in the 1966–67 survey to 36 percent in the 1980–81 survey of some 1,600 contracts, while worker coverage rose from 38 percent to 49 percent. Interplant transfer provisions increased from 32 percent to 35 percent, and worker coverage went from 46 percent to 49 percent. Agreements dealing with relocation allowances increased from 34 percent to 41 percent, while worker coverage went up from 60 percent to 65 percent.

On the issues of the major technological change, work transfer, or plant closings, some major contracts have a variety of provisions.[1] For example, the United Automobile, Aerospace and Agricultural Implement Workers of America International Union AFL–CIO (U.A.W.)–General Motors contract provides for advance notice to the union in cases of technology-related permanent layoffs, a special union/company committee to deal with technology layoffs, and company transfer of work. Workers have the right to train for a new job in cases of technology-related permanent layoff. In the case of plant closings, department closings, and transfer of work, workers have the right to bump to another job in the same plant, transfer to a replacement facility, or transfer to a new plant. They will receive preferential hiring at another plant, keep seniority with respect to fringe benefits, receive moving expenses up to $1,355, take layoff with recall rights, and get severance pay.

The United Steelworkers' of America AFL–CIO (USW) contract with Kennecott Copper includes a no-layoff clause and attrition protection for workers affected by technology changes that will permanently eliminate their jobs. Under this contract, workers have the right to bump to another job in the same plant or in another plant. The Amalgamated Transit Union AFL–CIO (ATU) contract with the New York City transit system and the Newspaper Guild AFL–CIO (TNG) contract with the *New York Times* also have no-layoff contract protection.

The Steelworkers' contract with American Can Company calls for a twelve-month advance notice of permanent layoffs related to technological change. The United Food and Commercial Workers International Union AFL–CIO (UFCW) contract with Armour calls for six-month notice and the Guild–*New York Times* agreement calls for four months. There are contracts with advance-notice requirements as short as seven days and contracts with advance-notice requirements but no specified time period.

A broad range of labor/management cooperation is already included in many other labor/management agreements with negotiated specific procedures for adjusting to technological change. One method of easing the human costs of new technology is assuring advance information to workers and their unions about management plans for future innovation that will affect workers with job loss or other serious problems. Major technology changes result from management decisions taken long before the new technology is actually introduced, often years earlier. Certainly there should be long advance notice before any technological change that results in layoffs or plant shutdown. The failure of management to institute worker safety, health, and environmental protections should not be the way that workers learn about intended plant shutdowns or major layoffs.

An early-warning system of advance notice helps make it possible to ease the problems of affected workers. Such early-warning provisions have long been standard in many union contracts. With advance notice and labor/management cooperation, workers can look for or train for a new job, perhaps with the same employer in the same plant or at another location. Employer-paid retraining is an important part of any adjustment-to-innovation program.

There are other methods and techniques for labor/management cooperation to cushion adverse effects from changing technology. These include income maintenance with work and/or pay guarantees. One way is through no-layoff attrition to reduce the work force by natural turnover, deaths, retirements, and voluntary quits, thus protecting the jobs and earnings of those workers who remain with the company. Of course, attrition alone is not an adequate solution. Red-circle earnings protection for workers downgraded through no fault of their own attaches a wage rate to an individual instead of to the job itself and thus protects workers against loss of income that might result from innovation-induced downgrading.

Seniority is a key principle in protecting workers against layoffs and downgradings. This rewards long service but does much more — properly reflecting the worker's investment in the job and the company's investment in the worker. Early retirement is an option that older workers should have available when major technological change wipes out their jobs. But the option should be available as a free choice, not as a requirement. Many older workers cannot afford to retire early, and others prefer to continue working.

Transfer and relocation rights and mobility assistance to workers are other ways to provide job and income protection. Intra- and interplant transfers, relocation assistance, severance pay, pension rights, seniority protections, and supplemental unemployment benefits can all help cushion adverse effects on workers and their families when industrial innovation occurs. Shorter workweeks and reduced time per year on the job, including longer paid vacations and sabbatical leaves, also can ease the negative employment effects of technology.

Electrical machinery manufacturing is an industry where extensive use of robots is expected in the future. The June 1982 General Electric agreement with the International Union of Electrical, Radio, and Machine Workers AFL–CIO (IUE) includes these protections for workers who lose jobs to robots and automation (Bureau of National Affairs 1982: F-1):

> A production employee whose job is directly eliminated by a transfer of work, the introduction of a robot or of an automated manufacturing machine and who is entitled to transfer or displace to another job shall basically retain the rate of the eliminated job for a period of up to 26 weeks.
>
> The company shall give the union advance notice of a minimum of six months of plant closing or transfer of work and of a minimum of 60 days of the installation of robots or automated manufacturing machine for production.
>
> An employee who is terminated because of a plant closing will be assisted to find new jobs and learn new skills under an employment assistance program which will include job counselling as well as job information services.
>
> An employee with two or more years of service who is terminated as a result of a plant closing will be entitled to receive education and retraining assistance, including reimbursement of $1,800 for authorized education expenses.

Obviously, these provisions do not constitute total protection, but they offer some protection and some help to displaced workers.

INDUSTRIAL DEMOCRACY

The potential for misuing technology is great, but the possibility of human progress through the wise and humane use of technology is equally great. The opportunity for new technology to be introduced with minimal social disruption will be greatly enhanced if workers and employers have an equal opportunity for discussion and joint decisionmaking on the subjects of changing technology and the quality of working life.

Collective bargaining, an established institution in our democratic society, has been a fair and workable process for joint labor/management decisions on wages, working conditions, and other major issues. It is therefore a logical mechanism for increasing the involvement of workers in such areas of decisionmaking as adjustment to new technology.

New technology and rising expectations that work should be humane for workers as well as profitable to business are forcing transformations in the work place. Human and social values must be more highly esteemed in the production process — not only when the process is producing goods and services and jobs but also when it is producing cultural and social effects, including leisure and unemployment. The human desire for greater autonomy and greater participation in decisionmaking on the shop floor, in the corporate boardroom, and in national economic policy making must recieve higher priority. Improvements in the quality of work life (QWL) include better occupational safety, health and work organization, improved work environment, better long-run investment, employment, and training decisions, and the introduction of new technology. These QWL issues are logical subjects for joint labor/management negotiation and decision. But employers must not use QWL as a disguise for union busting.

Irving Bluestone (1979: 249–50), a former UAW vice-president, has been a strong proponent of increased worker participation in corporate decisions. He warns that the joint labor/management programs now in existence have not proved themselves in any permanent sense and must be constantly reviewed. Based on successes to date, certain ingredients should be present. First, programs should be voluntary, and workers must have the free opportunity to decide whether or not to participate in the program. They should be assured that participation will not erode job security and that they will share the gains of improvements made. Bluestone also stresses the need to engineer job functions to fit the worker, contrary to the current system, which is designed to make the worker fit the job on the theory that this is more efficient.

The conflict theory of labor relations is a sound basis for worker representation, worker participation, and worker gains. Conflict is institutionalized in our political system, in our legal system, and in our economic system, and we have institutionalized conflict in labor/management relations through the American system of collective bargaining.

But the adversary role, which is appropriate to the conflict of collective bargaining, should be limited to the period of contract negotiation. During the life of the contract, the adversary relationship can very logically and appropriately be replaced by cooperation aimed at improving the quality of work life and at maximizing the potential success of the enterprise, the company, or the establishment. The labor-relations cycle should be one of periods of conflict during the negotiating period followed by the longer contract period of cooperation.

Labor unions today jointly participate with management in thousands of safety committees, apprenticeship committees, community-wide labor/management committees, quality-of-work-life committees, quality circles, and other joint labor/management efforts. As a result, labor/management committees are joining together to deal with matters of mutual interest such as foreign trade, federal, state, and local programs, community philanthropic purposes, and revitalization and strengthening of their industries and their communities. Some committees give workers a direct voice in the issues of the work place, including investment and innovation with new technology (Siegel and Weinberg 1982; U.S. Department of Labor, Labor Management Services and Bureau of Labor Statistics 1982).

Only the collective bargaining stature of their unions establishes workers as real partners in those labor/management committees. Actions that weaken a union, distort the balance in its relationship to management, or weaken the union's ability to represent its membership will damage that union's ability and desire to participate in committees of any kind with a particular management. Programs that strengthen the union's ability to grapple with the new issues that union members want addressed, including technology change issues, and programs that hold out real promise for the expansion of work place democracy will get sympathetic attention from workers and their unions. Every union must continue asserting its rights and those of its members to be accepted as legitimate equals in a partnership with management, with collective bargaining as the essential foundation for labor/management cooperation.

INCOME DISTRIBUTION

The shift in U.S. employment from goods-producing industries to service-producing industries is producing a downward shift — a relative lowering of the overall wage base and a debasing of the nation's wage structure. In 1960 manufacturing accounted for one out of every four jobs. By 1980 it was responsible for one out of five, and by 1990 it will be only one out of six. Even in manufacturing the proportion of nonproduction service jobs will increase as automation and robots replace blue-collar production workers.

The service-producing sector will continue to be the major source of new jobs. From 1940 to 1980 business and personal-service industries such as health care, education, wholesale and retail trade, repair and maintenance, government, transportation, banking, and insurance increased their share of total employment from about 45 percent to about 70 percent. Business services have shown the biggest job gains.

The decline of jobs in manufacturing and the increase of jobs in the service sector have significant implications for earnings and income. In 1983 average weekly earnings in manufacturing were $354. By contrast, weekly earnings were $263 in finance, insurance, and real estate, $237 in personal and business services, and $207 in wholesale and retail trade.

Service occupations will increase in goods-producing industries as well as in service-producing industries. In the 1970s about 90 percent of all new jobs added to the economy were in service occupations. By 1990 service industries will employ 72 percent of the labor force — about 90 million workers. Unfortunately, job growth in the 1980s will be biggest in traditionally low-pay, high-turnover jobs like sales, clerical, janitorial, and food service work. Too often these jobs lack career-opportunity ladders leading to higher-skill, higher-pay jobs. Higher-skill, higher-pay jobs do not increase as fast as high technology is spreading through the U.S. economy into almost every sector and every industry. There are now some 6,000 robots and 2 million desk-top computers in use in the United States. By 1990 there may be up to 100,000 robots and 20 million computers in use.

As computers and robots take over more and more functions in the factory and the office, a two-tier work force is developing. In some cases, jobs are being upgraded. In many other cases, jobs are being downgraded. (In some production processes, computerization may lead to a narrowing of skill differentials between supervisors and production workers when both need detailed knowledge of a relatively complicated process.) At the top will be a few executives, scientists and engineers, professionals, and managers performing high-level, creative, high-paid full-time jobs in a good work environment. And the executives among them will decide whether the work will be done by people or by robots, and whether the work will be done in Terre Haute or Taiwan. At the bottom will be low-paid workers performing relatively simple, low-skill, dull, routine, high-turnover jobs in a poor work environment. These jobs will often be part-time and usually lacking job security and opportunities for career advancement. Too often these jobs are oversupervised and devoid of employee control over the pace of work.

Between these two major tiers will be fewer and fewer permanent, well-paid, full-time, skilled, semi-skilled, and craft-production and maintenance jobs, which in the past have offered upward mobility to workers who start in low-paid, entry-level jobs. Many middle-management jobs will also be gone. The loss of middle-level, good-pay jobs raises serious questions about inadequate growth of consumer buying power in the future and about loss of opportunities for upward economic and social mobility. It also raises serious questions about social stability if middle-class America becomes relatively smaller and has less job security and lowered income expectations.

Office and clerical work has been a huge source of jobs for millions of woman workers. But automation, data processors, and word processors have invaded the office. Some jobs are being upgraded, but more jobs are being de-skilled and downgraded. Office automation in a fixed work situation will reduce growth in office and clerical job opportunities in the future. The net effect of office automation will probably slow growth in office and clerical job opportunities in the future.

Other white-collar jobs, including supervisory, managers, and professional jobs, are facing de-skilling, downgrading, and displacement as a result of new technology. There are estimates of 500,000 surplus college graduates in 1990—people who cannot find jobs that use their education and skills. Of course, some of the new white-collar jobs will require new skills that bring upgrading and higher pay. At this stage of industrial evolution, these new skills are not yet fully recognized or identified. The danger is that existing patterns of education and training will perpetuate and widen employment and earnings gaps in this more polarized, two-tier occupational structure.

Below the two-tier work force is the labor surplus underclass, the workers without jobs and without job prospects. There is some movement in and out of this labor surplus underclass, but upward movement essentially is limited to the bottom level of the two-tier work force.

What happens to a society increasingly polarized by wide earnings and income gaps between those who work? What happens to a society in which income gap between low-pay workers and the jobless, labor-surplus underclass becomes smaller and smaller? Workers and their unions don't have the answers but are certainly concerned about these questions (AFL–CIO 1983a).

INDUSTRIAL POLICY

In addition to collective bargaining and work-place democracy as key institutional vehicles for dealing with technological change, the American labor movement increasingly is looking to conscious, institutionalized national industrial policy—including effective employment and training programs—that would deal in a comprehensive way with industry shifts, public and private investment, international trade and capital flows, slow economic growth and persistent high unemployment, and the impact of technological change. Recognition of the need for a national industrial policy is widespread.[2] America needs an industrial policy to meet the nation's goals for full employment and expanded noninflationary production and humane adjustment assistance to help workers and communities adversely affected by economic and technological change.

The AFL–CIO has proposed the creation of a tripartite National Reindustrialization Board—including representatives of labor, business, and the government—which would develop a balanced program to ensure the revitalization of the nation's basic industries and decaying communities. At the same time this board would encourage the development of new industries with promise for the future. The board would encourage productivity growth, dissemination of research and development findings, and a balanced use of the nation's resources. It would target industrial sectors and regions for special assistance. A resolution adopted at the October 1983 convention of the AFL–CIO (1983b: 7) declared

To modernize and revitalize the American economy, business, labor, and government should participate in a tripartite Reindustrialization Board. Under this board, a Reconstruction Finance Corporation would invest public and private funds in necessary reindustrialization projects.

The urban infrastructure of sewers, water systems, streets, and bridges needs to be renewed and the nation's transportation network must be upgraded for people and goods to move more efficiently. Railroads, highways, port facilities and airports are in desperate need of rehabilitation. Urban mass transit systems need support and modernization.

Private pension funds could be encouraged to make investments in such financing arrangements to support and expand industrial employment in the United States. Too often the nation's tax laws encourage investment abroad rather than in the United States and thus undermine domestic job opportunities.

The AFL–CIO has urged that all obligations of the RFC that are purchased by employee pension-benefit plans should be guaranteed with the full faith and credit of the United States. Organized labor considers it highly desirable that pension funds should be used for reindustrialization and expansion that would provide employment with adequate security for the pension funds.

There should be added a requirement for an analysis of the effect on areas that will be affected and on the work force employed in the affected industries. There will, no doubt, be a need to retrain people to work with advanced technological production methods. There may also be displacement of people in some industries. Provision must be made for advance warning, adequate compensation to those affected, retraining, job placement assistance, relocation assistance, and a pension supplement where age and other factors make it appropriate. Such training and retraining as may be necessary could be done during the period of plant and equipment modernization and retooling to enhance growth in productivity.

A reindustrialization policy must include international trade and investment policies that deal effectively with the adverse effects on American workers, on American industries, and on U.S. national security resulting from international trade and international capital movements and the export of American technology.

U.S. tax laws encourage investment abroad and technology outflows. At a time when the nation must rebuild its industrial base and improve its competitiveness, the newest technology is up for sale to the closed economies of the world. New technological processes invented in the United States are sold or licensed for production and use abroad. Employment is often created for foreign workers who make products such as steel and auto parts that compete in U.S. markets with firms and industries that do not invest in new production here in the United States. Tax and trade policies must be changed to slow the outflow of technology, capital, production, and jobs and to control imports that raise unemployment and further weaken the U.S. industrial base.

PUBLIC POLICY AND LABOR DISPLACEMENT

New technology often eliminates some jobs and changes the job content, skill requirements and work flow of others. Technology often causes changes in industry location—shutdowns of departments and entire plants and shifts to new locations in suburban or outlying areas and sometimes overseas. No industry is immune to such changes, which are constantly shifting the structure of skills, occupations, jobs, and earnings of American workers.

More information is needed on the effects of technology on workers. Federal action is needed to set up a clearinghouse to gather information on a continuing basis on innovation and technological change and its effects on the welfare of the American people, on jobs, skills, training needs, and industry location. There are few economic studies of the effect of technological shifts because there is no systematic data gathering relating to the changing technology of American production. With more complete information, public and private adjustment programs can better avoid needless human hardship and suffering, which too often result from the disruptive impact of changing technology. Through this clearinghouse, the federal government could provide unions and employers with comprehensive information and service, on request, to help develop labor/management solutions for the complex problems caused by technological change at the work place.

Technology-caused economic dislocation and other kinds of dislocation—including plant shutdowns caused by corporate merger mania and by recession, job loss from trade policies, and production shifts away from defense-related industry—require cooperative labor/management efforts and also national programs to deal with these complex problems. Further exploration is needed of programs that deal with plant shutdowns and plant relocation and with reconversion of defense-related industry.

Occupational training and retraining may perhaps help displaced workers acquire new skills and new jobs—but such new jobs may provide lower skill levels and pay. Furthermore, the loss of an industry and the skills that go with that industry diminish the essential diversity and pluralism required for a health economy and society.

In 1982 Congress enacted new federally supported job-training legislation, but the scope of the program was too small to help the millions of workers who have lost their jobs to technological change and economy shifts. The recession sharpened union pressures to secure retraining commitments from employers ("Retraining Displaced Workers" 1982: 178–85).

For example, in 1982 the United Auto Workers together with Ford and General Motors set up training programs financed with 5-cents-per-hour payments that will put about $10 million a year into the UAW–Ford training fund and about $40 million a year into the UAW–GM funds. The August 1983 settlement of the Communications Workers of America AFL–CIO (CWA) and Electrical Workers with AT&T included a $36 million career-development training program. This program will open opportunities for both general training for upgrading currently employed workers and also for training workers whose jobs have been identified for potential dislocation. The contract sets up a joint labor/management committee to identify the skills that will be needed in the future and the kind of training that will be required for these skills. The committee will also monitor the effectiveness of training to make sure that it is properly related to job opportunities. Besides in-house training for telephone-company workers, the August settlement provides for a tuition-refund program so that workers can maintain and upgrade their skills to meet the needs of changing technology and industry structure.

Workers who lose jobs because of plant closings may not be able to find new ones or may be forced to work at reduced pay. Family life is often disrupted. The mental and physical health of displaced workers often declines at a rapid rate. Research over a thirteen-year period indicates that the suicide rate among workers displaced by plant closings is almost thirty times the national average (Bluestone and Harrison 1980: 78–82; Brenner 1976). Such workers also suffer a far higher than average incidence of heart disease, hypertension, and other ailments.

Bills to deal with this grave economic and social problem have been introduced in Congress.[3] Although these bills differ in some respects, they would do much to counteract the devastating effects of shutdowns and relocations. Unfortunately, they do not address the problems caused by the relocation of governmental facilities. Among other things, these bills would

1. require firms to provide advance notice of their intentions to close or relocate a major facility;
2. advocate programs to support troubled business, including incentives to promote employee ownership;
3. call for the issuance of economic impact statements and federal investigation of the circumstance; and
4. require employers, whenever existing jobs cannot be saved, to provide minimal protections to their workers in such matters as transfer rights, relocation expenses, severance pay, pension protection, health care, and job training.

Four states—Wisconsin, Maine, Massachusetts, and Michigan—have laws relating to plant shutdowns, and some fifteen other states have proposals pending with state labor organizations pressing for action on protective plant shutdown legislation at the state level. However, because of "competitive laxity" among the states in their efforts to attract new and runaway business, federal legislation with national plant closings standards is essential.

Until 1982 there was no centralized, comprehensive information on plant closings and major layoffs. There was no information on the number of workers affected or the cause of plant closings. However, in 1982 the Bureau of National Affairs, a private information service, began a quarterly report on layoffs, plant closings, and concession bargaining. Later in 1982 Congress passed the Job Training Partnership Act, which includes a requirement that the secretary of labor collect and make public information on permanent layoffs and plant closings once a year. The law (section 462(e)) specifies that the secretary's annual report include the number of plant closings, the number of workers displaced, and location of the affected plants, and the types of industries involved.

For labor it is crucially important to require employers to recognize responsibilities to their employees and communities before they shut down a plant and to provide economic protections to workers and their families who must suffer the consequence of too hasty corporate action. There is nothing radical or unusual about national legislation that requires advance notice and other worker and community protections. In other nations, private business firms—including affiliates and subsidiaries of many American firms — find they can live with laws requiring advance notice and other protections for workers and communities against the adverse effects of economic dislocation and plant shutdowns.

In terms of international comparisons, Sweden requires six months notice when more than 100 workers are involved, four months notice for twenty-six to 100 workers, and two months notice for five to twenty-five workers. Under Swedish law, no dismissals may take place until the unions have been contacted and granted an opportunity to negotiate concerning the issues and consequences of the dismissals. In the United Kingdom, ninety-day notices must be given where 100 or more workers are involved and thirty days in plants employing ten to ninety-nine workers. Failure to communicate with the unions and to give the appropriate notice can make the employer liable for continuing the pay of the workers during the required notice period. In France, Greece, and the Netherlands, prior to making large-scale dismissals, the firm must have permission of the government to lay off the workers, and in actual practice the advance notice period is as long as half a year to a year, depending on the specific circumstances.[4]

These examples indicate that advance notice is a practice that firms can live with. It must also be remembered that in most foreign countries the benefits paid workers are generally two-thirds of lost earnings for up to a year after the layoff.

Unfortunately, in the United States there are a number of tax advantages provided for corporations that close even viable, money-making plants. Congress should look into these plant closings very carefully to determine if there is indeed an array of tax incentives encouraging businesses to close plants. Legislation must be created that will stop such incentives and will prevent tax-related plant shutdowns. Legislation must also be created that will establish basic job and income protections for workers and protection of workers' pension and health-care and other benefits to deal in an effective and humane way with the economic and social dislocation resulting from plant closings.

CONCLUSION

Workers and their unions have reasonable concerns about loss of jobs and loss of income. They also have reasonable and legitimate concerns about the nation's economic strength, national security, and social equity or fairness. If these concerns are met adequately and effectively, workers will be much more willing to accept and adjust to changing technology.

There are no simple solutions to the task of protecting workers against the adverse impacts of changing technology. In thousands of labor/management contracts covering millions of workers in both the public and private sectors, unions and management have adopted a wide variety of provisions to cushion workers against these adverse impacts. These provisions fall into a few general categories — job protection, income protection, safety and health protection, retraining, and relocation assistance. The specifics include attrition or no-layoff protection, early warning of technological change, seniority protections, early retirement opportunities, red-circle pay protection, shorter work-weeks or work-years, relocation rights to follow transferred operations, severance pay, negotiated safety and health protections supplementing safety and health laws and regulations, and many other specific labor/management collectively bargained responses to technological change.

Without full collective bargaining — no matter how enlightened or benevolent management may be — working men and women simply don't have a sense of participation in the basic decisions that govern their jobs, income, and lives. Collective bargaining helps workers share the benefits of technological progress and meet the challenge of technological change with a minimum of social and human dislocation.

A healthy, expanding, full-employment economy is an essential environment for collective bargaining to be effective in protecting workers against adverse effects of technological change. Workers and unions, therefore, have an interest in national economic policies that will modernize and revitalize the American economy. And workers want the dignity and enhancement of human values that come from income protection, training and advancement opportunities, and productive jobs.

NOTES

1. The following contract provisions are listed in Industrial Union Department (1979).
2. For a discussion of industrial policy, see Wachter and Wachter (1981).

3. For example, see H.R. 5040 (introduced by Congressman Ford of Michigan); S. 1608 (introduced by Senator Riegle of Michigan); S. 1609 (introduced by Senator Williams of New Jersey); and S. 2400 (introduced by Senator Metzenbaum of Ohio), 96th Cong., 1st Sess. (1979).

Title III of the Job Training Partnership Act passed by the Ninety-seventh Congress in 1982 authorizes employment and training assistance for "displaced workers" facing permanent layoffs and plant closings, including prelayoff assistance, relocation assistance, and encouragement for joint labor/management early cooperative intervention in the event of plant closings and permanent layoffs.

In 1983 a Ninety-eighth Congress bill dealing with plant closings, H.R. 2847, sponsored by Congressman Ford of Michigan with sixty-five cosponsors, was approved by the Labor/Management Relations subcommittee of the House Committee on Education and Labor. This bill requires advance notice of plant closings and permanent layoffs and sets forth a range of employer responsibilities in such situations.

4. For discussion of European experience, see Chamot and Dymmel (1981). For additional discussion of the two-tier work force, see Thierry and Stanback (1983).

Two studies reported by Pear (1983: I, 28, 1) indicate that

> The economy is creating high-income jobs in high-technology industries and lower-paying jobs for workers such as building custodians and guards, cooks, waiters and waitresses and nurses' aides. But the number of middle-income jobs in the automobile, steel, machinery, construction and other manufacturing industries had dropped sharply.

Baltimore economist Stephen J. Rose (1983: 11) finds that "the middle middle class" (intermediate income between a low budget line and a high budget line) fell from 55 percent of the population in 1978 to 40 percent in 1983, while the percentage of those below the low budget line rose from 30 to 40 percent.

REFERENCES

American Federation of Labor and Congress of Industrial Organizations (AFL–CIO), *The Future of Work: A Report by the AFL–CIO Committee on the Evolution of Work* (Washington, D.C.: AFL–CIO, August 1983a).

———, *Policy Resolutions Adopted October 1983 by the 15th Constitutional Convention* (Washington, D.C.: AFL–CIO, December 1983b).

Bluestone, Irving, "Emerging Trends in Collective Bargaining," in Clark Kerr and Jerome M. Rosow, eds., *Work in America: The Decade Ahead* (New York: Van Nostrand Reinhold, 1979), ch. 12.

Bluestone, Barry, and Bennett Harrison, *Capital and Communities: The Causes and Consequences of Private Disinvestment* (Washington, D.C.: Progressive Alliance, 1980), pp. 78–82.

Brenner, Harvey, *Estimating the Costs of National Economic Policy: Implications for Mental and Physical Health, and Criminal Aggression* (Washington, D.C.: Joint Economic Committee, October 26, 1976).

Bureau of National Affairs, *Daily Labor Report* no. 125 (June 29, 1982): F-1.

Chamot, Dennis, and Michael D. Dymmel, *Cooperation or Conflict: European Experiences with Technological Change at the Workplace* (Washington, D.C.: AFL–CIO, 1981).

Industrial Union Department, *Comparative Survey of Major Collective Bargaining Agreements, Manufacturing and Non-Manufacturing, March 1979* (Washington, D.C.: AFL–CIO, December 1979).

McLaughlin, Doris B., *The Impact of Unions on the Rate and Direction of Technological Innovation* (Ann Arbor, Mich.: Institute of Labor and Industrial Relations of the University of Michigan and Wayne State University, February 1979) (report to the National Science Foundation, grant no. PRA 77–15268).

National Commission on Technology, Automation, and Economic Progress, *Technology and the American Economy,* vol. 1 (Washington, D.C.: U.S. Government Printing Office, February 1966).

Pear, Robert, "Middle Class Shrinking as More Families Sink into Poverty," *New York Times,* December 11, 1983, sec. I, p. 28, col. 1.

"Retraining Displaced Workers: Too Little, Too Late?," *Business Week* (July 19, 1982): 178–85.

Rose, Stephen J., *Social Stratification in the United States,* 3rd ed., (Baltimore: Social Graphics Co., 1983).

Siegel, Irving H., and Edgar Weinberg, *Labor–Management Cooperation: The American Experience* (Kalamazoo, Mich.: Upjohn Institute, 1982).

Slichter, Summner, James J. Healy, and Robert Livernash, *The Impact of Collective Bargaining on Management* (Washington, D.C.: Brookings Institution, 1960), ch. 12.

Thierry, Noyelle, and Thomas Stanback, Jr., *Cities in Transition* (Totowa, N.J.: Allenheld, Osmun, 1983).

U.S. Department of Labor, Bureau of Labor Statistics, *Collective Bargaining and Technological Change* (Washington, D.C.: U.S. Department of Labor, BLS Report No. 266, March 1964).

———, *Major Collective Bargaining Agreements: Plant Movement, Interplant Transfer and Relocation Allowances* (Washington, D.C.: U.S. Department of Labor, Bulletin 1425–10, July 1981).

———, *Major Collective Bargaining Agreements: Plant Movement, Transfer, and Relocation Allowances* (U.S. Department of Labor, Bulletin 1425, July 1969).

U.S. Department of Labor, Labor Management Services and Bureau of Labor Statistics, *Labor–Management Cooperation: Recent Efforts and Results* (Washington, D.C.: U.S. Department of Labor, BLS Bulletin 2152 (readings from the *Monthly Labor Review*), December 1982).

Wachter, Michael L., and Susan M. Wachter, eds., *Toward a New U.S. Industrial Policy?* (Philadelphia: University of Pennsylvania Press, 1981).

9 WORKER ADJUSTMENT TO CHANGING TECHNOLOGY: TECHNIQUES, PROCESSES, AND POLICY CONSIDERATIONS

Larry M. Blair

Results of the work reported in this book, as well as most earlier studies of employment effects of technical change, indicate that technical change alone has not created aggregate labor displacement. However, technical change or other structural shifts can lead to dislocations for some groups (such as workers in particular localities, industries, or occupations) and more generally requires adaptation of the work force to shifts in the composition of labor demand. Adjustment mechanisms in the private and public sectors facilitate worker adaptation to new technology on the job; assist workers with geographic, occupational, or industry moves if such are necessary; and once employment moves are made, help workers to find satisfaction in their jobs, lifestyles, and future prospects.

This chapter provides a comprehensive review of private and public mechanisms that have been or might be used to aid worker adjustment to technical change. Private and public mechanisms are detailed

Any opinions, findings, conclusions, or recommendations are those of the author and do not necessarily reflect the views of Oak Ridge Associated Universities.

Editor's note: This chapter covers an enormous body of literature for which no comparable survey has been published. Therefore, we have employed an alternative referencing system whereby cited works are listed as numbered endnotes rather than appearing in-text. Full citations will follow the endnotes per convention.

in the first two parts. Criteria for choosing among alternative policy strategies and policy implications are discussed in the last two parts.

PRIVATE-SECTOR ADJUSTMENT MECHANISMS

For discussion purposes private-sector adjustment mechanisms are grouped into six broad categories: (1) training, transfer, and mobility; (2) job protection; (3) work sharing; (4) income security measures; (5) reemployment aids; and (6) bargaining procedures.

Training, Transfer, and Mobility

Basic adjustment techniques include retraining to meet revised job requirements and intraplant or interplant job transfers with the same firm with or without retraining. Workers who solve their employment problems in this manner will probably not require any special policy considerations, unless the change involves a lowering of wages or other hardships that affect the worker's well-being. The transfer may be to a like job, or it may be to a job that is very similar and requires only a slight retraining of the workers. This may be through informal, on-the-job training (OJT) or formalized programs sponsored by the firm or union. Of course, the affected workers could be faced with a significant job change within the firm, which requires considerable retraining by the union or firm.

While most private-sector retraining programs are for jobs within the same firm, it is possible for private companies and unions to establish retraining programs for displaced workers that are designed to provide them with job opportunities with new employers. It would be expected that private-company retraining programs would normally be designed (in terms of content and what workers are included) within the limits of what is the best profit-maximizing approach for the firm unless special considerations and arrangements (such as union agreements or company-specified benefits package) have been made.

The amount of worker adjustment to technological change that is handled by a combination of in-plant transfers, transfers between plants and relocation, and by on-the-job and formal company-provided retraining appears to be considerable.[1] These approaches — while not receiving the attention that the popular literature has given to some of the more dramatic mechanisms such as early retirement, guaranteed annual wages, extended vacations, profit sharing, and so forth—seem to be handling a large amount of the adjustment process. Retraining by itself probably has the most advocates and is the most widely used single adjustment mechanism in the private sector. Related issues are maintenance of paygrades and seniority with job transfers and allowances to encourage transfer and relocation.

One of the deterrents encountered in getting workers to use interplant transfers involving relocation is the cost incurred in moving. This cost is both psychological and financial. The psychological costs involve leaving family, friends, and a known community in return for the uncertainty of a new job and a new community. The financial costs and perhaps part of the psychological costs can be fully or partially offset by the use of relocation allowances by the firm. A number of past studies have discussed the value of relocation allowances[2] to stimulate and aid relocation in response to technological change that has reduced employment opportunities. The firm in return for this outlay should encounter less worker (and union) resistance to change and retains experienced workers with training specific to the firm's activities.

Seniority rules also affect workers' acceptance and use of transfers and relocation options. Plant- or companywide seniority units promote transfers by more experienced workers because it gives them the highest priority for job transfer (of course this increases the likelihood of "bumping out" workers with less seniority). Several past studies[3] have discussed the importance of seniority transfer as related to job transfers and relocations. Another method by which workers may be encouraged to accept job transfers (intra- or interplant) and by which worker and union resistance to change may be lowered is for labor and management to agree on the maximum number of paygrades a worker may be lowered if he accepts transfer to a new work activity.[4]

The amount of literature giving evidence of private retraining and/ or advocating private retraining as a method to substantially cushion the impact of technological change on workers is extensive.[5] Several analysts[6] conclude that informal on-the-job training that takes place as technological change occurs (during the process of innovation, installation, and debugging of the new equipment) to be a much better source of acquiring skills for specific jobs than are vocational schools, apprenticeships, the armed forces, or company classroom training.

However, several areas of disagreement concerning the use of retraining do exist in the literature. Several writers[7] argue that company training (formal and OJT) should be coordinated with public education and vocational training in order to have an effective training component for all workers and to meet the economy's needs for new skills required for new technologies. Also, several writers urge greater retraining opportunities in the private sector for special groups of workers.[8] This includes greater opportunities for women in technical training and expanded training opportunities to aid older workers. Several studies[9] have cautioned that private-sector skill retraining programs may be too narrow, soon outmoded, or otherwise inadequate to meet the reemployment needs of displaced workers. This may be particularly true in the case where technologies greatly alter the content and structure of a large number of jobs.

Job Protection Techniques

Seniority systems and attrition schemes appear to be methods of reducing the displacement of experienced and especially older workers. Because older workers may have greater problems finding new employment and have fewer years to recover the costs of geographical moves and/or retraining, it may be appropriate to attempt to make these workers more secure in their current employment. The seniority system is of maximum benefit to the older worker when it extends over all plants owned by the firm. Systems that include only workers within a single section of the plant or across the single plant do not aid the older worker if the section or plant is eliminated by technological change.

The use of seniority as a basis for retention during periods of decreasing employment is a standard practice in much of the business and industrial world. Widening and broadening the seniority base appears to be a fairly commonly used and advocated method of maintaining the employment of older, more established workers when firms implement new technology that displaces workers.[10] This involves spreading the workers' seniority to include all sections of the plant or perhaps all plants owned by the firm.

On the other hand, some arguments have been raised against broader seniority, including the argument that seniority clauses protect white workers while they displace nonwhites who do not get to build up seniority sufficient to protect them. Younger workers may object to broader seniority systems because such systems allow older workers to take jobs even if the jobs are in plants or sections other than where the older workers are presently located.

Attrition schemes let the reduction in employment levels occur through normal retirements, deaths, job quits, and transfers rather than through layoffs. Attrition obviously protects jobs for all workers, not only older workers, and reduces the older/younger worker frictions that might occur under seniority systems where older workers can transfer in and "bump" younger workers. Also, under attrition schemes, if demand for the output grows over time and thus the derived demand for workers increases, the firm has a trained work force present. Workers do not have to switch employers and occupations, thereby losing skill experience and seniority rights and incurring job-turnover problems.

The use of normal attrition to reduce the work force to a new, lower required employment level is another apparently often used private-sector adjustment mechanism and is discussed widely in the literature.[11] The use of attrition plans to aid workers' adjustment to technological change is reported in Western Europe, Japan, Australia, and Canada.[12]

Attrition may lead to problems for the firm if workers or unions charge that the firm is attempting to increase work loads through the attrition scheme by releasing more employees than is needed.[13] It has also been pointed out that attrition due to automation is a threat to the labor force and organized labor if it reduces the numbers of jobs in the firm, industry, or occupation.[14]

An approach related to attrition schemes involves early retirement programs. These aid in maintaining the employment of younger workers by inducing (or perhaps forcing) senior workers to withdraw from the work force at an earlier than usual age or after employment of some specified number of years in the industry.[15] These retirement programs can be payments for nonparticipation in the industry or for complete cessation of labor-force participation. Early retirement programs would have to make nonwork attractive in order to be effective, unless a mandatory retirement age or maximum years of employment were established. To be attractive, the early-retirement programs would have to maintain income at a satisfactory level, ensure no great loss in social security benefits, and provide adequate health-insurance coverage that is often lost at retirement at an age too young for Medicare coverage.

One of the most controversial practices to protect jobs that has been discussed since at least the beginning of the factory system is the use of job requirements and work rules, or "featherbedding and work slowdown" as it is referred to by its opponents.[16] Labor agreements in several western European countries include clauses on job protection when new technologies are introduced.[17] The practice involves either an informal work slowdown or the establishment of formal job requirements detailing the actual duties of each particular job and the number of employees necessary to engage in any particular work activity. The extreme case would be guaranteed employment. Basic to many of the job security discussions is the concept of workers' "property rights" to their jobs.

This type of job protection has received a great deal of attention and has been attacked as inhibiting technological change, productivity improvements, and cost reduction. In this view, featherbedding is particularly harmful to the long-run growth and welfare of the economy. Workers and union spokesmen counter that individuals' welfare is of first priority, and loss of a job can be disastrous to individuals and their families. Furthermore, many job rules are defended as necessary in order to ensure the worker's health and safety[18] and to keep the job from becoming dehumanized due to excess demands on the worker. This last point has been stressed in several union/management agreements in Western Europe when negotiating over the introduction of new technologies.[19]

One of the results of automation appears to be an increased emphasis on job security in collective bargaining, including attempts at job freezes and at more restrictive work rules. However, reviews of specific organized-labor contracts conclude that the evidence indicates that in the great majority of cases the presence of work rules has not affected the rate of technological change. In fact, the evidence indicates that unions and workers often promote change in order to reduce job drudgery, improve health and safety, and increase incomes.[20]

The opposite of rigid work requirements systems are the various job flexibility concepts. Here the workers or their union spokesmen allow the firms more flexibility in job assignments and worker tasks in the expectation that this flexibility will produce cost and price reductions, resulting in greater output and helping to maintain employment. The literature points out several examples in the United States, Western Europe, and Japan on the use of job flexibility and job transfer as a means of promoting job protection as technology changes.[21]

One obstacle to union endorsement of job flexibility and job transfers is workers' fears of sizable cuts in their paygrades as job assignments vary. One way to minimize this is to establish a maximum on the number of paygrades a person may be lowered when he is transferred or when his job duties are redesigned.

Management may also aid in protecting jobs and in worker adjustment by its choice of the type of technology it implements or by the timing of the introduction of the new technology.[22] Union/management cooperative actions may affect this choice of type and timing of the innovation, as may the threat of union resistance to any change that greatly affects employment. In Western Europe unions often have a voice in, or even veto power over, the type and timing of new innovations.[23]

The choice of type of innovation may affect the labor/skill mix required and thus affect the employment of various groups. The innovation adopted may be one that better fits the existing workers' skills and capabilities for retraining. Also, the choice of type of innovation may affect the new optimum output level for the plant, which can affect total employment. If innovative changes in production are timed so as to coincide with economic growth periods, then the employment impact should be greatly reduced; and any workers displaced in the change will have a greater chance of finding reemployment. In addition, gradual introduction of new technologies is often advocated in order to permit easier worker adjustment and more time for informal OJT.

The formation of multicraft unions or union mergers is another possible technique to enhance labor's power to promote job protection and other adjustment mechanisms; this technique has been reported on or advocated in several articles.[24] One reason given for the wider union base is to overcome problems in union jurisdictional lines and functions created by new technologies when these problems tend to blur old craft and job distinctions. Another reason is if companies attempt to eliminate one plant or one skill craft group by the technological change and thus eliminate that union group, the use of multicraft or union mergers will counter this movement.

Work Sharing Arrangements

Another method of lessening any decrease in labor needs resulting from technological change is to share the remaining work load by reducing the hours worked by each employee. Historically, increases in worker productivity have been used jointly to increase workers' earnings and to reduce the number of hours worked. This type of adjustment is still discussed by many researchers and writers in the field.[25] However, the evidence available in the literature points to little actual use of work-sharing arrangements in the vast majority of businesses as a means to adjust to technological change.[26] It has been used in many instances over the last several decades as a method of combatting layoffs and unemployment caused by factors other than technological change in several unions and industries. The difficult issue is whether or not the reduction in hours worked is to be accompanied by offsetting wage increases to maintain earnings levels.

The average weekly hours of work has dropped little since 1929 (when it was approximately forty hours per week); however, the reduction in actual hours worked over the year has continued through the introduction of more holidays and longer vacation periods. Increased paid vacation time is discussed in several articles related to change in the United States and in Western Europe as a work-sharing method of easing any worker displacement.[27] However, outside of a few, well-publicized settlements, few references are found to the use of extended vacations as an adjustment to technological change.

Other methods that are related to sharing the work are attrition policies, early retirement (both discussed above), and reduction of overtime. Reduction of overtime may aid in continuing the employment of those already at work by spreading the work to more people. Employees who are displaced from one department may find work in another department which had been using considerable amounts of overtime.

Income Security Measures

Another type of private aid to adjustment involves workers sharing in the earnings from the new technologies through a supplemental-unemployment-benefits arrangement (SUB), a guaranteed annual wage (GAW), a profit-sharing/pay incentive arrangement, and/or a severance pay system for displaced workers. The guaranteed annual wage might be thought of as a job-protection scheme; however, the employees are paid the wage whether they work or not.

The GAW or SUB payments are usually established for workers who have been with the firm a minimum number of years and who meet other eligibility requirements. The SUB payments are paid for a given number of weeks of unemployment, while the GAW may be paid over a considerable number of years or even until normal retirement age is reached. Guaranteed annual wages, supplemental unemployment benefits, and to a lesser extent profit sharing and other pay-incentive approaches have received much publicity and have generated a considerable amount of controversy, as have the various "restrictive" work-rules approach to job security. Income security provisions are controversial because they extend employer/employee relations beyond the traditional wage payment for labor-services-rendered concept and affect the firms' cost-minimizing and resource-allocation decisions.

The general impression from the literature is that the use of income-security measures as technological-change-adjustment mechanisms is less than that of retraining, transfer, attrition, and wider seniority but far more than the use of work sharing and restrictive work rule arrangements. This would be true for all the income-security approaches except the guaranteed annual wage, where the publicity seems to far outweigh the use.

Many articles have discussed the use of and issues related to supplementary unemployment benefits (SUB).[28] The impression from the literature is that the use of SUB is much less frequent than the use of severance pay (although greater than guaranteed annual wages) but that use of SUB plans has increased substantially over the last fifteen to twenty years, especially in the heavily union-organized industries.

The use and misuse of a guaranteed annual wage (GAW) as an adjustment mechanism is often-discussed.[29] The GAW proposals are very controversial because they require employers to pay wages to a minimum number of employees, whether the employees are needed or not by the firm and regardless of whether the displaced worker can find reemployment elsewhere. As mentioned earlier, the actual use of GAW systems appears to be very limited.

Profit sharing and pay incentives are, of course, most beneficial to workers who remain employed with the firm. These are often implemented in connection with worker/union acceptance of greater managerial flexibility in setting work standards and job tasks when introducing technological improvements. For workers who become unemployed during a change process, the profit shares they have earned up to that time are an additional source of income, if needed, during their period of unemployment and adjustment. Thus, profit sharing may be used as a supplemental unemployment benefit, but at the discretion of each individual worker. Several studies provide evidence of the use of profit-sharing/pay-incentive programs to promote worker acceptance of job changes.[30]

Severance-pay plans have been established in various businesses as a method of maintaining workers' income after they have been laid off. Unemployment compensation (for those eligible) does not maintain earnings at the workers' old income levels; therefore, promoters of severance-pay systems argue that the extra funds allow the worker the time and money needed to seek reemployment in a job requiring similar skills with wages in line with his past earnings. The funds also give the worker a means of paying for geographical relocation or perhaps for retraining. The use of severance pay appears to be much more widespread and to have a much longer tradition than the other more glamorous income compensations for displacement.[31] This appears to be the case in most industrialized, capitalistic economies.

Reemployment Aids

When worker layoffs are required, various private sector procedures may be initiated by unions and management to aid the displaced workers in finding new employment. Among these procedures are advanced layoff notification, placement, and referral systems. If the firm gives employees notice of layoff several months before actual termination, the forewarned worker may begin to seek reemployment, prepare to undertake retraining, and/or adjust his expenditure pattern to accommodate a temporary break in regular earnings. By setting up job placement and referral systems, employers can provide labor-market information to displaced workers and refer workers to employers who have job vacancies matching the workers' skills. It is hoped that the worker will be able to shift more rapidly to a new job, and a better worker/job match will result.

There are many references to the use of advanced layoff notification and termination procedures to aid displaced workers.[32] Usually the advanced layoff notification is linked to a general advance notification of a coming technological change and to the plans for that change. The necessity and value of advance notification of technological change for adequate planning and for labor/management cooperation has been repeatedly stressed in the literature for over two decades.[33] In addition to the advance notification of layoffs, the soon-to-be displaced worker can be aided by private-sector-sponsored counseling, placement, and referral services established before dismissal time by management and unions.[34]

Another method of aiding the reemployment of displaced workers is to place them on a preferential rehiring or hiring list. Those last laid off are the first recalled by a firm under the preferential rehiring system. Preferential hiring arrangements allow displaced workers to have first choice at similar new jobs at other plants operated by their old employers or at other firms in the industry.

This system appears attractive to workers because it allows them a better chance of remaining in their old employment or regaining similar employment. By regaining employment with their old employer, workers may continue to be eligible for the seniority and benefits they have built up in the past. By continuing to work in the same industry with either their old firm or a new firm, the workers do not have to change occupations and perhaps unions. It may also be attractive to firms if they lay off workers in an order inversely related to their marginal products and then recall first those who were laid off last. Critics of preferential hiring or rehiring point out that the system causes workers to become immobile—that is, they wait for reemployment at their old place of employment rather than seek employment elsewhere. This represents a lessening of the resource-allocation functioning of the labor market and may reduce efficiency in the system.

Little mention of preferential rehiring as an adjustment mechanism for technological change is found in the literature; however, preferential rehiring practices are features of most collective bargaining agreements and of many managerial rehiring practices following layoffs. Workers displaced by technological change would be covered in these arrangements also.

Bargaining Procedures

The type of adjustment mechanisms available to workers and the specific effect of technological change can be influenced by the type of labor/management relations in use in the industry. Where labor (unions) and management cooperate, attempts are made to allow management to introduce technological change with flexibility in setting job requirements. This is done in return for various aids to workers who are displaced or otherwise affected by a change. For workers who remained employed with the firm after the technological change, shares in the increased returns may be established by such things as more benefits, higher wages, profit sharing, better working conditions, and so forth. Many articles have pointed out how collective bargaining has handled the effect of new technologies in specific industries. [35]

When labor/management relations are noncooperative, the results may be work stoppages, restrictive work rules, restrictions against technological change, and management efforts to totally eliminate the jobs of the troublesome workers. When this uncooperative attitude develops between workers and employers and it threatens to harm the economy and society, the use of third-party arbitration may be advocated. Several writers have discussed the use of third parties as participants in the bargaining process in order to promote smoother and more effective transitions to technological change. [36] These third parties may be arbitrators, mediators, or other neutrals, such as labor/management committees.

PUBLIC-SECTOR ADJUSTMENT MECHANISMS

In many areas of the economy, studies show collective bargaining and management/labor cooperation to have handled and to be handling adjustment problems fairly effectively. Many writers indicate or infer that all that is needed in order to establish effective worker-adjustment mechanisms for technological improvements is the private collective bargaining process (along with full employment growth). But the majority of American workers are not unionized, and not all unions are reported as being effective vehicles for establishing smoothly working adjustment mechanisms. [37] Also, some studies point out and caution that privately established adjustment mechanisms have or could have damaging effects on the economy, particular industries, and workers, at least in the longer run. [38]

Many writers have pointed out that public policies have been developed and need to be further developed in order to augment and strengthen private adjustment mechanisms that attempt to aid workers in regions, industries, occupations, and demographic groups that have suffered from technological displacement. These writers also wish to guard against private solutions that they believe are detrimental to the economy as a whole.

Discussed below are various public policies and programs that have been used or advocated to aid worker adjustment to technological change. Included is evidence concerning the contribution these public mechanisms have made to aiding displaced workers' adjustments.

For discussion purposes, the various public policies and programs to aid workers displaced or threatened by new technology are divided into five basic groups. The five groups are (1) aggregate demand and job creation; (2) labor-market information and placement programs; (3) education, training, and relocation; (4) income and work opportunities; and (5) union/management relations.

Aggregate Demand and Job Creation

The potential employment impact of technological change is obviously less in an economy experiencing full employment than in one suffering from slow-growth or no-growth problems. During strong economic growth, chances of being displaced are lessened, since most firms undergoing technological change would have expanding demand for their products or services. This increase in demand could partially or totally cancel out any reduction in employment involved in the change to new technology.

For workers who become unemployed, a rapidly expanding economy means more job vacancies and thus a greater likelihood of securing employment without suffering a long period of unemployment or without having to undertake retraining or relocation. Full-employment growth is viewed as a basic requirement to adjustment. Workers must have effective and approximately equal employment opportunities before labor mobility and adjustment mechanisms will function smoothly.[39] In fact, many analysts conclude that a full-employment-growth policy is essentially all that need be implemented by the public authorities to ensure adequate adjustment of workers displaced by technological change. They argue that the rest of the adjustment can be handled by private-sector actions.[40] Many other studies advocate the use of additional public adjustment mechanisms, along with stressing the importance of maintaining a full-employment growth policy.[41]

Full-employment policies involve a blend of fiscal, monetary, and perhaps income (that is, wage and price) policies.[42] The effect of various combinations of these policies on the employment of different worker groups (by occupation, industry, age, sex, ethnic group, and region) needs to be analyzed in relation to the amount of worker displacement likely to occur within each group, before any projections of reemployment can be made.

Regional, urban, and rural development policies may be used as the basis for implementing aggregate demand policies, or they may be instituted as complementary policies to aggregate programs.[43] In either case, these more localized programs may be able to take special problems of their areas into greater consideration than can national programs.[44] This means (conceptually at least) that the characteristics of the local labor force, especially those threatened by technological displacement, can be more closely identified and specific programs established to handle these potential labor-adjustment problems.

When other aggregate-demand policies fail to maintain full employment, the use of public employment programs has been discussed and advocated.[45] Public employment programs were implemented in the 1930s, again in 1971, and during 1974–83 under the Comprehensive Employment and Training Act. These programs have suffered in the public view due to being labeled "make work" or "government as the employers of the last resort" type programs.

Finally, government legislation can attempt to affect the aggregate demand for labor (in terms of workers) by establishing basic workweek hours and retirement age requirements. Legal requirements for the pay of overtime for over forty hours of work per week may promote more employment, as may laws restricting working more than some maximum number of hours per week. On the other hand, these measures may have a stifling effect. Also, governments as the employers of about one-sixth of the work force can help establish regional and national trends by changing their normal work week and vacation policies.

Several writers and studies have mentioned the use of shorter work weeks, job-sharing, and early-retirement programs established by the government to help maintain employment opportunities for all workers or for younger workers.[46] These writers usually assume that technological improvements lead to fewer job opportunities.

Labor Market Information Programs

Displaced workers may lack good information about the current state of the labor market. The government-operated Employment Security Offices serve as information sources for jobseekers and employers with job vacancies. This service, if effective, can reduce the search time for a person seeking employment and provide a better job match from both the worker's and the employer's viewpoint. Better job matches should result in fewer job turnovers from voluntary quits and dismissals. An active labor-market information program should have current information on technological trends in various industries and be prepared to handle the reemployment problems of workers likely to become displaced. This information service should also include testing services and counseling programs to provide workers with current labor-market information and with direction toward available retraining programs. The information service should also make available information concerning the potential for reemployment through relocation.

A large number of studies have discussed the need for and value of public counseling and placement programs to aid workers displaced by automation and mechanization.[47] Many of these studies point out that counseling and placement programs can be very effective in aiding the adjustment of displaced workers if full employment is being maintained. Several studies also conclude that early counseling conducted by trained, experienced personnel can do much for the morale and general welfare of displaced workers.[48] Several studies also point to the value of public labor-market information and counseling to aid specific groups of workers such as minorities and older workers.[49]

In order for placement, referral, and counseling to be effective for displaced workers who seek reemployment, advanced planning and information systems are important. Planning and information are basic components of successful manpower training and relocation programs (discussed next in this section). Several studies discuss planning and information flows;[50] others concentrate more on the planning aspect[51] or on the information system needs.[52]

Education, Training, and Relocation Programs

If technological change eliminates the need for certain skills in the economy, then some workers whose human capital consists mainly of those skills may need retraining in order to regain employment at a similar wage. The Manpower Development and Training Act of 1962, the Emergency Employment Act of 1971, and the National Training Partnership Act of 1982 specifically mention workers displaced by technological change as being among those eligible for funding.

A continuing question is whether public employment and training programs are of much value to displaced workers—that is, if present programs are geared more to supplying basic vocational skills and improving work habits, can they be of much value to experienced workers displaced by technological change? If the integration of displaced workers into vocational education programs and programs set up for the disadvantaged is not practical or effective, then how can the technologically displaced be serviced? Are there enough displaced workers in a region to permit special programs to be developed for them locally or should they be brought together at a national training center? Should an individualized system be established utilizing home study, private tutors, apprenticeship, and/or existing vocational and general education facilities?

A second question is more basic and relates not only to retraining programs but to all vocational and general education programs as well. The question is whether greater emphasis should be placed on the development of job-specific skills or on the development of the ability to adapt to changes in the work and leisure environment during a lifetime? If the future is to be one of accelerating rates of change, with continuous elimination or reduction of some skills and jobs, and the development of new work activities with new skills combinations, then training in only certain specific skills may be of value to the trainees for just the short run. Many writers who believe that the rate of technological change is accelerating emphasize the role of training and education programs in enhancing the individual's ability to adapt to his environment and to accept and adjust to change.

The relationship between technological change and the role of general education in aiding worker adjustment is one of the most discussed topics. In general, the recommended goal of education in relation to technological change is to provide a good basic, broad education in order to maximize each individual's potential for acceptance and successful adjustment to change.[53] However, several studies, while agreeing with the need for education to aid workers' adjustment, point out that there is little agreement as to whether the education should be broader, more comprehensive, more specialized, or some combination of these.[54] Some writers[55] have looked at vocational education programs as an aid for displaced workers and as a hedge against their displacement, but others have warned against the effectiveness of vocational education as an aid to adjusting to technological change.[56]

Many of the "futurists" recommend the use of education to adapt people to the successful use of their growing leisure time in the post-industrial society.[57] They feel education must become a continuous life-long process, both for job retraining and for personal fulfillment to make leisure more meaningful.

Training or retraining of workers whose jobs are affected by technological change is the most discussed adjustment mechanism. The role that the public sector should play in retraining of displaced workers is one of the most, if not the most, controversial and debated topics in the literature on technological change. Almost all of the literature concludes that the introduction of new technologies creates a need for training and retraining programs, but there is wide disagreement on whether public-sector involvement should be moderate or massive.

Most analysts who believe that major job disruptions and shortages of required skilled workers will occur as high technologies are introduced throughout the economy call for larger-scale programs including a substantial role for public planning and coordination.[58] Many of these writers also advocate the establishment of lifetime retraining programs for all workers because they believe that the rate of technological change in the future will accelerate and virtually everyone will require repeated retraining to keep their skills current for the needs of the economy. Some of the literature that advocates a large public role in retraining sees the major challenge of future technological change to be retraining and skills upgrading.

The assessments that conclude that the rate of introduction of the new high technologies into our economy will be more gradual and thus have a fairly moderate impact on workers usually advocate a smaller role for public training for displaced workers.[59] The controversy on public training goes beyond the degree of effect on employment and size of programs to questions about what types of skill development should be provided, what type of delivery systems should be used, how the programs should be financed, who should be eligible (and for what length of time), and what is the proper public role in planning and coordinating training programs for the displaced workers.

Some writers argue for a wholesale changing of the public-supported training system in order to meet their perceived needs for retraining for new technologies. These analysts charge that the present system doesn't meet the skills training needs of the new technologies, that it is ill-planned and poorly coordinated and in many cases actually detrimental to individuals and the growth needs of the economy.[60] Several of the writers who believe that the present public approach needs a major systematic change advocate the use of vouchers, the unemployment insurance fund, or prepaid employer/employee tuition funds for displaced workers that could be used for payment for training of the workers' choice, either public or private.[61]

Other writers believe that programs set up under the National Training Partnership Act mandates for displaced workers are the effective approach.[62] This includes several writers who feel that these employment and training programs are the best solutions for displaced minority group and older workers. The argument about what types of skill development to provide centers on how specific the skill training should be.[63] Some people argue for narrow training focused on a particular job, while other people advocate broader training that will not be quickly outdated and that will promote flexibility and an understanding of the implications of high-technology processes. One recent study concludes that the most effective training for displaced persons is job-search training rather than skill training.[64]

A number of studies have discussed the use of public relocation programs as an additional adjustment to technological change.[65] These studies point out that technological change and aggregate-demand stimulation affect job opportunities in an unequal manner among various regions; therefore, workers need to be mobile. When the literature that discusses public-supported relocation is reviewed, the relative lack of studies, especially for the United States, comes as somewhat of a surprise. In fact, relocation supported by public agencies and funds has been a rarely used adjustment mechanism in the United States and, based on present literature, appears still to have a low priority.

Income and Work Opportunities

Various discussions and proposals for income maintenance systems (negative income tax, guaranteed annual income, unemployment compensation) for workers displaced by technological change are found in the literature.[66] Many writers argue that technological change will cause unemployment, possibly for long terms or permanently, and that to help the ex-worker and stabilize the economy income maintenance is needed. Not only is income maintenance advocated for those unable to find employment, but it is proposed for those who are unable to be fully or adequately reemployed.

Unemployment compensation is often discussed as a measure to help maintain displaced workers' earnings as they search the labor market seeking reemployment and/or to aid displaced workers in meeting their spending needs during cyclical downturns in the economy.[67] Issues related to unemployment compensation concern the number of workers covered, the payment size, and the number of weeks the payments should be continued, including the use of any extended unemployment benefits periods.

Proponents of the use of unemployment benefits to aid the adjustment of laid-off workers argue for wider coverage of workers, higher benefit payments, and longer and more flexible use of extended benefits payments. It is argued that the longer payment periods and higher payments will allow recipients to maintain their accustomed level of living and pay debts outstanding (such as mortgage and installment loans) without undergoing severe hardships and that this will allow them to more adequately search the job market for a satisfactory job utilizing their skills and experience. This should provide for a longer-term, more productive work experience and less job turnover than if the unemployed person had to accept some job hastily because of present financial hardships.

Opponents of higher and longer unemployment benefits (or in some cases of any benefits) argue that the payment, especially at high levels, may impede the efficient functioning of the labor market. Workers receiving high payments may not aggressively search for new employment but may simply wait to be recalled to their old job. These workers may hold on to artificially high wage expectations and/or job expectations and keep searching the market rather than taking a more realistic view. Workers may not accept relocation as readily as they might have, even in the face of long-run declining employment opportunities in their present labor market area.

Much of the argument stems from the leisure/work tradeoff concept. The tradeoff concerns time used for work to produce income versus time used for leisure. The availability of nonwork income may cause a readjustment of the leisure/work time tradeoff. Opponents fear that nonwork income (unemployment benefits) may cause an option for full-time leisure over work.

Other types of possible income aids to displaced workers are the various income-maintenance programs and proposals. These programs can be a short-run aid to adjustment where the income maintenance programs would work much as unemployment compensation. In fact, it has been argued by some that one income-maintenance system encompassing the unemployed would be more efficient to administer. Income-maintenance programs also offer long-run compensation to displaced workers (and their families) who cannot find reemployment or who need fairly long retraining programs. For older workers whose skills are no longer needed because of technological change, some form of income maintenance may be the only answer. If private income-maintenance programs are missing or viewed as inefficient, then public programs may be the alternative. Again, the problem with income-maintenance programs of the guaranteed-income type is the effect on the individual's work/leisure tradeoff—that is, the guaranteed-income payment may lead to the individual's choosing leisure over work.

To promote "workfare" over "welfare" by giving incentives to seeking employment, various negative income-tax schemes have been proposed. Essentially all these proposals involve a basic guaranteed income at a fairly low level plus a payment that varies from a maximum according to the level of income earned. In this manner the individual receives more total income by working than by full-time leisure.

Income-maintenance programs may be especially important in aiding the adjustment of older workers displaced by technological change. The existing type of public retirement program (the social security system) can aid older workers to the extent that workers are covered, that the age requirements allow retirement, and that the income support levels make possible an adequate level of living by the recipients. This includes health-care insurance needs as well as income and income-in-kind payments.

The passage and enforcement of the equal employment opportunities legislation may help the adjustment problems of any groups facing discrimination in the labor market (such as minorities, females, and the aged) who are suffering employment problems because of technological displacement. If technological displacement has a relatively greater impact on the employment of specific groups who encounter hiring bias, fair-employment legislation may help in two ways: First, it may increase the number of job opportunities available to them; second, it may help make them more secure in their present employment.

A final topic for this section on public policies for work and income opportunities is the possible use of minimum-wage legislation to aid in worker adjustment to technological change. The use of minimum wages as an adjustment mechanism for technological change has not received a great deal of attention in the literature, although its use is proposed in a few articles.[68] Minimum wages might be used in the case where technological change is creating unemployment that could depress the wage rate. This may give those who remain employed more income security and make them more receptive to the idea of technological change that disrupts old job assignments and requirements. For those who are displaced but gain reemployment, minimum wages may help maintain earnings closer to their old levels.

The broader policy issue is whether minimum wage laws significantly affect aggregate and specific employment opportunities, real wages, and inflation. The impact of minimum-wage legislation depends on the level at which the minimum is established and on the fraction of the work force covered. The higher the basic wage is set, the greater is the number of jobs directly affected. Also, if any wage pyramids or differentials are based on the minimum wage, then the higher the minimum the greater the relative pyramiding of wage increases and price increases throughout the economy. If the full work force is covered by the legislation then the displaced have only two choices: remain unemployed while waiting for employment to increase or drop out of the labor force. If there is an uncovered segment of the economy then a third choice may exist: accept employment at lower wages.

A higher minimum wage may decrease or increase aggregate employment opportunities depending largely on the effect the higher wages have on consumer spending and aggregate demand. If the minimum wage leads to a significant inflation of prices, this may create other economic problems and hardships that must be faced by the policy maker.

Public Policies toward Labor/Management Relations

Several studies[69] have discussed public involvement in collective bargaining procedures and/or changes in the legislation affecting the bargaining process. Some analysts view technological change as necessitating a change in government policy toward union/management relations and collective bargaining procedures. It is argued that additional government intervention may be necessary if collective bargaining breaks down in attempting to handle technological change and severe work stoppages occur. Intervention may become necessary if the type of arrangements reached in private collective bargaining are deemed to be detrimental to society's welfare in the short run or long run (such as the stifling of economic growth).

Three possible forms of public intervention in the collective bargaining process are public representation, legislation covering bargaining areas, and compulsory bargaining. If collective bargaining is breaking down in the face of technological change, then perhaps public representatives acting as mediators may bring about agreements, or perhaps compulsory bargaining with no or limited work stoppages will have to be implemented. If collective bargaining is arriving at agreements viewed as less than optimal for the total economy and society, then maybe the presence of public representatives at the bargaining session will lead to more satisfactory results; perhaps legislation detailing the limits of collective bargaining agreements may be justified.

CRITERIA FOR CHOOSING AMONG ALTERNATIVE POLICY STRATEGIES

Principles developed in formal studies of welfare economics provide a conceptual approach for evaluating alternative policy strategies in terms of both production efficiency and overall social well-being. The starting point in this approach is that increases in output and hence in real economic income are desirable[70] — that is, increases in economic output are usually assumed to bring about greater levels of welfare in society.[71] The type of adjustment mechanisms used by labor and management and introduced by government obviously may have a significant effect on the production possibilities frontier in the short run as well as the direction and the rate of growth of the production frontier over the longer run. Early retirement, attrition schemes, seniority, guaranteed annual wages, supplemental employment benefits, changes in hours of work, relocation, retraining programs, and work rules all affect the quantity and the quality of manpower available in the economy (regionally, and by industry and occupation). These adjustment mechanisms, then, determine or influence the actual level of output relative to the production possibilities frontier in the short run and influence the rate and direction of growth of the production frontier over the longer run by affecting the type of manpower inputs available (skill levels and mix) and the expected rates of return on investment.

In an ideal setting when technological improvements occur, society would move in a Pareto optimal manner to the new production possibilities frontier and have more output, full employment, and a higher level of welfare (that is, a move in which at least part of society is better off and no one is worse off). However, any move due to technological change to a new production frontier means that the production function for one or more products has been changed. This probably means that the skill mix needed in production has varied or that the content of jobs has been altered. If either or both of these events occur, then the welfare of some workers may be diminished, *even though they remain employed*.

The well-being of some workers may be lowered because of decreased earning power after the change due to a shift in absolute demand for various skills. If this occurs, then the increase in output under the new technology could not be proved to have increased society's welfare without some sort of weighting of the improvements of the gainers relative to the losses of the losers. Allowing "the market to work" could give this result; and if it is foreseen as a likely outcome by the potential losers, they may work to stop the change or delay it (with inflexible work rules, attrition schemes, and so forth).

A shift of the type described above causes a windfall loss in the return to human investment for the individuals whose incomes are reduced. The implementation of education and training programs as adjustment mechanisms may aid workers in accepting and more rapidly adjusting to technological change by providing an investment hedge in human capital.

In the "real world" the economy is, more often than not, inside its production possibilities frontier before and after a technological change occurs. Here Pareto optimal moves to the production frontier are possible *within* the context of the new real incomes of the individuals. Private adjustment mechanisms may or may not facilitate a rapid move to the production frontier because of poor information, misconceptions of what the move would entail, and so on. Public programs then might bring about a more rapid movement to the production frontier, somewhat improving the welfare of each individual. However, this type of Pareto optimal move is within the context of the new state of technology and reveals nothing about the equity or welfare of the final real-income distribution as compared to the one that existed before the technological change occurred.

In addition to changes in welfare due to shifts in real earnings of workers, technological change may also change workers' welfare by changing job duties and activities, social relationships, residence, feelings of security, and so forth. Recognizing that workers receive satisfaction (or dissatisfaction) from work itself and circumstances related to their jobs means that technological change that varies job content, location, work setting, and career ladders may cause workers' welfare to vary. In this case worker well-being could be lowered, even though the purchasing power of all individuals is increased, because of changes in employment and job activities.

If it is assumed that the goal of policy is to increase the overall feelings of well-being rather than just improvements in one or two measurable dimensions such as income and employment, then qualitative judgments must be made along with quantitative judgments for all factors associated with individual and societal well-being. I.M.D. Little has written: "Getting rid of value judgements would be throwing the baby away with the bathwater. The subject is one about which nothing interesting can be said without value judgements, for the reason that we take a moral interest in welfare and happiness."[72]

This broader view of the relation between job and welfare means that economic welfare studies based on the neoclassical view of the production function as the best technical efficiency standards[73] must be expanded. Meaningful welfare analysis can be developed only if worker job satisfaction is incorporated into the model—that is, the external costs and benefits to the workers of any production technique must be considered along with the internal costs and benefits to the firm.

When discussing the welfare aspects of technological change, it can not be assumed that interpersonal comparisons are not made by individuals when calculating their welfare. This appears to be a realistic consideration since ". . .comparisons of real income must be, in part at least, of mental states or changes in mental states."[74] And as Little points out, mental states are affected by interpersonal comparisons that must be expected to occur. If the relative distribution of income, job opportunities, work settings, working conditions, and so forth shift as technology changes and a higher production frontier is created, some individuals may feel worse off (have a lower level of welfare). This can occur even if the absolute level of income has increased for everyone and if other job attributes are viewed as having improved.

Thus, proposed adjustment mechanisms and policies may flounder because inadequate attention is being given to the relative share of the gains going to different groups of workers. This is an important consideration since one of the often-expressed goals of labor unions is to get a fair share of the gains for labor.

The introduction of interpersonal comparisons in utility functions allows for the possibility that the economy is not on the new production frontier but that society is still maximizing welfare. This "inefficiency effect" (which has been developed by J. de V. Graaff[75]) results from the presence of external effects that may arise from the interpersonal comparisons of income or earnings. As Graaff has demonstrated, an infinite number of optimum welfare positions are possible with this inefficiency effect, only one of which is likely to be on the production frontier. The presence of interpersonal comparisons in utility functions means that a distribution after a technological change of the gains in output (and other job-related attributes such as working conditions and advancement opportunities) that includes "more" for each worker still may not result in an increase in society's welfare. Interpersonal comparisons provide another possible explanation for the demands for adjustment mechanisms such as inflexible work rules, broader seniority, continued pay differentials, and others that appear to restrict output below its potential by not allowing the best technical combination of inputs and outputs.

As discussed in earlier sections, technological change may lead to increased unemployment, at least in the short run and in some occupations, industries, or regions. Immobility of labor, inability to adapt to change by retraining, discrimination, monopoly power, and income distributions leading to insufficient purchasing power or insufficient capital development may all result in the economy's operating off the production frontier (that is, with some unemployment). Technological change may increase these problems in some areas.

Since all the institutional imperfections do exist that make attainment of the competitive equilibrium on the production and welfare frontier difficult if not impossible, Graaff argues that the actual welfare positions that society can reach, given the institutional constraints present, should be the ones of most immediate interest. This locus of welfare positions he terms the "efficiency locus."[76] Technological change may shift the welfare frontier and efficiency locus in the same direction or in opposite directions, or may twist one or both of the curves (change the slope of the curve). In a like manner, adjustment may cause the locus to shift inward by giving one group more at a considerable real loss to others in society.

The presence of imperfect institutions on the producers' side and in the labor market negates the competitive efficiency arguments on which attainment of the welfare frontier through competitive market mechanisms rests. To reach a maximum efficiency position in this environment, Scitovsky argues that bargaining between labor and management is needed.[77] Thus, the development of private adjustment mechanisms based on labor/management agreements may be viewed as required in order for efficiency to be reached in an imperfectly competitive economy. Graaff has presented similar arguments that would support the "efficiency" of public adjustment mechanisms, even if the mechanisms created situations in which the real price of labor was not equal to its marginal product (that is, the situation is not one of *production* efficiency).[78]

The introduction of unemployment resulting from technological change points out another conceptual (and definitional) problem encountered in discussing workers and society's welfare. Some technologically displaced workers may simply withdraw from the labor force rather than become long-term unemployed. This represents a contraction of the labor supply, and it leads to underestimates of the number of people affected if only changes in the official unemployment rates are used to measure displacement. Many of the displaced workers who drop out of the labor force are probably part of "the hidden unemployed" who would like to work and would reenter the labor force if they felt sufficient job opportunities were available.

The concept of "hidden employment" is, however, a slippery one: If people voluntarily withdraw from the labor force, it means the best wage offer available to them (possibly zero) is below their reservation wage. One way of interpreting the labor-force behavior of these so-called marginal workers is that on average they have "better" non-market uses of time and thus have relatively higher reservation wages than other workers. If so, it is not clear that they should be singled out for any special policy consideration.

In addition to the possibility of creating hidden unemployment, technological change may create underemployment. The underemployed are persons who are displaced and can find only part-time employment (though they might prefer full-time jobs), plus persons employed at jobs requiring much lower skill levels than they possess. Both of these represent loss of output to the total economy and probable loss of individual welfare due to lower income levels and/or lower job satisfaction. Even if this underutilization of skills is only temporary, it has longer-run implications when skills are dulled by nonuse and/or new techniques are not learned.

An additional complicating aspect is the possible effect that imperfect knowledge and uncertainty may have on a worker's view of technological change and on preference among adjustment mechanisms. No individual nor any group has access to perfect knowledge concerning the final outcome of technological change on welfare. Even if individuals can agree on what are the proper goals for society, they may disagree on the usefulness of different mechanisms to reach these goals, on the likelihood of certain events' occurring, and on the impact of these events on different individuals.

Differences may result from different individuals' preferences to handle or allow for uncertain outcomes. Some may react in a risk-taker approach expecting or hoping to gain; others may be extreme risk-averters, fearing any change in work tasks and opportunities brought on by technological change.

Private and public adjustment mechanisms that include better information flows and more research concerning probable future events resulting from technological change may help bring about more agreement on what are proper adjustment mechanisms. No system can provide perfect knowledge about the future, so uncertainty must be considered in any policy or planning system. "Anticipations and the confidence with which they are held...enter quite directly into the determination of welfare. Our hopes and fears for the future should enter our utility functions quite explicitly—for they certainly affect our choices."[79]

The establishment of mechanisms (such as income maintenance, wider seniority, and relocation and retraining programs) that guarantee compensation from unforeseen future events may help to reduce fears arising from uncertainty and aid the implementation of adjustment mechanisms which encourage change and growth.

The preceding discussion has outlined several reasons, in relation to technological change, that cast doubt on the ability of our economy to move in a Pareto optimizing fashion (at least one person better off, no one else worse off) to an equilibrium position where the community-welfare frontier is tangent to a production frontier (that is, to a point of overall social efficiency). These reasons include interpersonal utility comparisons, utility derived from work itself and other job-related factors, uncertainty, imperfect competition in business and labor supply, and unemployment resulting from imperfect factor mobility and insufficient aggregate demand.

All of these lead to the possibility — in a realistic model on which public policy must be based — of changes occurring in the economy that make some individuals better off and some worse off. Thus, the policymaker is often, if not always, faced in decisions on facilitating technology change and adjustment mechanisms with the problem of weighing the gains in welfare for some members of society against the losses in welfare for other members of society. One method by which this problem may be circumvented is by using what E.J. Mishan calls the conservative principle of compensated adjustment. Mishan suggests "We must suppose. . .that any degree of welfare redistribution is feasible, and on this principle, redistribute in order that no one is left worse off, though some are better off. . ."[80]

Many private adjustment mechanisms appear to be based on the compensation approach (such as supplementary unemployment benefits, profit sharing, guaranteed annual wages, shorter workweeks with no loss of income, and early retirement). Where these private adjustments appear to be working in the best interest of the public at large, the government policy may need to consist largely of measures to improve the speed at which these agreements are reached. In areas where private mechanisms do not appear to be working well, public policy may attempt to compensate potential welfare losers (such as with extended unemployment benefits, relocation allowances, and re-training and income maintenance programs). When compensation is impossible, then the difficult task of analyzing and summing net changes in individuals' welfare must be resolved.

Graaff notes that decisionmaking based on what appears possible leads to what Paul A. Samuelson calls the feasibility locus. Samuelson's feasibility locus tells us how well-off it is politically feasible to make any one individual, given the levels of well-being enjoyed by the others.[81] Society can move the existing efficiency locus closer to the welfare frontier (that is, to a higher welfare level) by movements along the current feasibility locus. Proper government programs in training, counseling, information, and education and in curbing monopoly power shift actual efficiency and feasibility locus positions closer to the maximum welfare frontier.

Finally, in contemplating or advocating compensation and redistributed programs and other moves along the feasibility locus, it must be remembered that the institutional form of the social organization needed to make the move may itself be an input into the community's welfare function—that is, the institutions that are used to generate end results for the system may be ends in themselves. Graff considers the market mechanism to be a good example. An individual may feel that the market's decisions are in some sense impersonal and unbiased and may thus prefer to have prices determined and income distributed by the market rather than by some bureaucrat whom the individual does not trust.[82] So evaluation of movements to improve welfare along the feasibility locus will also have to take into account any gains or losses in welfare generated by changes in social institutions and/or mechanisms set up to handle applications of the compensation principle. At present only a start has been made toward using the principles of welfare economics in empirical assessments of alternative adjustment strategies.

Much of the literature on worker adjustment discusses in detail the kinds of adjustment mechanisms found in labor contracts and in other agreements. Even though considerable work has been done to determine what adjustment techniques are most used and preferred by various worker groups, there still is room for much more research to determine which adjustment mechanisms are most effective to use before technological innovations actually occur and which are the most effective mechanisms to use in the short run and in the long run after the innovations have taken place. In addition, more research is needed on the benefits and costs of the various private and public adjustment mechanisms to individuals, organizations, and society. This must be done before quantitative assessments of the cost and welfare effectiveness of alternative policy strategies can be made. In the meantime, decisions about policy strategies must be based primarily on analytical rather than quantitative arguments.

POLICY IMPLICATIONS

Policy recommendations by different analysts for aiding worker adjustment to technological change reflect the analysts' assessments of the degree of impact that new technology is likely to have on employment opportunities, job content, and skill mix requirements.[83] As might be expected, writers who believe technological change will have a large impact on workers, job content, and aggregate employment tend to conclude that existing private and public adjustment mechanisms are inadequate and need to be greatly expanded, perhaps in a radical manner.[84] At the other extreme, writers who foresee little or no significant impact on employment and workers as new technologies are introduced believe little is needed in the way of special adjustment mechanisms beyond full employment policies and the continued use of existing private sector adjustment mechanisms.[85]

At the risk of some overgeneralization, the great majority of the literature does not foresee new technologies alone causing any general increase in aggregate unemployment or the rapid wholesale elimination of occupations given the maintenance of full employment growth and existing adjustment mechanisms. However, this majority viewpoint does conclude that the introduction of new technologies will affect the required job content and skill mix for a substantial number of occupations and workers and that some job displacement and unemployment will occur, at least in the short run.[86] Also, many analysts believe that some groups of workers are likely to be affected relatively more, including the unskilled, minorities, women, older workers, and, in the opinion of some, younger workers.[87]

The most widely expressed view is that new technologies will be introduced at a gradual rate in coming years, as has occurred in the past. A gradual rate of innovation into the general economy should permit normal market adjustment factors, economic growth, and mobility to handle most of the worker impact. Based on this expected gradual rate of innovation, the continued use of existing public and private worker-adjustment mechanisms, perhaps with some limited expansion, is the basic policy recommendation expressed in the majority of the literature.

This includes the continued application of the existing, commonly used private-sector adjustment mechanisms including pay incentives, retraining, transfer, seniority, advanced notification of change and layoffs, severance pay, private counseling, placement, and referral, and gradual diffusion of innovations.[88] Most of this literature concludes that these private-sector approaches have worked fairly effectively and will continue to do so in the future, with some suggested expansion of planning activities and broadening of the use of these adjustment aids to include all sectors of the economy.

Training or retraining programs are the most commonly recommended private sector adjustment mechanisms,[89] with on-the-job training often cited as the best method to develop specific new skills.[90] Provision of training in the private sector is advocated in order to accommodate worker adjustment and to generate the skill mix required for the introduction of high-technology equipment, processes, and systems. This includes improving the capabilities and commitment of management and personnel department staffs in planning for retraining for worker adjustment,[91] along with some expansion of worker participation in the planning process.[92]

Private-sector adjustment mechanisms — such as the occasional use of work restrictions, guaranteed job and income provisions, and the sometimes difficult labor/management negotiations — have not been found to have impeded the past introduction of new technologies and are not thought likely to do so in the future. Thus, there does not seem to be a need to advocate a major change in public policy toward these private sector activities.

A full-employment policy is the public adjustment mechanism that is advocated almost universally as the basic requirement for the effective functioning of all other public adjustment mechanisms as well as private mechanisms.[93] In addition, some improvement in public information and planning activities is advocated in order to enhance counseling and placement, retraining, education, and relocation programs as worker-adjustment mechanisms for technological change.[94] These public activities are advocated in order to speed up the adjustment process and reduce the cost to the affected workers and society.

The greatest divergence between policy recommendations and actual use of adjustment mechanisms appears to be in the design of public supported retraining and education programs. Some analysts call for public-operated programs, while other analysts advocate publicly funded assistance (such as vouchers) for worker participation in private programs. Moreover, there exist rather widespread differences as to how broad and comprehensive versus specialized the content of public retraining and education programs should be.[95] Even among authors who agree that education should be changed to help workers become more flexible in responding to change, there is no consensus as to the kind of education program this requires.

To summarize, existing private-adjustment mechanisms as well as policies of full-employment and labor/management cooperation, including advance planning for change, should be able to handle the vast majority of worker-adjustment problems, although some improvement is needed to handle pockets of displaced workers. Multiple private adjustment mechanisms should be used to provide workers several options in order to best fit their needs and preferences. Public adjustment mechanisms recommended include more retraining and education to help workers adapt to technological change; however, just what kind of training and education — broad or narrow — will best aid worker adjustment is not clear. A substantial number of analysts argue that public adjustment programs also should be expanded to aid particular groups in the work force, including minorities, women, older workers, and the unskilled.

A final caveat is important. Many analysts' generally sanguine assessments of the capacity of existing adjustment mechanisms are based on the underlying assumption that new technology will not be introduced at an accelerated pace or at the same time as other sources of labor dislocation appear. Consequently, continued monitoring of emerging structural change and the capacity of existing adjustment mechanisms is an appropriate component of the mix of programs employed to facilitate worker adjustment to technical change.

NOTES

1. Burack and McNichols 1968; Canada Dept. of Labour 1967, Nov.; Carnevale and Goldstein 1983; "Cooperation a Key...," 1983; Crispo 1968; Delamotte 1971; Freedman 1968; Herman, 1970; Hunt and Hunt 1983; Killingsworth 1970; Levin and Rumberger 1983; Levitan and Johnson 1982; Martin 1982; Off. Tech. Assessment 1983; O.E.C.D. 1966; Perline and Tull 1969; Prasow and Massarik 1969B; Robinson 1971; Rothberg 1969; Stern 1971; Stern 1969; U.S. Congress 1983; U.S. DOL 1965; Ullman 1969; and Wolfbein 1970.
2. Kassalow 1970; Kheel 1966; Killingsworth 1963; Nelson, Peck and Kalachek 1967; and U.S. DOL 1972.
3. Aronson 1965; Davey 1972; "High-Tech Panel..." 1983; Killingsworth 1963; Nelson, Peck and Kalachek 1967; Off. Tech Assessment 1983; and U.S. DOL 1965.
4. Nelson, Peck and Kalachek 1967; and U.S. DOL 1965.
5. "Adjustment to Tech..." 1966; Canada Dept. of Labour 1967, Nov.; Carnevale and Goldstein 1983; Choate 1982; Davey 1972; Freedman 1968; "High-Tech Panel..." 1983; Hudson 1982; Kassalow 1970; Kelber and Schlesinger 1967;Kheel 1966; Killingsworth 1970; Levin and Rumberger 1983; Levine 1969; Levitan and Johnson 1982; McNiff 1970; Meshel 1970; Nat. Com. Tech. 1966; Nelson, Peck and Kalachek

1967; Off. Tech. Assessment 1983; Robinson 1971; Stern 1971; U.S. Congress 1982, June; U.S. Congress 1983; U.S. Congress 1982, March; U.S. DOL 1972; U.S. DOL 1968; Weber 1968; Weinberg 1970; and Weinberg and Ball 1967.

6. Carnevale and Goldstein 1983; Choate 1982; Levin and Rumberger 1983; Mueller 1969; and Off. Tech. Assessment 1983.

7. Choate 1982;"Cooperation a Key...," 1983; Cross 1983; Gilchrist and Shenkin 1982; "High-Tech Panel..." 1983; Levin and Rumberger 1983; and Off. Tech Assessment 1983.

8. Agassi 1972; Dalton and Thompson 1971; and Dunlop 1966.

9. Cross 1983; Fitzgerald 1982; Gilchrist and Shenkin 1982; Off. Tech Assessment 1983; O.E.C.D. 1966; U.S. Congress 1982, June; U.S. Congress 1983; and U.S. DOL 1968.

10. Barkin 1967; Canada Dept. of Labour 1967, March; Freedman 1968; Gen. Acct. Off. 1982; Goldberg 1968; Goldberg 1971; Golodner 1973; Killingsworth 1963; Killingsworth 1970; King 1972; Levine 1969; Macdonald 1967; McNiff 1970; Mueller 1969; Nelson, Peck and Kalachek 1967; Prasow and Massarik 1969B; Rehmus 1971; Shils 1970; and Zeisel 1968.

11. "Automation Halts...," 1973; Barkin 1967; Critchlow 1970; Davey 1972; Delamotte 1971; Freedman 1968; Gen. Acct. Off. 1982; Horrigan 1970; Macdonald 1967; Nelson, Peck and Kalachek 1967; Off. Tech. Assessment 1983; Rehmus 1971; Robinson 1971; Rothberg 1969; Shils 1970; U.S. Congress 1982, March; Weber 1968; and Weinberg 1970.

12. Early and Witt 1982; and Walker 1967.

13. "Automation Halts...," 1973.

14. Kheel 1966; and Wolfbein 1970.

15. "High-Tech Panel..." 1983; Hunt and Hunt 1983; Levitan and Johnson 1982; Off. Tech. Assessment 1983; and U.S. Congress 1982, March.

16. Davey 1972; Gen. Acct. Off. 1982; "High-Tech Panel..." 1983; Jensen 1971; Kassalow 1970; Kelber and Schlesinger 1967; Macdonald 1967; Moore 1970; Mueller 1969; Nat. Assoc. Mfg. 1967; Off. Tech. Assessment 1983; U.S. Congress 1982, June; U.S. DOL 1972; and Weinberg 1970.

17. Early and Witt 1982.

18. U.S. DOL 1969.

19. Early and Witt 1982.

20. Goldberg 1971; Hartman 1969; Herding 1972; Killingsworth 1963; Killingsworth 1970; King 1972; Rehmus 1971; and U.S. Congress 1982, June.

21. Early and Witt 1982; Goldberg 1971; Hartman 1969; Killingsworth 1963; and Off. Tech. Assessment 1981.

22.   Barkin 1967; Crispo 1968; Hartman 1969; Herman 1970; Kelber and Schlesinger 1967; Mueller 1969; Nat. Assoc. Mfg. 1967; Prasow and Massarik 1969B; U.S. DOL 1970; and Weinberg and Ball 1967.

23.   Early and Witt 1982.

24.   Critchlow 1970; Golodner 1973; Kheel 1966; Meshel 1970; Shils 1970; and Weber 1968.

25.   Chamot 1983; Delamotte 1971; Dunlop 1966; Froomkin 1966; "High-Tech Panel..." 1983; Jensen 1971; Kheel 1966; Levitan and Johnson 1982; McNiff 1970; Nat. Com. Tech. 1966; Reisman 1971; Sheppard 1966; Siemiller 1970; U.S. DOL 1970; Walker 1967; and Weber 1968.

26.   Aronson 1965; Canada Dept. of Labour 1967, Nov.; "High-Tech Panel..." 1983; and Mueller 1969.

27.   Early and Witt 1982; Froomkin 1966; "High-Tech Panel..." 1983; Levitan and Johnson 1982; Sheppard 1966; Siemiller 1970; and Weber 1968.

28.   "Adjustment to Tech..." 1966; Aronson 1965; Bolz 1966; Canada Dept. of Labour 1969; Canada Dept. of Labour 1967, March; Critchlow 1970; Early and Witt 1982; Goldberg 1971; Hartman 1969; Kheel 1966; Killingsworth 1970; Levine 1969; Macdonald 1967; McNiff 1970; Nat. Com. Tech. 1966; Perline and Tull 1969; Stern 1971; U.S. DOL 1972; U.S. DOL 1966; and Weber 1968.

29.   Barkin 1967; Bolz 1966; Delamotte 1971; Goldberg 1968; Goldberg 1971; Jensen 1971; Macdonald 1967; Nat. Com. Tech. 1966; Perline and Tull 1969; Rehmus 1971; Stern 1971; and Weber 1968.

30.   Burack and McNichols 1968; Early and Witt 1982; Mueller 1969; Walker 1967; and Weber 1968.

31.   "Adjustment to Tech..." 1966; Barkin 1967; Canada Dept. of Labour 1967, March; Canada Dept. of Labour 1967, Nov.; Davey 1972; Delamotte 1971; Freedman 1968; Gen. Acct. Off. 1982; Gilchrist and Shenkin 1982; Golodner 1973; Herding 1972; Horrigan 1970; Kheel 1966; King 1972; Levine 1969; Moore 1970; Nat. Assoc. Mfg. 1967; Nat. Com. Tech. 1966; Nelson, Peck and Kalachek 1967; Off. Tech. Assessment 1983; Siemiller 1970; Stern 1971; Stern 1969; U.S. DOL 1966; and Weber 1968.

32.   Aronson 1965; Bolt 1966; Calif. Com.... 1964; Canada Dept. of Labour 1969; Canada Dept. of Labour 1967, March; Canada Dept. of Labour 1967, Nov.; Early and Witt 1982; Gen. Acct. Off. 1982; Horrigan 1970; Kheel 1966; Killingsworth 1970; Levine 1969; Nat. Com. Tech. 1966; Rehmus 1971; Shils 1970; U.S. DOL 1972; and Zciscl 1968.

33.   "Adjustment to Tech..." 1966; Barkin 1967; Crispo 1968; "Displaced ...Stress," 1983; Freedman 1968; "High-Tech Panel..." 1983; Hudson 1982; Levitan and Johnson 1982; McNiff 1970; Off. Tech. Assessment 1983; Perline and Tull 1969; Prasow and Massarik 1969B; Rothberg 1969; Stern 1971; Stern 1969; U.S. Congress 1982, June; U.S. DOL 1965; Ullman 1969; and Weinberg 1970.

34. Dalton and Thompson 1971; "Displaced...Stress," 1983; "High-Tech Panel..." 1983; Kheel 1966; Nat. Assoc. Mfg. 1967; Nat. Com. Tech. 1966; Prasow and Massarik 1969B; Rothberg 1969; and Ullman 1969.

35. "Cooperation a Key...," 1983; Critchlow 1970; Cross 1983; Goldberg 1968; Goldberg 1971; Hartman 1969; Hunt and Hunt 1983; Kahn 1971; Levine 1969; Levinson 1971; O'Carroll 1971; Off. Tech. Assessment 1983; Rehmus 1971; and U.S. DOL 1965.

36. Canada Dept. of Labour 1967, Nov.; Kassalow 1970; Killingsworth 1963; Levinson 1971; Rehmus 1971; and Shils 1970.

37. Aronson 1965; "Displaced Worker...," 1983; Herding 1972; and King 1972.

38. Choate 1982; Davey 1972; Gilchrist and Shenkin 1982; and Mortimer 1971.

39. Bolz 1966; Chamot 1983; Critchlow 1970; Goodwin 1965; "High Tech Hype...," 1983; "High-Tech Panel..." 1983; Jaffe and Froomkin 1968; Levitan and Johnson 1982; Sheppard 1966; U.S. Congress 1982, June; U.S. Congress 1982, March; and Weinberg 1970.

40. Aronson 1965; Choate 1982; Davey 1972; "High Tech Hype...," 1983; Macdonald 1967; Off. Tech. Assessment 1983; Perline and Tull, 1969; and Weber 1968.

41. Barkin 1966; Bell 1971; Chamot 1983; Crispo 1968; Froomkin 1966; "High-Tech Panel..." 1983; Kassalow 1970; Leontief 1983; Nat. Com. Tech. 1966; Nat. Ind. Conf. Board 1966; and Wolfbein 1970.

42. Some authors argue that manpower programs fit in one or more of these groups. For example, see Ulmann 1973.

43. Nat. Com. Tech. 1966; Nat. Ind. Conf. Board 1966; and Sheppard 1966.

44. Goodwin 1965; and Salner 1965.

45. Calif. Com.... 1964; Chamot 1983; Gen. Acct. Off. 1982; Jaffe and Froomkin 1968; Leontief 1983; Michael 1967; Nat. Com. Tech. 1966; Nat. Ind. Conf. Board 1966; Puryear 1966; Sexton and Sexton 1971; and Sheppard 1966.

46. Dunlop 1966; Nat. Com. Tech. 1966; and Rosenberg 1966.

47. Bolz 1966; "Displaced Worker...," 1983; "High-Tech Panel..." 1983; Nat. Com. Tech. 1966; "Review Six Displaced...," 1983; Salner 1965; "Study: Choosing...," 1983; U.S. Congress 1982, March; U.S. DOL 1966; Weinberg and Ball 1967; and White House Conf. 1983.

48. Goodwin 1965; Stern 1969; and White House Conf. 1983.

49. Dunlop 1966; Nelson, Peck and Kalachek 1967; Puryear 1966; and Zeisel 1968.

50. Goodwin 1965; Nat. Com. Tech. 1966; and Puryear 1966.

51. Barkin 1966; Bell 1971; Reisman 1971; Salner 1965; and Stern 1969.

52. Aronson 1965; Nat. Ind. Conf. Board 1966; Nelson, Peck and Kalachek 1967; and Wolfbein 1970.

53. Dunlop 1966; Kassalow 1970; Levin and Rumberger 1983; Nat. Com. Tech. 1966; Off. Tech. Assessment 1983; Off. Tech. Assessment 1981; U.S. Congress 1982, June; U.S. Congress 1982, March; U.S. DOL 1966; and U.S. DOL 1968.

54. Bright 1966; Burack and McNichols 1968; Drucker 1973; "High-Tech Panel..." 1983; Mueller 1969; Off. Tech. Assessment 1983; Prasow and Massarik 1969B; Puryear 1966; Rosenberg 1966; U.S. Congress 1983; and Vrooman 1980.

55. Choate 1982; "Displaced Worker...," 1983; Levine 1969; Martin 1982; "Study: Choosing...," 1983; and U.S. Congress 1982, March.

56. "Adjustment to Tech..." 1966; Cross 1983; Fulco 1969; and Mueller 1969.

57. Laucks 1966; Michael 1967; and Reisman 1971.

58. Choate 1982; "Cooperation a Key...," 1983; "Displaced Worker...," 1983; "Displaced...Stress," 1983; Gilchrist and Shenkin 1982; "High-Tech Panel..." 1983; Kassalow 1970; "Study: Choosing...," 1983; U.S. Congress 1982, June; U.S. Congress 1983; U.S. Congress 1982, March; and White House Conf. 1983.

59. Levitan and Johnson 1982; Nat. Com. Tech. 1966; U.S. DOL 1968; Weinberg 1970; and Wolfbein 1970.

60. "Displaced Worker...," 1983; Fitzgerald 1982; Gilchrist and Shenkin 1982; and Off. Tech. Assessment 1983.

61. Choate 1982; Choate, Summers and Bishop 1983; "Cooperation a Key ...," 1983; "Displaced Worker...," 1983; "High-Tech Panel..." 1983; U.S. Congress 1982, March; and White House Conf. 1983.

62. "Displaced Worker...," 1983; Dunlop 1966; Fulco 1969; Goodwin 1965; "High-Tech Panel..." 1983; Meshel 1970; Nat. Com. Tech. 1966; Nelson, Peck and Kalachek 1967; Puryear 1966; "Review Six Displaced...," 1983; White House Conf. 1983; and Zeisel 1968.

63. Bright 1966; Martin 1982; and Off. Tech. Assessment 1981.

64. "Highlights," Feb. 1983.

65. Aronson 1965; Choate 1982; Dunlop 1966; Gilchrist and Shenkin 1982; "High-Tech Panel..." 1983; Nat. Com. Tech. 1966; Nat. Ind. Conf. Board, 1966; O.E.C.D. 1966; and Puryear 1966.

66. Gen. Acct. Off. 1982; "High-Tech Panel..." 1983; Jaffee and Froomkin 1968; Leontief 1983; Levitan and Johnson 1982; Michael 1967; Nat. Com. Tech. 1966; Nat. Ind. Conf. Board 1966; and Seligman 1966.

67. Crispo 1968; Dunlop 1966; Gen. Acct. Off. 1982; Goodwin 1965; Kassalow 1970; Leontief 1983; Levitan and Johnson 1982; Nat. Com. Tech. 1966; O.E.C.D. 1966; and Zeisel 1968.

68. Barkin 1966; Calif. Com.... 1964; and Nat. Com. Tech. 1966.

69. Calif. Com.... 1964; Levinson 1971; Nat. Com. Tech. 1966; and Nat. Ind. Conf. Board 1966.

70. Off. Tech. Assessment 1981; and U.S. Congress 1982, March.
71. These growth oriented assumptions have been questioned by some since the energy problems and in light of such assessments as *The Limits to Growth* (Meadows 1972).
72. Little 1957, 80.
73. Scitovsky 1971, 480–1.
74. Little 1957, 55–6.
75. Graaff 1967, 58–9.
76. Graaff 1967, 76.
77. Scitovsky 1971, 472.
78. Graff 1967, 85.
79. Graaff 1967, 120.
80. Mishan 1969, 14.
81. Graaff 1967, 79.
82. Graaff 1967, 79.
83. Choate 1982; Fitzgerald 1982; Gilchrist and Shenkin 1982; Kassalow 1970; Leontief 1983; Sexton and Sexton 1971; and Siemiller 1970.
84. Bloice 1972; Ferkiss 1969; Lee and Lancaster 1971; Melechanik 1969; and Reisman 1971.
85. Jaffe and Froomkin 1968; Levin and Rumberger 1983; Levitan and Johnson 1982; U.S. Congress 1982, March; and Weinberg 1970.
86. Fechter 1982; Gen. Acct. Off. 1982; Hudson 1982; *Manpower Comments* 1982; Martin 1982; Off. Tech. Assessment 1983; and Off. Tech. Assessment 1981.
87. Agassi 1972; *Age, Work and Auto....*, 1970; Cargill and Rosemiller 1969; Dalton and Thompson 1971; Fulco 1969; Goldberg 1968; Levine 1969; Mueller 1969; Young 1970; and Zeisel 1968.
88. Burack and McNichols 1968; Carnevale and Goldstein 1983; Critchlow 1970; Freedman 1968; Gen. Acct. Off. 1982; Herman 1970; "High-Tech Panel..." 1983; Kahn 1971; Levine 1969; Levitan and Johnson 1982; Meshel 1970; Mueller 1969; Off. Tech. Assessment 1983; Perline and Tull 1969; Prasow and Massarik 1969B; Rezler 1972; Rothberg 1969; Stern 1969; U.S. Congress 1982, June; U.S. DOL 1972; U.S. DOL 1968; Ullman 1969; Weber 1968; and Wolfbein 1970.
89. Burack and McNichols 1968; Carnevale and Goldstein 1983; Critchlow 1970; Gen. Acct. Off. 1982; "High-Tech Panel..." 1983; Levine 1969; Martin 1982; Mortimer 1971; O'Carroll 1971; Off. Tech. Assessment 1983; Prasow and Massarik 1969A; Rothberg 1969; Stern 1969; U.S. Congress 1982, June; U.S. Congress 1983; U.S. Congress 1982, March; U.S. DOL 1972; Ullman 1969; and Vickery 1972.
90. Burack and Pati 1970; Carnevale and Goldstein 1983; Mueller 1969; Off. Tech. Assessment 1983; and Prasow and Massarik 1969A.
91. Hudson 1982; O'Carroll 1971; Rezler 1972; Rothberg 1969; Stern 1969; and U.S. Congress 1982, March.

92.   Burack and Pati 1970; Davey 1972; Freedman 1968; Hudson 1982; and Prasow and Massarik 1969B.
93.   Chamot 1983; Fechter 1982; Gen. Acct. Off. 1982; "High Tech Hype . . . ," 1983; "High-Tech Panel. . ." 1983; Leontief 1983; Levitan and Johnson 1982; U.S. Congress 1982, June; and U.S. Congress 1982, March.
94.   Bell 1971; Burack and Pati 1970; Canada Dept. of Labour 1969; Cargill and Rosemiller 1969; Choate 1982; Fulco 1969; Gen. Acct. Off. 1982; Gilchrist and Shenkin 1982; "High-Tech Panel. . ." 1983; Martin 1982; Mortimer 1971; Off. Tech. Assessment 1981; "Review Six Displaced. . . ," 1983; Rothberg 1969; Stern 1969; "Study: Choosing. . . ," 1983; U.S. Congress 1982, March; U.S. DOL 1968; Ullman 1969; White House Conf. 1983; Wolfbein 1970; and Zeisel 1968.
95.   Bell 1971; "Displaced Worker. . . ," 1983; Drucker 1973; "High-Tech Panel. . ." 1983; "Highlights," Feb. 1983; Lee and Lancaster 1971; Martin 1982; Mueller 1969; Off. Tech. Assessment 1983; Prasow and Massarik 1969B; U.S. Congress 1983; U.S. DOL 1968; Ullman 1969; and Vrooman 1980.

REFERENCES

"Adjustment to Technological Change within the Firm: One Aspect of Active Manpower Policy," *OECD Observer* no. 22 (1966): 34–35.

Agassi, Judith B., "Women Who Work in Factories," *Dissent* 19 (Winter 1972): 233–39.

Age, Work and Automation (report of an International Colloquium at Semmering, Austria, June 1966) (Basel: S. Karger AG, 1970).

Appelbaum, Eileen, "High Tech and the Structural Unemployment of the Eighties (paper presented at the American Economic Association Meetings, December 28, 1981, at Washington, D.C.) (mimeographed).

Aronson, Robert L., *Jobs, Wages and Changing Technology,* bulletin 55 (Ithaca, N.Y.: New York State School of Industrial and Labor Relations, Cornell University, July 1965).

"Automation Halts the St. Louis Dailies," *Business Week* (September 1, 1973): 19.

Barkin, Solomon, "Programming of Technical Changes and Manpower Adjustments," in Jack Stieber, ed., *Employment Problems in Automation and Advanced Technology* (New York: St. Martin's Press, 1966).

Barkin, Solomon, ed., *Technical Change and Manpower Planning, Coordination at Enterprise Level* (Paris: Organization for Economic Cooperation and Development, 1967).

Bell, Daniel, "Notes on the Post-Industrial Society," in Jack D. Douglas, ed., *The Technological Threat* (Englewood Cliffs, N.J.: Prentice-Hall, 1971).

Bloice, Carl, "The Black Worker's Future Under American Capitalism," *The Black Scholar* 3 (May 1972): 14–22.

Bolz, Robert W., *Understanding Automation, Elements for Managers* (Cleveland, Ohio: Penton, 1966).

Bright, James R., "The Relationship of Increasing Automation to Skill Requirements," in *The Employment Impact of Technological Change, Technology and the American Economy,* appendix vol. 2 (Washington, D.C.: U.S. Government Printing Office, February 1966).

Burack, Elmer H., and T.J. McNichols, "Management and Automation Research Project" (Chicago: Illinois Institute of Technology, February 1968).

Burack, Elmer H., and Gopal C. Pati, "Technology and Managerial Obsolescence" *Michigan State Business Topics* 18 (Spring 1970): 49–56.

California Commission on Manpower, Automation, and Technology, *Report to the Governor and to the Legislature* (Sacramento, Calif.: 1964).

Canada Department of Labour, "Automation and Mobility: Is the Price Too High?," *Labour Gazette* 69 (June 1969): 331–32.

Canada Department of Labour, "Human Adjustment to Industrial Conversion," *Labour Gazette* 67 (March 1967): 174–75.

Canada Department of Labour, "Technological Change Provisions in Collective Agreements," *Labour Gazette* 67 (November 1967): 687.

Cargill, B.F., and B.E. Rosemiller, eds., *Fruit and Vegetable Harvest Mechanization, Policy Implications* (East Lansing, Mich.: Rural Manpower Center, Michigan State University, 1969).

Carnevale, Anthony, and Harold Goldstein, *Employee Training: Its Changing Role and An Analysis of New Data* (Washington, D.C.: American Society for Training and Development, 1983).

Chamot, Dennis, New Researchers Conference reported in *Employment and Training Reporter,* November 9, 1983, pp. 257–58.

Choate, Pat., *Retooling the American Work Force: Toward a National Training Strategy* (Washington, D.C.: Northeast–Midwest Institute, 1982).

Choate, Pat, Lawrence Summers, and John Bishop, U.S. Congress Joint Economic Committee Hearings, reported in *Employment and Training Reporter,* November 9, 1983, pp. 256–57.

"Cooperation a Key Word for GM/UAW/CAL Dislocated Worker Retraining Program," *Employment and Training Reporter,* September 28, 1983, pp. 70–71.

Crispo, John H.G., "Human Adjustment to Industrial Conversion: A Canadian Experiment," in B.C. Roberts, ed., *Industrial Relations: Contemporary Issues* (New York: St. Martin's Press, 1968).

Critchlow, Robert V., "Technological Changes in the Printing and Publishing Industry," *Monthly Labor Review* 93 (August 1970): 3–9.

Cross, Michael, *Changing Requirements for Craftsmen in the Process Industries,* interim report (London: Technical Change Centre, April 1983).

Dalton, Gene W., and Paul H. Thompson, "Accelerating Obsolescence of Older Engineers," *Harvard Business Review* 49 (September/October 1971): 57–67.

Davey, Harold W., "Job Security," in Harold W. Davey, ed., *Contemporary Collective Bargaining.* 3d ed. (Englewood Cliffs, N.J.: Prentice-Hall, 1972.

Delamotte, Yves, *The Social Partners Face the Problems of Productivity and Employment* (Paris: Organization for Economic Cooperation and Development, 1971).

"Displaced Worker Programs Discussed, Explained at Joint Economic Hearings," *Employment and Training Reporter,* September 28, 1983, pp. 67–68.

"Displaced Worker Programs Should Come at Time of Greatest Stress, Study Says," Review of University of Michigan Study, *Employment and Training Reporter,* November 2, 1983, pp. 237–38.

Drucker, Peter, "Evolution of the Knowledge Worker," in Fred Best, ed., *The Future of Work* (Englewood Cliffs, N.J.: Prentice-Hall, 1973).

Dunlop, John T., "Technological Change and Manpower Policy — The Older Worker," in Juanita Kreps, ed., *Technology, Manpower, and Retirement Policy* (Cleveland, Ohio: World, 1966).

Early, Steve, and Matt Witt, "How European Unions Cope with New Technology," *Monthly Labor Review* 105 (September 1982): 36–38.

Fechter, Alan, Statement before the Subcommittee on Employment and Productivity, Senate Labor and Human Resources Committee, 97 Cong., 2 Sess. (March 26, 1982).

Ferkiss, Victor C., *Technological Man: The Myth and the Reality* (New York: George Braziller, 1969).

Fitzgerald, Pat, "Economic Revolution Has Left Midwest Reeling," *USA Today,* November 18, 1982, p. 48.

Freedman, Audrey, *Manpower Planning for Technological Change, Case Studies of Telephone Operators,* U.S. Department of Labor Bulletin no. 1574 (Washington, D.C.: U.S. Government Printing Office, 1968).

Froomkin, Joseph N., "Implications of Technological Change for Jobs," in Juanita Kreps, ed., *Technology, Manpower, and Retirement Policy* (Cleveland, Ohio: World, 1966).

Fulco, Lawrence J., "How Mechanization of Harvesting is Affecting Jobs," *Monthly Labor Review* 92 (March 1969): 26–32.

General Accounting Office, *Advances in Automation Prompt Concern Over Increased U.S. Unemployment,* a staff study, GAO/AFMD-82-44 (Washington, D.C.: U.S. Government Printing Office, May 25, 1982).

Gilchrist, Bruce, and Arlaana Shenkin, "Results of studies reported in 'All Parties to Worker Layoffs Found Deficient in Providing Retraining,'" *Employment and Training Reporter,* October 6, 1982, pp. 118–19.

Goldberg, Joseph P., "Containerization as a Force for Change on the Waterfront," *Monthly Labor Review* 91 (January 1968): 8–13.

———, "Modernization in the Maritime Industry," in *Collective Bargaining and Technological Change in American Transportation,* pt. 3 (Evanston, Ill.: The Transportation Center, Northwestern University, 1971).

Golodner, Jack, "Professionals Go Union," *The American Federationist* 80 (October 1973): 6–8.

Goodwin, Robert C., "The Labor Force Adjustment of Workers Affected by Technological Change," *Manpower Implications of Automation* (Washington, D.C.: U.S. Department of Labor, September 1965).

Graaff, J. de V., *Theoretical Welfare Economics* (London: Cambridge University Press, 1967).

Hartman, Paul T., *Collective Bargaining and Productivity, The Longshore Mechanization Agreement* (Berkeley: University of California Press, 1969).

Herding, Richard, *Job Control and Union Structure* (Rotterdam: Rotterdam University Press, 1972).

Herman, Arthur S., "Manpower Implications of Computer Control in Manufacturing," *Monthly Labor Review* 93 (October 1970): 3–8.

"High Tech Hype on Employment Impact Out of Proportion, House Panel Told," (review of hearings before the House Small Business Subcommittee on General Oversight and the Economy) *Employment and Training Reporter,* May 25, 1983, pp. 1204–06.

"High-Tech Panel Seeks Middle Ground: How to Get the Good and Miss the Bad" (report on Joint Hearings, U.S. Congress) *Employment and Training Reporter,* June 29, 1983, pp. 1435–38.

"Highlights," *Employment and Training Reporter,* August 17, 1983, p. 1.

"Highlights," *Employment and Training Reporter,* February 16, 1983, p. 1.

Horrigan, George, "The Management of Automation: Issues and Responsibilities," *Material Handling Engineering* 25 (August 1970): 72–80.

Hudson, C.A., "Computers in Manufacturing," *Science* 215 (February 12, 1982): 818–25.

Hunt, H. Allen, and Timothy L. Hunt, *Human Resource Implications of Robotics* (Kalamazoo, Mich.: The W.E. Upjohn Institute, 1983).

Jaffe, A.J., and Joseph Froomkin, *Technology and Jobs: Automation in Perspective* (New York: Praeger, 1968).

Jensen, Vernon H., *Decasualization and Modernization of Dock Work in London* (Ithaca, N.Y.: New York State School of Industrial and Labor Relations, Cornell University, 1971).

Jondrow, James M., Robert A. Levy, and Louis Jacobson, "Labor Adjustment to Technical Change in Steel and Related Industries" (paper presented at the American Economic Association Meeting, December 28, 1981 at Washington, D.C.) (mimeo).

Kahn, Mark L., "Collective Bargaining on the Airline Flight Deck," in *Collective Bargaining and Technological Change in American Transportation,* pt. 4 (Evanston, Ill.: The Transportation Center, Northwestern University, 1971).

Kassalow, Everett M., "Automation and Labor Relations," in Simon Marcson, ed., *Automation, Alienation, and Anomie* (New York: Harper & Row, 1970).

Kelber, Harry, and Carl Schlesinger, *Union Printers and Controlled Automation* (New York: Free Press, 1967).

Kheel, Theodore W., "The Changing Patterns of Collective Bargaining in the United States," in Jack Stieber, ed., *Employment Problems of Automation and Advanced Technology* (New York: St. Martin's Press, 1966).

Killingsworth, Charles C., "Cooperative Approaches to Problems of Technological Change," in Gerald G. Somers, et al., eds., *Adjusting to Technological Change* (New York: Harper & Row, 1963).

————, "Industrial Relations and Automation," in Simon Marcson, ed., *Automation, Alienation, and Anomie* (New York: Harper & Row, 1970).

King, Geoffrey R., "Arbitration of Technological Change," Ph.D. Dissertation, University of Southern California, 1972.

Laucks, Irving F., "The Future Society," in Alice Mary Hilton, ed., *The Evolving Society* (New York: The Institute for Cybercultural Research, 1966).

Lee, John W., and J. Lancaster, "The Maintenance Training Gap," *Training and Development Journal* 25 (November 1971): 46–49.

Leontief, Wassily, "Technological Advance, Economic Growth, and the Distribution of Income," *Population and Development Review* 9 (September 1983): 403–10.

Levin, Henry M., and Russell W. Rumberger, *The Educational Implications of High Technology,* report No. 83–A4 (Palo Alto, Calif.: Institute for Research on Educational Finance and Governance, Stanford University, February 1983).

Levine, Morton, "Adjusting to Technology on the Railroads," *Monthly Labor Review* 92 (November 1969): 36–42.

Levinson, Harold M., "Collective Bargaining and Technological Change in American Transportation: An Integrative Analysis," in *Collective Bargaining and Technological Change in American Transportation,* pt. 5 (Evanston, Ill.: The Transportation Center, Northwestern University, 1971).

Levitan, S.A., and C.M. Johnson, "The Future of Work: Does It Belong to Us or to the Robots?," *Monthly Labor Review* 105 (September 1982): 10–14.

Little, I.M.D., *A Critique of Welfare Economics,* 2d ed. (London: Oxford University Press, 1957).

Macdonald, Robert M., "Collective Bargaining in the Postwar Period," *Industrial Labor Relations Review* 20 (July 1967): 553–77.

Machlup, Fritz, George Bitros, and Kenneth Leason, *Effects of Innovation on Demand for and Earnings of Productive Factors* (a report to the National Science Foundation) (New York: New York University, 1974).

Manpower Comments (review of the study *California's Technological Future: Emerging Economic Opportunities in the 1980's*) 19 (December 1982): 10.

Martin, Gail M., "Industrial Robots Join the Work Force," *Occupational Outlook Quarterly* 26 (Fall 1982): 2–11.

McNiff, John J., "Implementing Automation," in *Automation Management: the Social Perspective* (Athens, Ga.: The Center for the Study of Automation and Society, 1970).

Meadows, D.H., *The Limits to Growth* (New York: Universe Books, 1972).

Melechanik, G., "Social Costs of the Scientific–Technical Revolution under Capitalism," *Problems of Economics* 12 (December 1969): 3–22.

Meshel, Yerucham, "The Social Role of the Unions," in *Technological Change and Human Development* (Ithaca, N.Y.: New York State School of Industrial and Labor Relations, Cornell University, 1970).

Michael, Donald N., "The Impact of Cybernation," in Melvin Kranzberg and Carroll W. Pursell, Jr., eds., *Technology in Western Civilization,* vol. 2 (New York: Oxford University Press, 1967).

Mishan, E.J., *Welfare Economics,* 2d ed. (New York: Random House, 1969).

Moore, Wilbert E., "Technological Change and the Worker," in Simon Marcson, ed., *Automation, Alienation, and Anomie* (New York: Harper & Row, 1970).

Morrison, David L., Richard H. Snow, and John R. Lamoureux, "Advances in Process Control," *Science* 215 (February 12, 1983): 813–18.

Mortimer, J.E., *Trade Unions and Technological Change* (London: Oxford University Press, 1971).

Mueller, Eva, et al., *Technological Advance in an Expanding Economy: Its Impact on a Cross-Section of the Labor Force* (Ann Arbor: Institute for Social Research, University of Michigan, 1969).

National Association of Manufacturers, Industrial Relations Division, *The Challenge of Automation* (New York: National Association of Manufacturers, 1967).

National Commission on Technology, Automation, and Economic Progress, *Technology and the American Economy* (Washington, D.C.: U.S. Government Printing Office, February 1966).

National Industrial Conference Board, *The Report of the President's Commission on Automation — A Critique,* Public Affairs Conference Report No. 4 (New York: National Industrial Conference Board, 1966).

Nelson, Richard R., Merton J. Peck, and Edward D. Kalachek, *Technology, Economic Growth, and Public Policy* (Washington, D.C.: The Brookings Institution, 1967).

Nicosia, Francesco N., et al., *Technological Change, Product Proliferation, and Consumer Decision Processes* (a report to the National Science Foundation) (Berkeley: Institute of Business and Economic Research, University of California, 1974).

O'Carroll, Floyd T., "Technology and Manpower in Nonelectrical Machinery," *Monthly Labor Review* 94 (June 1971): 56–63.

Office of Technology Assessment, U.S. Congress, *Automation and the Workplace: Selected Labor, Education, and Training Issues* (Washington, D.C., March 1983).

———, *Exploratory Workshop on the Social Impacts of Robotics: Summary and Issues* (Washington, D.C., July 31, 1981).

Organization for Economic Cooperation and Development, *Manpower Aspects of Automation and Technical Change* (Paris: OECD, 1966).

Perline, Martin M., and Kurtis L. Tull, "Automation: Its Impact on Organized Labor," *Personnel Journal* 48 (May 1969): 340–44.

Prasow, Paul, and Fred Massarik, *A Longitudinal Study of Automated and Nonautomated Job Patterns in the Southern California Aerospace Industry*, vol. 1 (Los Angeles: Institute of Industrial Relations, University of California, April 1969).

———, *The Impact of Automation on Individuals and Jobs, A Review of Recent Literature (1956–1967)*, vol. 2 (Los Angeles: Institute of Industrial Relations, University of California, April 1969).

Puryear, M.T., "Technology and the Negro," in *Adjusting to Change, Technology, and the American Economy*, appendix vol. 3 (Washington, D.C.: U.S. Government Printing Office, February 1966).

Rehmus, Chalres M., "Collective Bargaining and Technological Change on American Railroads," in *Collective Bargaining and Technological Change in American Transportation*, pt. 2 (Evanston, Ill.: The Transportation Center, Northwestern University, 1971).

Reisman, David, "Leisure and Work in Postindustrial Society," in Jack D. Douglas, ed., *The Technological Threat* (Englewood Cliffs, N.J.: Prentice-Hall, 1971).

"Review of Six Displaced Worker Demonstration Projects Shows Pitfalls," *Employment and Training Reporter* (review of a progress report by ABT Associates, August 24, 1983), pp. 1693–94.

Rezler, Julius, "Automation," in Joseph J. Famularo, ed., *Handbook of Modern Personnel Administration* (New York: McGraw-Hill, 1972).

Robinson, L.A, "Office Automation: Stimulus or Deterrent to Clerical Growth," *Personnel Journal* 50 (November 1971): 846–55.

Rosenberg, Jerry M., *Automation, Manpower, and Education* (New York: Random House, 1966).

Rothberg, Herman J., "A Study of the Impact of Office Automation in the IRS," *Monthly Labor Review* 92 (October 1969): 26–31.

Salner, Edward, "The Manpower Problems of Automation," *Employment Service Review* 2 (October 1965): 48, 51–54.

Scitovsky, Tibor, *Welfare and Competition,* rev. ed. (Homewood, Ill.: Richard D. Irwin, 1971).

Seligman, Ben B., *Most Notorious Victory – Man in an Age of Automation* (New York: Free Press, 1966).

Sexton, Brenda, and Patricia Sexton, "Labor's Decade – Maybe," *Dissent* 18 (August 1971): 365–74.

Sheppard, Harold L., "Implications of Technological Change for Leisure," in Juanita Kreps, ed., *Technology, Manpower, and Retirement Policy* (Cleveland, Ohio: World, 1966).

Shils, Edward B., "Clerical Automation and White-Collar Organizing Drives," in Simon Marcson, ed., *Automation, Alienation, and Anomie* (New York: Harper & Row, 1970).

Siemiller, P.L., "The Future of Collective Bargaining and the Resolution of Industrial Conflict," in *Technological Change and Human Development* (Ithaca, N.Y.: New York State School of Industrial and Labor Relations, Cornell University, 1970).

Spinrad, R.J., "Office Automation," *Science* 215 (February 12, 1983): 808–13.

Stern, James L., "Collective Bargaining Trends and Patterns," in *A Review of Industrial Relations Research* (Madison, Wis.,: Industrial Relations Research Association, 1971).

———, "Evolution of Private Manpower Planning in Armour's Plant Closing," *Monthly Labor Review* 92 (December 1969): 21–28.

"Study: Choosing between Retraining and Job Search Still an Open Question," *Employment and Training Reporter* (review of ABT Associates study), September 28, 1983, pp. 69–70.

Tornatzky, Louis G., et al., *The Process of Technological Innovation: Reviewing the Literature* (Washington, D.C.: National Science Foundation, May 1983).

U.S. Congress, House Subcommittee on Investigations and Oversight of the Committee on Science and Technology, *Robotics,* 97th Cong., 2nd sess. (June 23, 1982).

U.S. Congress, Subcommittee on Economic Goals and Intergovernmental Policy of the Joint Economic Committee, *The Impact of Robotics on Employment,* 98th Cong., 1st sess. (March 18, 1983).

U.S. Congress, Subcommittee on Monetary and Fiscal Policy of the Joint Economic Committee, *Robotics and the Economy,* 97th Cong., 2d sess. (March 26, 1982).

U.S. Department of Labor, Bureau of Labor Statistics, *Manpower Planning to Adapt to New Technology at Electric and Gas Utility,* report No. 293 (Washington, D.C.: U.S. Government Printing Office, April 1965).

U.S. Department of Labor, Bureau of Labor Statistics, *Railroad Technology and Manpower in the 1970s,* bulletin 1717 (Washington, D.C.: U.S. Government Printing Office, 1972).

U.S. Department of Labor, Bureau of Labor Statistics, *Technological Trends in Major American Industries,* bulletin 1474 (Washington, D.C.: U.S. Government Printing Office, February 1966).

U.S. Department of Labor, "Exploring Restrictive Building Practices," *Monthly Labor Review* 92 (July 1969): 31–39.

U.S. Department of Labor, Manpower Administration, *Work Force Adjustments in Private Industry — Their Implications for Manpower Policy,* Manpower Automation Research Monograph No. 7 (Washington, D.C.: U.S. Government Printing Office, 1968).

U.S. Department of Labor, Wage and Labor Standards Administration, Women's Bureau, *Automation and Women Workers* (Washington, D.C.: U.S. Government Printing Office, February 1970).

Ullman, Joseph C., "Helping Workers Locate Jobs Following a Plant Shutdown," *Monthly Labor Review* 92 (April 1969): 35–40.

Ulmann, Lloyd, ed., *Manpower Programs in the Policy Mix* (Baltimore, Md.: John Hopkins University Press, 1973).

Vickery, Mary L., "New Technology in Laundry and Cleaning Services," *Monthly Labor Review* 95 (February 1972): 54–59.

Vrooman, John, "Technology and Labor Market Segmentation" (Austin, Tex.: 1980) (mimeo).

Walker, K.F., "Automation and Non-Manual Workers," *Labor and Automation,* bulletin No. 5 (Geneva: International Labor Office, 1967).

Weber, Arnold R., "Collective Bargaining and the Challenge of Technological Change," in Charles Walker, ed., *Technology, Industry, and Man, the Age of Acceleration* (New York: McGraw–Hill, 1968).

Weinberg, Edgar, "Some Manpower Implications," in *Automation Management: The Social Perspective* (Athens, Ga.: The Center for the Study of Automation and Society, 1970).

Weinberg, Edgar, and Robert L. Ball, "The Many Faces of Technology," *Occupational Outlook Quarterly* 2 (May 1967): 7–10.

White House Conference on Productivity, September 22–23, 1983, Reported in *Employment and Training Reporter,* September 28, 1983, pp. 66–67.

Wolfbein, Seymour L., "The Pace of Technological Change and the Factors Affecting It," in Simon Marcson, ed., *Automation, Alienation, and Anomie* (New York: Harper & Row, 1970).

Young, Whitney M., "Technology and the Dispossessed," in *Technological Change and Human Development* (Ithaca, N.Y.: New York State School of Industrial and Labor Relations, Cornell University, 1970).

Zeisel, Rose N., "Technology and Labor in the Textile Industry," *Monthly Labor Review* 91 (February 1968): 49–55.

INDEX

ABOUT THE CONTRIBUTORS

Peter S. Albin is Professor of Economics at John Jay College, the Center for the Study of Systems Structure and Industrial Complexity, and the Graduate Center of the City University of New York. He is the author of *Analysis of Complex Socioeconomic Systems, Progress without Poverty, Economic Structure and Complexity,* and numerous papers in leading economic journals. He received the Ph.D. in economics from Princeton University and the B.A. from Yale University.

Eileen Appelbaum is a member of the economics faculty at Temple University, and of the editorial board of the *Journal of Post-Keynesian Economics.* She is the author of *Work Attitudes and Labor Market Experience, Back to Work: Determinants of Women's Successful Re-entry,* and many articles about post-Keynesian labor theory and employment policy issues. Her current research focuses on technology and employment in the office industries. Professor Appelbaum received the Ph.D. in economics from the University of Pennsylvania.

Larry M. Blair is the Director of the Labor and Policy Studies Program at Oak Ridge Associated Universities. His program conducts employment, education, and training studies as well as public policy analysis. His current research interests include labor market analysis, employment-education linkages, workers and technical change, labor productivity, and applied microeconomics. Before joining Oak Ridge Associated Universities, he was a member of the economics faculty and Associate Director of the Human Resources Institute at the University of Utah. He received the Ph.D. in economics from Claremont Graduate School.

Marianne Bowes has been an economist at the Public Research Institute of the Center for Naval Analyses since 1978. Her research interests include spatial economics, regulation, and the effects of regulation on productivity growth. Her current work is focused on the differential way in which experience rating for unemployment insurance influences small and large businesses. She received the Ph.D. in economics from the University of Illinois.

Faye Duchin is Senior Research Scientist and Associate Director of the Institute for Economic Analysis at New York University. She has recently coauthored a detailed study of structural change in the U.S. economy and the potential effects of computer-based automation on employment. She has also studied and written about the implications of military spending for the U.S. and world economies. Prior to joining the Institute for Economic Analysis, Duchin worked for several years as an economist at Mathematica, Inc. She received the B.A. in psychology from Cornell University and the Ph.D. in computer science from the University of California at Berkeley.

James M. Jondrow received the Ph.D. in economics from the University of Wisconsin, and has been an economist at the Public Research Institute of the Center for Naval Analyses since 1973. He has directed econometric studies of how the demand for American labor has been affected by international competition and, more recently, a study of labor market distinctions between full- and part-time work. His current research interests include the effects of technical change on labor—firm by firm—and the microeconomics of highway speed limits.

Robert A. Levy received the Ph.D. in economics from Northwestern University, and has been an economist at the Public Research Institute of the Center for Naval Analyses since 1976. He directed a recent econometric study of the employment effects of technical change from which results were drawn for the paper in this volume. That work applied new econometric techniques for estimating input adjustment to technical change when some input stocks are fixed in the short run. His current work is focused on the effects of government labor policies, including minimum wage laws and the Davis–Bacon Act, on private-sector productivity growth.

Kenneth McLennan is Vice President and Director of Industrial Studies of the Committee for Economic Development. Prior to joining the Committee, he was Division Chief, Social Affairs and Industrial Relations, Organization for Economic Cooperation and Development; Deputy Assistant Secretary for Policy Development, U.S. Department of Labor; and Chairman, Department of Economics, Temple University. He has written many articles on industrial relations and productivity issues and is a contributor and coeditor with William F. Baumol of a forthcoming book *Productivity Growth and U.S. Competitiveness*. He received the B.Sc. in economics from the University of London, the M.B.A. from the University of Toronto, and the Ph.D. in industrial relations at the University of Wisconsin.

Markley Roberts is an economist at the American Federation of Labor and Congress of Industrial Organizations. A member of The Newspaper Guild for thirty years, he has published numerous articles and studies about employment, unemployment, productivity, and technology issues. He received the B.A. from Princeton University and the Ph.D. from American University.

John Vrooman is a member of the economics faculty at the University of Utah where he teaches labor economics, and heterodox political economy. His research interests and published work center on human resource economics and econometric analysis of labor market phenomena. He received the Ph.D. in economics from the University of Texas.

ABOUT THE EDITORS

Eileen L. Collins is a staff economist and program manager (for studies of the employment effects of technical change and studies of the impacts of tax policy on innovation) in the National Science Foundation's Division of Policy Research and Analysis. Her work includes an edited volume *Tax Policy and Investment in Innovation* and shorter papers in the employment and tax areas. Prior to joining the National Science Foundation, she was a member of the economics faculty of Fordham University, Barnard College, and the University of Waterloo. She received the Ph.D. in economics from the University of Wisconsin and the B.A. from Bryn Mawr College.

Lucretia Dewey Tanner is the Executive Director of the Advisory Committee on Federal Pay. Her government posts have included Deputy Assistant Director, Office of Pay Monitoring, Council on Wage and Price Stability; Director of Research, Federal Mediation and Conciliation Service; and labor economist at the Bureau of Labor Statistics and the Cost of Living Council. Earlier she was with the American Federation of Labor and Congress of Industrial Organizations, the Service Employees International Union, and the American Nurses Association. She has written numerous articles about collective bargaining, mediation, and industrial relations. She received the B.S. in political science from the University of Connecticut and the M.S. in industrial relations from the University of Wisconsin.

HD 5724 .A56 1984

American jobs and the
changing industrial base

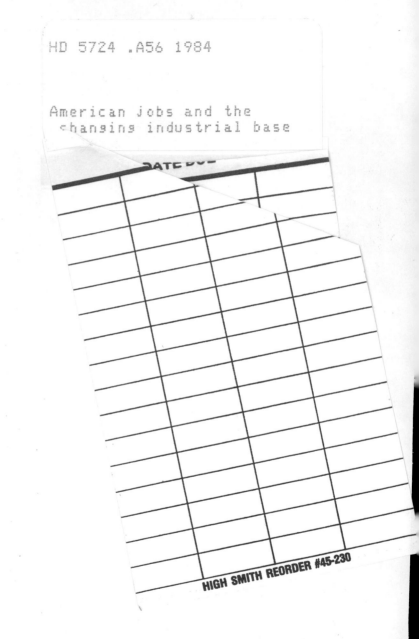

DATE DUE

HIGH SMITH REORDER #45-230